Elvis Presley couldn't read music. He was working at $1 an
hour as a stock clerk when he sent in an audition tape to Sun
Records in 1953. It cost him $3.98 to make the tape. The song
**My Happiness** was the start of a career that brought him
earnings of over **$4.3 Billion Dollars**. He died in 1977 at
age 42. In the seven months before his death, his doctor had
prescribed **5,300** pills and vials for Elvis to take. *How tragic
that he never found true happiness in life!*

## Excerpt from **WHAT IS THE RAPTURE ?**

The moment we are raptured, we will never age...**TIME**
will actually stand still!   Do you realize that every
light image reflected off this earth is <u>right now</u> out
there in space!   As you pass through these light
images at the Rapture...it will be quite possible you
will be able to see events as they were happening
during the ministry of Christ

## Excerpt from **WHAT IS HELL ?**

Hell is a place of consciousness, a place of torment, a
place of darkness, eternal separation from loved ones,
with not the slightest hope of release. It is also a place
where one will experience the torment of <u>unsatisfied</u>
lustful cravings plus the torment of a memory in hell!

## Excerpt from **WHAT IS HEAVEN ?**

Heaven is a prepared place for prepared people.  It is a
place where Mansions have already been prepared for
us...where all our saved loved ones will be...where we
will see God... where we will have new bodies...where
we will receive rewards. In Heaven...there is no need
to carry photographs of those we love...because all the
Saints of all the ages will be there...and we will
recognize each other in Heaven!

## **Over 50 Photographs, Illustrations and Charts!**

# WHAT IN THE WORLD WILL HAPPEN NEXT?

By
**Salem Kirban**

ISBN 0–89957–905–1

FUTURE
EVENTS
PUBLICATIONS

Published by Future Events Publications, an imprint of
AMG Publishers, P. O. Box 22000, Chattanooga, TN 37422.

*Printed in the United States of America*
02 01 00 99 98 97 –D– 7 6 5 4 3 2

# SALEM KIRBAN

# WHAT IN THE WORLD WILL HAPPEN NEXT?

**ANSWERS TO LIFE'S FOUR MOST IMPORTANT QUESTIONS**

**WHAT IS LIFE!   RAPTURE!   HELL!   HEAVEN!**

# IN DEDICATION

To My Wife, **KATE JERNIGIGAN**, who stands by me!

Rev. Robert Jernigan


To My Wife, **AGNES SIMPKINS**, who loves the Lord!

W.J. Simpkins


In Honor of my Parents, **LEATHA and WILLARD BURCHARD** who raised me in Christian Faith.

Joyce A. Burchard


To The Loving Memory of our Daughter **BONNIE JEAN BENSON** whom the Lord called home to be with Him, December 23, 1985.

Barb and Steve Holmes


In Loving Memory of my wonderful Dad, **HUGO LEVANDER**, and precious brother, **HUGO, Jr.**, who together now dwell within Heaven's gates with our most gracious Saviour.

Muriel Harvey


In Memory of our loved ones who are now with the Lord...

| | |
|---|---|
| **CARL and EDITH HOLMGREN** | Father/Mother [Grandparents] |
| **LLOYD W. HOLMGREN** | Brother [Uncle] |
| **TERRY HOLMGREN** | Nephew [Cousin] |

From the Dale Holmgren family, Dale, Helen, Tammy & Gina


In Memory of our daughter who was lovingly dedicated to her Lord and her Family.

Kenneth and Marian Alberding

## In Dedication to my wife MARY

*"Who can find
a virtuous woman?
For her price
is far above rubies.*

*A virtuous woman
is a crown
to her husband"*

[Proverbs 31:10; 12:4]

Mary's life is a constant
inspiration to me.
Without her unfailing
love and support, I
could have never
written **51** books.

## In loving Memory of my mother, OLGA KIRBAN

My mother was Olga Kirban. Her
maiden name was Olga Shoucair. She
was born in Schweifat, Lebanon.

Lebanon, historically, was a part of Syria
and originally was controlled by the
Ottoman Empire. In 1915, the Turks
rounded up Lebanese and put them in
the front lines. My mother's father
owned a large sheep ranch but the
Turks robbed him of everything he had
and he died of starvation.

My mother, Olga, was one of 12 children. As a young child, she worked
long hours each day by candlelight doing crocheting. At 18 she and her
sister, Linda, took a ship headed for the United States. However, because of
her poor eyesight brought about by years working under a dim light...she
was turned back at Marseilles, France. About four months later her sister
was able to gain Olga entry into the United States.

# CHARTS and SPECIAL FEATURES

## WHAT IS THE RAPTURE LIKE?

## WHAT IS HELL LIKE?

## WHAT IS HEAVEN LIKE?

## What In The World Will Happen Next?                309

# WHAT IN THE WORLD WILL HAPPEN NEXT ?

## Table of Contents

This book is divided into five sections as noted below.
The complete Table of Contents for each section
is found at the beginning of that section.

[The section **WHAT IS LIFE** is set in typewriter type.
The reason:   to convey the fact that life on
this earth is only a temporary dwelling place and
individuals must decide [while living] whether to
spend an eternity in Hell or in Heaven!]

## IN GRATEFUL ACKNOWLEDGMENT

**To my wife, Mary and our daughter, Doreen Frick**
who both devoted many hours proofreading the text.

**To my brother, Lafayette Kirban**
who helped make possible the printing of this book.

**To my sister, Elsie Corey**
for her faithful prayer support through the years.

**To Dr. Gary G. Cohen**
for his guidance and invaluable suggestions and input.

**To Walt Slotilock, Chapel Hill Litho**
for superior craftsmanship in making the negatives for this book.

**To Dave Koechel of Koechel-Peterson Designs**
for providing an excellent cover design.

**To Vern DeWeerd of Dickinson Press**
for his caring concern and printing of this book.

**To AMG Publishers**
who gave permission to print excerpts and charts from my previous books including **666/1000**. **AMG Publishers** of Chattanooga, Tennessee is the distributor of my books to bookstores worldwide.

# WHAT IS LIFE?

Most people go through life never knowing what life _really_ is!

Why did God put you on this earth?
What is the purpose of your life?
   A house, a family, a good church, retirement?
Is this _all_ there is to life?

Now! Discover for yourself why life is _much more_ than all these. Discover how to have true happiness, joy, peace and contentment. It's all _yours_ when you understand WHAT IS LIFE!

# SALEM KIRBAN

# Presented to

_____

# By

_____

_____

_____

# Date

_____

# WHAT IS LIFE ?

## Table of Contents

This book is divided into five sections.
This is the **First** Section
### WHAT IS LIFE ?

The section **WHAT IS LIFE** is set in typewriter type. The reason:  to convey the fact that life on this earth is only a _temporary_ dwelling place and you must decide **[while living]** whether to spend an eternity in Hell or in Heaven!

Back in the **1930's**...as a young boy...this was my
dream house...my castle on the hill!  It was the
home of Keith and Alma Grover in Schultzville,
Pennsylvania...just a few miles from Clarks Summit.

How often I would longingly look at it from my
vegetable stand in the small valley below...and
hope some day to own such a "mansion"!

See Page 37

1

# WHAT IS LIFE?
## [How Most People View Life]

Have you ever wondered exactly **WHAT IS LIFE?**

Physically...you are 70-85% water!

**You have:**

50,000 miles of blood vessels and capillaries...
206 bones / nearly half in the hands and feet
100 joints / and as you age, they may ache!
17 to 20 square feet of skin / of which you grow
    1000 completely new outer skins in a lifetime!

**And while you are sleeping:**

Your fist-size heart pumps
    80 gallons of blood per hour!
And your heart beats about
    **2.8** billion times during an average lifetime!

But is that all there is to YOU?

Of course not! That is your body. But you also
have a soul and spirit. However, very few people
are even aware of what makes up their body...let
alone discovering anything about their soul and
spirit. They could care less and rush through life
as though the secret of living is in financial
security, unbridled sex, possessions and power!
How tragic will be their end...for an eternity!

13

# Test most cars can't pass

**BEFORE A CAR leaves Yahya Minkara's repair shop, it is sprayed with at least 50 machine-gun bullets as the customer watches carefully.**

Yahya makes cars bulletproof in war-torn Beirut, Lebanon. The seemingly endless violence that has plagued the city has made him a millionaire.

"People here seem to like the idea of making their cars bulletproof," the mechanic says. "There is also a lot of imitation going on.

## How to Succeed in Business By Polishing Your Manners

**Wear the right clothes, take appropriate gifts when going abroad, never have more than one drink at lunch—steps such as these will help make you a winner at work, says an expert.**

## U.S.—$212 Billion Deeper in the Hole

World trouble spots will be a major topic during Geneva talks, but the outlook for defusing conflicts is dim.

## China, Iran Playing Nuclear Footsie?

---

## World

PUBLIC HEALTH

# A Scourge Spreads Panic

*As AIDS reaches around the globe, governments are galvanized into action*

CARL FISCHER

# What Entertainers Are Doing To Your Kids

ROCK MUSIC PUBLIC ENEMY #1

DARRYL HEIKES—USN&WR

While children are drawn to lurid shows and songs, protesters call for action.     The nationwide controversy is embroiling parents, politicians and popular stars in a debate over free speech.

## A Window of Time

In the days of Julius Caesar, the average life
expectancy was **36**.  [In much of Africa today, the
average life expectancy is also **36** years].

Sweden has the <u>highest</u> life expectancy...**73.1** for
men and **79.1** years for women.  [The United States
figures are:  **71.2** for men and **76.2** for women]

Looking at the above figures...you can see that
compared to an eternity...we physically on this
earth are only given a <u>very brief</u> moment of time
to get our priorities in line.  Understanding this,
<u>where in the world are you spending your time</u>?

> Is it in watching soap operas on TV?
> Is it in filling your body
> > with junk foods
> > with alcohol
> > with drugs...legal and illegal
> > with tobacco...
> > to shorten this "window of time"?
> Is it in holding down two jobs to make a
> > living...but not a life?
> Is it placing your job above your marriage
> > so you can advance up the corporate
> > ladder?
> Is it placing your child in a day care center
> > so you can have more "things"?
> Is it wallowing in the filth of sexual
> > excesses?
> Is it fanatically struggling for power and
> > prestige so you become respected?
> Is it devoting your adult life working for a
> > political power thinking <u>your</u> leader
> > will solve all the ills of the world?

<u>None of the above</u> will be of any value whatsoever
in light of eternity!  Take time now to discover
what is really lasting in this "window" of time!

### Is This Life?

Her stage name was <u>Pola Negri</u>.  She was an exotic
silent screen star of the 1920's.  She twice
married wealthy men and was linked romantically to
Charlie Chaplin and Valentino.  She was immensely
proud of her movie career.  Her close friend,
Gilbert Denman said:

> She was always quite vain about her looks,
> even at her decrepit old age.
>
> If I was late,
> she could make me wait for 20 minutes
> while she put her fake eyelashes on.

Two months before she died in August, 1987, a young
doctor in the hospital was examining her.  He had
no idea who she was.  Pola Negri raised herself up
in her bed and cried out:

  "I was the greatest film actress in the world!"

<u>From eternity's view...is this Life?</u>

* * *

<u>John B. Connally</u>...ex-Governor of Texas...at age **65**
was reportedly worth **$6 Million!**  In August, 1987,
he went into bankruptcy with <u>liabilities</u> of some
**$37 Million** because of real estate ventures.  In
his career he was a business tycoon, he owned a
radio station and was a Director of many large
corporations including Ford Motor Company.  A
lifetime of building assets suddenly crumbled
almost overnight.  And one day in 1987, he watched
as other "possessions seekers" bid on desks,
chairs, china and hundreds of antiques and
memorabilia in his home!

<u>From eternity's view...is this Life?</u>

Elvis Presley, couldn't read music yet he started singing at 10 years of age in 1945. He was working at $1 and hour as a stock clerk when he sent in an audition tape to Sun Records in 1953. [It cost him $3.98 to make the tape]. The song was **My Happiness**. From $3.98 in 1953 till the time he died...his career earnings topped **$4.3 Billion Dollars!**

[How tragic that he never found
true happiness in this life!]

In the **4** weeks Elvis appeared at the International Hotel in Las Vegas in 1969, he outdrew Frank Sinatra, Dean Martin and Barbra Streisand. A total of **101,500** people saw him. Not one seat remained unsold, a record that still stands!

His TV special, Aloha From Hawaii, was watched worldwide by more than **1 Billion** people...more than watched man's first walk on the moon!

Elvis Presley lived and died at his mansion in Memphis, Tennessee called "Graceland". It is reported he sometimes made late night visits to a local funeral home to ponder the dead.

He died on August 16, 1977 at age 42. Found in his body were some **8** prescription drugs and significant amounts of three sedatives and codeine plus Demoral [a narcotic analgesic] and Valium [a tranquilizer]. His doctor was charged by the Tennessee Board of Medical Examiners with "indiscriminately prescribing **5,300 pills** and vials for Elvis in the seven months before his death."

Each year on the anniversary of his death, some **50,000** fans make a pilgrimage to Graceland. Some even worship him as a god and pray to him as their intercessor.

From eternity's view...is this Life?

### A Big Mac

In August, 1987, Joan Kroc,
  [widow of McDonald's founder, the late Ray Kroc,
  who is reportedly worth some $640 Million]
gave **$1 Million** to the Democratic Party in hopes
that the Democrats will provide

> "...principled leadership...
> to restore America
> to its proper place as
> the foremost champion of
> peace and justice in the world."

From eternity's view...is this Life?

* * *

In 1987, celebrated pianist Liberace died.  He
lived in a 10,000 square foot palace.  It has a
Roman marble bath, lit by a chandelier.  The master
bedroom has a mirrored fireplace.  The ceiling is
covered with copies of Sistine Chapel frescoes.
At his death, all this luxury estate was put up for
sale at **$2.8 million**.

From eternity's view...is this Life?

* * *

In the early 1980's, rock star Michael Jackson
released his album titled THRILLER.  It became the
best selling album in history...with worldwide
sales of 38.5 million!  In 1987 he released his
album titled BAD.  It contained such "memorable"
lyrics as: "I just can't stop loving you, and if I
stop, just tell me what will I do."  He has become
a multi-millionaire but lives a life in seclusion.
At one time his companion was a chimpanzee.

From eternity's view...is this Life?

Dennis B. Levine had everything.  At age 27 he
found himself on Wall Street.  Just 6 years later
he was paid $1 Million a year.  He lived in an
exclusive $500,000 Park Avenue co-op.  He drove in
a $80,000 red Ferrari on weekends and on weekdays
was chauffeured in a limousine.

On May 12, 1986, he was summoned to the U.S.
Attorney's office where he was handcuffed and
accused of alleged illegal trading by using
nonpublic information to make a reported $12.6
million killing on 54 different stocks.  This greed
for wealth ruined his career at a time when he had
a 5-year-old child and a pregnant wife.

From eternity's view...is this Life?

* * *

A 32-year-old woman is head of a $200 Million
money-management firm.  She is a chain smoker.  Her
personal net worth is over $5 Million.  Her aim now
is to reach $10 Million in personal assets.  She is
a workaholic.  She arrives at her office at 6:30 AM
and leaves about 10:30 PM.  She states:  "My
business is my life...I want to be the richest
woman in the USA."

From eternity's view...is this Life?

* * *

In Tokyo, Japan, Norio Dotsuta and his wife, Junko,
together earn some $55,000 a year.  They have no
children and hoped to move from their two-room
apartment into a home,  But homes in Tokyo start at
$1 Million in desirable areas and two-bedroom
apartments are $280,000.  Japan is a land where a
pound of beef can cost over $200!

From eternity's view...is this Life?

MAY 16, 1988 $2.00

# TIME

Are U.S. Aircraft Safe?

EXCLUSIVE

# Astrology in the White House

Excerpts From Don Regan's Explosive Memoirs

Plus Reagan's Laid-Back Management Style

An Insider's

**COVER: An explosive memoir exposes some embarrassing White House secrets**    **24**

In exclusive excerpts from his forthcoming book, former White House Chief of Staff Donald Regan tells how Nancy Reagan's astrologer all but controls the President's schedule—and how the First Lady controls much besides that. ▸ Mrs. Reagan's "Friend" with the star charts is Joan Quigley, a Nob Hill socialite with several books to her credit. *See* NATION.

# Scheduling by Horoscope

Our days were busy. The President had decided to speak to the nation about the findings of the Iran-contra report, hold a press conference and deliver a major foreign-policy speech, all in March. As usual, no dates for these events were set in conversations with President Reagan. I discussed the schedule with Mrs. Reagan, who consulted her Friend. She reported back that March 4, the Reagans' wedding anniversary, and March 5 were "good days." But the press conference had tentatively been scheduled for March 9, and this date was not among the auspicious ones that had been certified by the Friend. According to a list provided by Mrs. Reagan, the Friend had made the following prohibitions based on her reading of the President's horoscope:

| | |
|---|---|
| **Late Dec. thru March** bad | **March 16** very bad |
| **Jan. 16-23** very bad | **March 19-25** no public exposure |
| **Jan. 20** nothing outside WH—possible attempt | **March 21** no |
| **Feb. 20-26** be careful | **March 27** no |
| **March 7-14** bad period | **April 3** careful |
| **March 10-14** no outside activity! | **April 11** careful |
| **March 12-19** no trips exposure | **April 17** careful |
| | **April 21-28** stay home |

## A Star Gazing Affair

In May, 1988, Former White House aide Don Regan
dropped a bombshell when he alleged in his memoirs
that Nancy Reagan influenced her husband's schedule
based on astrology.

> [Astrology is a pseudo-science
>  claiming to foretell the future
>  by studying the supposed influence
>  of the relative positions
>  of the moon, sun and stars
>  on human affairs]

It was reported that President Reagan and his wife
daily read the horoscopes and Nancy regularly
consulted with a California astrologer.  Her
interest in astrology became serious after the
attempted assassination attempt on the President.

She apparently exhibited a fear of the future and
looked to the stars for guidance.   She still seeks
guidance through astrology.

From eternity's view...is this Life?

                         *  *  *

Look at your own life!  Why not get a piece of
paper right now.  Draw a line down the center and
place the below headings atop each column:

**That Which Is TEMPORARY**          **That Which is ETERNAL**

Then, examine your daily routine and list under the
appropriate column the activities and goals that
occupy your time.  You will discover that most of
your entries will be in the left column.

**Realizing this...remember it is not too late to
change your PRIORITIES!**

Pictured above is the Chapel at Girard College in
Philadelphia.  This photo was taken in 1986 during
the annual Founder's Day in May.

Running in front is our grandson, Joel. And behind
him [left to right] is my wife Mary, my sister,
Elsie and our daughter, Doreen.

This Chapel was built before the so-called
progressive "disposable society."  It was built in
1933 at a cost of **$1.5** Million dollars.  It is
over 200 feet long, 140 feet wide and 103 feet
high...much larger than the famed Solomon's Temple.
For more details on this, see page 30 and 31.

## LIVING IN A DISPOSABLE SOCIETY
### [The More Man Progresses...the More He Regresses]

### Do "things" Have Any Value?
That's the headline of a column by James Brady in
<u>Advertising Age</u>, April 20, 1987.

Brady comments:

> There's this terrible new idea.
> The disposable camera...
> You pay $7 to $10 for the camera,
>     including a roll of film,
> and after you've snapped off your shots
> you turn the camera in,
> the film is developed
> and they throw the camera away!
>
> Cameras used to be wonderful, serious things,
> items of delicacy and craftsmanship...
> Now we throw them away...

Brady is saddened by the fact that his old Smith
Corona typewriters...when they broke down...were
considered worthless junk by a typewriter
shop...another sign of this disposable age.

Today you can buy a quartz watch for $2.97.   But
sending it for repairs will cost $4.95 for postage
and handling.

Brady concludes:

> There's too much progress.
> Too much junk.
> Too many clever machines.
> Too little craft and care.
> We throw away too much
>      and cherish too little.
> Turn in your camera?
> Junk a Smith Corona?
> We might as well scrap those we love.

And James Brady could not have said it better!
Isn't that just what we do?  In our race for
success, security and spoils we forget the real
meaning of life!  Everything is disposable!

John S. Lang, Assistant Managing Editor of U.S.
& World Report, wrote in an editorial in June,
1987:

> The heavens, too,
>      are littered with our leavings...
> So an astronaut may ride on lunarscape,
>      we make a "moon rover."
> It costs tens of millions of dollars.
> It is ridden once.  It is left behind.
> For eternity,
>      the moon is a used-car lot.

> A colleague [from England] comes here
>      with a radio-cassette player
>      bought for $30.  She wants the
>      volume knob fixed and goes to a number
>      of electrical shops.

> "We don't fix things;
>      we just throw them away and replace them...
> You are in America now."

And so the race goes on in a disposable society!

## There Will Be No Cars In Heaven!

And for this we can be thankful.

It is simply remarkable how the apostle Paul covered so much territory and accomplished so much without a car!

> [One way to reduce auto accidents is to build cars so they can't go any faster than the average person thinks! Some cars have fluid drives; others just have a drip at the wheel!]

You get a pretty good idea of eternity when you start paying for a $25,000 car on the installment plan!

Whoever called them "pleasure cars" never drove them in traffic! A rumor is afloat that we have a new trade agreement with Russia. We will send them 10,000 automobiles from Detroit...if they will send us 50,000 parking spaces from Siberia!

Los Angeles has **730 miles** of freeway. In just **24** hours, **2.5 million** vehicles carry **4.3 million** people on **8.3** million trips...covering a grand total of **224 million miles a day!**

Automobiles have contributed to the increasingly fast speed of living. We now live in a disposable society and a breakdown of the family unit. We buy things, use them briefly and discard them. We toss away so much that it takes **30,000** trash trucks to take away **133 million tons** of waste annually!

We now have disposable marriages with divorces almost equaling the number of marriages. Add to this...disposable people with abortions soaring into the millions! And they call this an advanced and sophisticated progressive society!!!

Pictured is a **1929** Willys Eight coupe with a rumble
seat!  Standing in front of car is motion picture
actor Neil Hamilton.  He last appeared as Police
Commissioner Gordon on TV's "Batman" series (1960).


Close-up detail of rumble seat on a **1927** Packard.

## Life Becomes A Race

Ever watch how people drive?  They are always in a
hurry.  If you are on an interstate where repair
work is going on...and two lanes of traffic
suddenly have to merge into one lane...drivers will
smash their gas pedal to the floor just to pass you
before the single lane traffic begins...just to get
one car length ahead of you.

Remember the good old days when the speed limit was
50 miles per hour?  [I can remember when it was 25
miles per hour!]

    My stepdad used to take me for a ride
        in his Model A Ford.

    It had a rumble seat.
        Did you ever ride in a rumble seat?
        If you did,
            you know what Heaven is going to be like!

    And we would go barreling down the highway
        at the breakneck speed of 25 miles per hour!

    I was 9 and I had my heart in my mouth.

    I remember those old Burma Shave signs...5 signs
        spaced 100 feet apart on the highway.  And
        at 25 miles per hour...you could read them!
        One sign read:

            Don't stick your elbow out so far...
            It may go home...in another car!

But today we have gone mad!  The speed limit is now
65 miles per hour.  So we speed up to 75 miles per
hour...whizzing by beautiful wildflowers, trees,
buttercups and butterflies.  We never see them at
that speed.  And we whiz past our little window of
earth's time allotted to us.  How tragic!

## Is This Life?

In the famous Pennzoil-Texaco lawsuit of the late 1980's...estimated <u>legal fees</u> generated each <u>month</u> averaged **$5 Million Dollars** alone!

Americans pay some **$28 Billion** each year just for the <u>packaging</u> that their food comes in! [What happened to the old fashioned days when you simply went out to the garden and plucked a tomato from the vine and clipped some romaine lettuce, squash and cucumbers. The incidence of cancer, heart disease and high blood pressure was much lower!]

Where has our sanity gone? In just 6 years the Air Force spent **$115,634** on matchbooks and playing cards for Presidential planes Air Force One and Two!

In one year in New York City, marriage license fees totaled $806,090. Divorce fees were **$3,637,095.**

We are living in a disposable society.

The air is unfit to breathe. The water from your faucet is unfit to drink. The cities are unfit to live in. The water at the beaches is unfit to swim in. Most of that which we call food in our large supermarkets is unfit for human consumption.

It can take an hour to go 10 miles in rush hour traffic!

To those who do not know Jesus Christ as their personal Saviour and Lord...they may agree with Samuel Johnson who wrote around 1750 that "Human life is everywhere in a state in which much is to be endured, and little to be enjoyed."

Examine your own daily activities and priorities. Is this really what is lasting in that small window of earthly time you call life?

## 3

## IF IN THIS LIFE ONLY...
## [There's More to Life than This Life]

It was Dan Jansen's big chance...the Winter
Olympics of 1988 in Calgary, Canada.

Ahead of him was a 500-meter speedskating race...a
race that could earn him a Gold medal.  But just a
few hours before, he learned that his sister had
died of leukemia.  His three nieces are now without
a mother.  Suddenly the years of striving for this
single Olympic occasion to win a Gold medal...
suddenly these years of training are no longer
important.  The Gold medal is just another trinket!

Dan Jansen discovers there is more to life than
this life.

* * *

In the summer of 1987, Rev. Robert Davis said
goodbye to his Miami congregation.  It was a moment
of stunning emotion.  Men and women wept and gave
him a standing ovation.  Davis, 53, 6-foot-7, was a
former two-time All-American football player.  As
Pastor of a Presbyterian Church he saw his church
grow from 46 when he arrived in 1972 to a 2400
congregation.  But Rev. Davis now has Alzheimers...
an incurable disease that wastes away the brain,
taking memory, judgment and bodily control.  He can
no longer read a book.  His math ability is on a
third-grade level.  He once had a genius-level IQ!
Davis knows there is more to life than this life!

## A Promised Expectation!

God's Word, the Bible, is very clear in telling us
that there is more to life than this present life!
The apostle Paul, in telling the Corinthians about
the importance of Christ's resurrection states:

> If in this life only
>     we have hope in Christ,
> we are of all men
>     most miserable.     [1 Corinthians 15:19]

What God is telling us in the above Scripture verse
is that... if, being a Christian is of value to us
only in this present life...we would be the most
miserable people on earth.  We as believers have an
eternal inheritance awaiting us!  "Our citizenship
is in Heaven, from which also we look for the
Saviour, the Lord Jesus Christ who shall change our
lowly body, that it may be fashioned like His
glorious body..." (Philippians 3:20).

On the other hand, Christians, have a sure hope.
Our hope is "...an anchor of the soul, both sure
and steadfast...a lively hope...an inheritance...
that fadeth not away, reserved in heaven for you.
(Hebrews 6:19 and 1 Peter 1:3,4)

Those who do not accept Jesus Christ as their
personal Saviour have **no hope** beyond the grave.
Whatever life they have is only the few years they
exist on this earth.  A very small window of time.
Their final destination is an eternity in constant
torment in the Lake of Fire. (Revelation 20:11-15).
Is it really worth it to trade 70 or 80 years
living for self without God to spend eternity in
Hell!  Remember, eternity is never-ending time!

On this present earth's small "window of time".
even Christians have periods of trials, testings
and suffering.

**Second Coming, Inc.** is a non-profit literature missionary ministry. I began this worldwide outreach in 1968. Our goal is to supply Bibles and books on Bible prophecy and Christian living to seeking souls in foreign countries. It seems that almost every day we receive a letter from some friend of Second Coming's ministry concerning a problem or trial in their life. These are from Christians. But God does not promise to take us <u>above</u> our circumstances in this temporary earthly life. He does promise to take us triumphantly <u>through</u> every circumstance. Let me give you a few examples from letters sent me.

## When Life Seems Useless

A self-employed person in a service trade accepted Christ as his personal Saviour and Lord in 1974. He is now 50. He is torn between living in a northern state or moving down south to be near his daughter and granddaughter. He is so desperate for direction. Because of his situation he says he has

> "...just about lost all of the power
> of God in my life. I just can't find
> direction for my life. I feel like these
> are the most useless years of my life
> and most unhappy...even though our
> marriage is a happy one. I have the
> greatest helpmate in the world. But
> where would I find a place to lay my
> head down when I am old...if I sold my
> house and moved down south?"

I wrote him suggesting he not make hasty decisions about moving...that he cannot run the life of his children and grandchildren...and worrying will not help the situation. He should leave them in God's hands and daily ask God for guidance.

If in this life only we have hope...

## "I Still Miss Him"

A widow from the mid-west writes:

It was two years ago today
that my beloved husband
left this earthly home
to be with the Saviour he loved.

Oh, how I still miss him
  and all that we had shared together.
My married life was great
  and very satisfying and rewarding.
I have asked God
  for another special someone
  to love and be loved by...
Someone who loves the Lord
  and wants to spend the rest of the time
  we each would have
  serving the Lord...

Sometimes I feel
  as if I can't take it much more...
Satan tries to tell me
  how worthless I am
And that if God really loved me,
  he wouldn't have taken my husband from me.
He also suggests I end it all
  and get rid of my hurting.

I have worked through most of that now...
  and found victory in Christ's shed blood...
Now its the lonely nights and days
  without someone to love and care for
  and someone to love and care for me.
I'm short on patience at times.
God is so patient and forgiving of me.

<u>If in this life only we have hope in Christ</u>!  How
wonderful to know that heaven for an eternity will
wipe out each sorrow, each tear in triumphant joy!

## "A Bleak Future"

Another writes:

> I am 53 years old and presently unemployed.
> I have had 4 jobs since the manufacturing
>    plant I worked at closed.
> My wife is so distressed,
>    she talks about pulling the plug.
> My financial future looks bleak.
> We simply don't know
>    how we are going to survive after age 65.
> Neither of us has a pension plan.

## "A Biblical Wife"

A distraught wife wrote me:

> Please continue to pray, Brother Kirban.
> It looks like I'll have to file bankruptcy
>    to pay off my ex-husband's debts.
>
> I signed my property over to him to pay
>        his debts while we were still married.
>
> I tried to be a Biblical wife
>        and do as he said.
> When I left him four years ago,
>        our financial statement was about
>        $4 Million dollars.
> Now I have lost everything
>        except a few personal pieces of jewelry.
> I have so many bills I cannot pay.

In Jeremiah 12:1, the prophet of God...persecuted
by his own people...asked the question: "...Why
does the way of the wicked prosper? Why do all the
faithless live at ease?" However, it is only in
this very small 70-80 year "window of earth's time"
that they prosper. For an endless eternity they
will be separated from God in a burning hell.

### "That Bothers Me More Than Anything"

An 83-year-old widow writes:

> This past week has been a very trying one
> for me.  I feel the need of writing you.
>
> Last Saturday,
>   we buried one of my sons.  He was 57.
> He suffered from chronic asthma and cancer.
>
> My son had not made a commitment for Christ
>   and that bothers me more than anything.
>
> I live alone.
> I would appreciate your prayers.

As Mary and I travel throughout the United States
speaking in churches...one common concern grips
many Christians.  A loved one dies and the
survivors are troubled, asking the question:  "Did
that loved one ever accept Christ as Saviour and
Lord?"  One Pastor's wife has been worrying for the
past three years...wondering if her mother who
died, had ever accepted Christ.

The  "window of earth's life" is so temporary.  How
often we are guilty of rushing through life placing
our priorities of time on the unimportant while
sacrificing that which is truly real and lasting!

If there is such a thing as a universal human
experience...it is pain.  Physical pain affects
some **40** million American adults annually.  And some
**30 Billion** aspirin tablets are swallowed each year.
But beyond physical pain there are the scars left
by emotional pain.  Christians can rest on the
promise found in 1 Corinthians 15:57:

**But thanks be to God, who giveth us the victory
through our Lord Jesus Christ**

# 4

## WHAT LIFE IS NOT!
### [You Mean My Financial Portfolio Is Worthless?]

In 1933, in the heart of the Great Depression, it became necessary for my mother to place me in a home for fatherless boys. My father, Lafayette, had died when I was one year old. My mother [Olga] and sister [Elsie] and brother [Lafayette...named after our father]...lived in Scranton, a coal mining town in Pennsylvania.

The home for fatherless boys was Girard College. Located in Philadelphia...it was not a college but rather an elementary and high school. At that time they had some 1500 students. My brother had already been in Girard for five years when I arrived.

We only were able to go home during the two months of summer. By this time my mother had moved several times in the Pennsylvania area...from Tunkhannock, to Clarks Summit, to Schultzville. And it was in Schultzville that I have my fondest memories.

If you blinked your eyes while you were driving on Route 307...you would be past Schultzville. It was a small country town [and still is]...uncluttered by the so-called progress of time.

35

This photo taken in **1938** shows Mrs. Card standing
in front of her home.  It was here that I often
would longingly look up at that "mansion" on the
hill.  When I grew up, I discovered this "castle"
was just a small cottage.

The photo below was taken in 1970.  It shows my
old homestead in Schultzville, Pennsylvania.  We
occupied the left half.  Shown in front are Diane,
Dawn and our youngest son, Duane.

## The Bungalow On The Hill

We lived in one part of a double house on a large
acreage of farmland facing the highway. The owner,
who we called "Teenie" was an industrious farm
lady. The house had no indoor plumbing. But often
I would go into "Teenie's" living room and pump her
old piano player. The piano roll would magically
fill the room with "I wish I had wings like an
angel...o'er these tall prison walls I would fly."

My stepdad...who had a Model A Ford [with a rumble
seat] would often drive us about a mile down the
road to friends of his, Mr. & Mrs. Card. They
lived in an equally old house. I would spend my
time there as a 10-year-old "fixing" clocks and
baking cakes. I recall having a vegetable stand by
the side of the road and doing quite well.

Often as I stood at that stand...I would look to my
right at a fascinating attraction on a small hill.
Just about a half mile away was a bungalow. Today
I guess you would call it a cottage. But to me
that bungalow seemed like heaven! Someday, I
thought to myself, I want to own that! It was to
me the symbol of everything this world could offer.

One day I walked up to the bungalow on the hill.
To a 10-year-old it was a palace! Keith Grover and
his wife, Alma lived there. The year 1935. Alma
was very kind to me and showed me through her
home...complete with indoor plumbing! In the next
few years we became very good friends. This
friendship continued for many years...even after I
graduated from Girard. Then Alma died.

And just last year, I passed that "castle on the
hill". But from the perspective of time...that
dream house now appeared to be just a small, rustic
cottage. Those things we count precious now will
fade into insignificance when we see Heaven!

The Girard College Chapel was built in the Great
Depression of 1933 at a cost then of **$1.5 Million**.
It is actually larger than Solomon's Temple!  The
Chapel is **201** feet long, **140** feet wide and **103** feet
high.  In the ceiling there is **12,000** square feet
of decorated gold.  Yet all the gold used weighs
less than **5 pounds**!  The Chapel seats 2500 people.
While Solomon's Temple took **7** years to build, the
Girard College Chapel was built in just **2 years**!

## Memories of Girard College

I can recall as a child we had a music teacher with
marvelous capabilities. I can still remember the
songs he taught us. His name was Dr. Bruce Carey.
All 1500 boys from 7 to 17 would gather daily in
the Girard College Chapel. And Bruce Carey would
lead us in singing rounds and memorable songs.

One of the rounds was:

> Life is a vapor,
>   Full of woes
> Man cuts a caper
>   Down he goes...
>   Downy, downy, downy, downy, down he goes!

The Girard College Chapel I consider one of the
seven wonders of the world. If you ever get a
chance to hear an organ recital or Christmas
concert in this Chapel...by all means take
advantage of that opportunity! Girard College is
located in Philadelphia near 21st and Girard
Avenues. The phone number is [215] 787-2600.
When that pipe organ peals forth...reverberating
through that vast gold-ceiling chapel...it gives
you a small insight into the music of heaven!

Anyway, the point I want to make is that from my
early days at Girard singing that round, I came to
discover that verse in James 4:14 which reads:

> Whereas ye know not what shall be
>   on the next day.
> For what is your life?
> It is even a vapor
>   that appeareth for a little time,
>   and then vanisheth away.

If we discover what life is **not** it is our first
step to understanding what life really **is**!

## Learning From Solomon

Solomon was the tenth son of King David and the second son of Bathsheba. He lived about 961-922 B.C. It is recorded in 1 Kings 3:7-12 that God granted his wish for wisdom and that none before him nor none after him would possess as much wisdom as Solomon.

Solomon spoke 3000 proverbs and wrote 1005 songs. See 1 Kings 4:32. Solomon's major accomplishment was the construction of the Temple in Jerusalem.

In his latter years he began to move away from his initial zeal in serving the Lord...probably because of his oversize harem. He had accumulated **700** wives and **300** concubines (1 Kings 11:3). He allowed many of these women to worship pagan gods.

Solomon passed through a time of disillusionment, frustration and despair. He soon found that all of his accumulated knowledge about life meant nothing if he did not know the Creator of life!

Solomon learned the truth the hard way. And he gave us his experiences in the book in the Bible called Ecclesiastes. In his search for what life really is, he discovered that:

## A Full Stomach Is Not The Answer

As the richest man in the world, Solomon had the very best in foods and he was a connoisseur of fine wines. Yet he concluded in Ecclesiastes 6:7:

> All the labor of man is for his mouth,
> and yet the soul is not satisfied.

Yet, how many today think that abundant food is what life is really all about. They gorge themselves only to end up with a tragic illness.

## Sex Is Not The Answer

Solomon's quest for sexual pleasure was certainly
not hindered by a lack of partners. As previously
stated, he had 700 wives and 300 concubines. And
many of them enticed him away from God. He soon
found these temporary pleasures meaningless leading
him to despair and defeat.

## Great Works and Riches Not The Answer

In the second chapter of Ecclesiastes we find that
Solomon exhausted life seeking an answer to Life's
real meaning.

In this quest, he:

```
1.   Built houses
2.   Planted vineyards, trees and gardens
3.   Built reservoirs and aqueducts
4.   Had hundreds of servants and maids
5.   Had thousands of cattle
6.   Had musicians to entertain him
7.   Was the world's wealthiest man
```

Yet when he looked back on all of this he finally
came to the conclusion:

> Yet when I surveyed all
>     that my hands had done
>     and what I had toiled to achieve,
> everything was meaningless,
> a chasing after the wind;
> nothing was gained under the sun.
> (Ecclesiastes 2:11)

Remember this was written almost 3000 years ago.
And we haven't changed much since Solomon's time!
We are obsessed with the same things that
controlled Solomon...food, sex, music, real estate,
wealth and power. Isn't it time to wake up?

### When POSSESSIONS Become POSSESSIVE

Solomon had it all...women, wealth and power!
After all this he came to the conclusion:

> I hated all the things
>   I had toiled for under the sun,
> Because I must leave them
>   to the one who comes after me.
> [Ecclesiastes 2:18]

Each year Solomon received gold that weighed **666**
talents.  [**$20 Million**]  In today's economy this
$20 Million would probably be equal to **$7 BILLION**.
Solomon's priorities were wrong.

It took just **7** years to build the Temple.
  But
He devoted 13 years to building his own house!
    [See 1 Kings 7:1 & 37]

Solomon allowed his possessions to possess him!
This is one of Satan's most successful and
cleverest tools to **[1]** keep unbelievers from God
and **[2]** to defuse the effectiveness of Christians.
Solomon had:

**[1]**  A kingdom free from external danger.
**[2]**  Virtually unlimited power.
**[3]**  He had unlimited wealth
        [even foreign kings paid taxes to him]
**[4]**  He had **700** wives
        [and he built a shrine for each one]

Even today people try to find pleasure in "things."
Sweepstakes, lotteries, TV game shows all promise
instant wealth.  But Solomon, who had it all,
reminds us:  "He who loves silver will not be
satisfied with silver, nor he who loves abundance,
with increase" [Eccl. 5:10].  From an eternal
standpoint your financial portfolio is worthless!

**5**

## UNDERSTANDING <u>NATURAL</u> AND <u>ETERNAL</u> LIFE
## [70 Years or Forever...The Choice Is Yours]

This natural life is much too short to satisfy us. God stated in Genesis 6:3 that the very most that He would allow man to live is **120** years. However, few live to be a hundred.

Psalm 90 gives us real insight into the eternal God and the mortal man.

To the eternal God...

> A thousand years are but as yesterday.
> [Psalm 90:4 & 2 Peter 3:8]

To the natural man, God reminds us...

> We spend our years as a tale that is told...
> The days of our years
>     are threescore and ten [70],
> and if, by reason of strength,
>     they be fourscore years [80],
> yet is their strength
>     labor and sorrow;
> for it is soon cut off, and we fly away.
> [Psalm 90:9,10]

Verse 12 reminds us to "...number our days, that we may apply our hearts unto wisdom."

The film was **CASABLANCA**...made in **1942**.  The actors
were Humphrey Bogart and Ingrid Bergman.  In the
motion picture, Bogart and Bergman are sweethearts,
separated in Paris because of World War **2** and an
intriguing set of circumstances.

They finally meet up in Casablanca, the capital of
Morocco only to find they must say goodbye again.
The last scene is on a foggy, rainy night at the
Casablanca airport where the last plane is about to
leave for Portugal.

Humphrey Bogart turns to Ingrid and says:

> "It's never easy to say goodbye.
>  So think of something else,
>      like
>  'We'll always have Paris.'"

As one grows older...somethings the only joy and
escape from loneliness they receive...are the
pleasant memories of yesterday.  This life is a
"mist".  It is never satisfying.  How important
that each of us get our priorities in line in light
of an eternity!

## A Revealing Comparison

What does God say about our earthly <u>natural</u> life?

1. <u>It is a SHADOW</u>
     Our days on earth are like a shadow...
                              [1 Chronicles 29:15]

2. <u>It is FULL OF TROUBLE, a FLOWER and a SHADOW</u>
     Man born of woman
         is of a few days and full of trouble.
     He springs up like a flower
         and withers away;
     Like a fleeting shadow,
         he does not endure.
                              [Job 14:1,2]

3. <u>It is a MIST</u>
     ...You do not even know
         what will happen tomorrow.
     What is your life?
     You are a mist
         that appears for a little while
         and then vanishes.
                              [James 4:14]

4. <u>It is NEVER SATISFYING</u>
     Everyone that drinketh of this water
         shall thirst again...     [John 4:13]

5. <u>It is like GRASS</u>
     All men are like grass,
     and all their glory
         is like the flowers of the field;
     The grass withers
     and the flowers fall.
                              [1 Peter 1:24]

Understanding this...why is so much (if not all) of
our time spent on those things which are temporary!

## Our Eternal Life

Your life comes from God:

> For with Thee is the fountain of life;
>   in Thy light shall we see light.
>                                    [Psalm 36:9]

Through Jesus Christ:

> I am <u>the</u> way, <u>the</u> truth and <u>the</u> life;
> No man cometh unto the Father,
>   but by Me.
>
>                                    [John 14:6]

With the Holy Spirit as our guide:

> I will put my Spirit in you
>   and you will live...
>                                    [Ezekiel 37:14]

To the those who accept Jesus Christ as their
personal Saviour and Lord...their life will be:

1. <u>Imperishable</u>

> Whosoever liveth and believeth in me
>   shall never die.    [John 11:26]

2. <u>Transforming</u>

> When Christ who is our life, shall appear,
>   then shall ye also appear with Him
>   in glory.         [Colossians 3:4]

If you <u>reject</u> Him as your personal Saviour and Lord
of your life...you will meet Him as your Judge
[Revelation 20:11-15] and spend an eternity in the
Lake of Fire.

## WHAT IS LIFE?
[Look At Life Beyond What You Plan To Do Tomorrow]

Most of our thoughts about life revolve about what we plan to do tomorrow or the day after. About the only area in which there is any long range planning is in the field of financial investments.

However, we should look at life with Eternity's values in view!

100 years from now...
it will not matter
whether you had a nice bank account,
a portfolio of stocks,
a savings account,
an IRA or retirement account!

What will count for an eternity is

WHAT DID YOU DO FOR JESUS CHRIST!

The great use of life is to spend it for something that outlasts it! Alexander the Great, when he discovered there were no more lands to conquer... sat down and wept!

A psychiatrist, who was a full professor in a prestigious medical school in the South was successful and wealthy. Yet at age 45, he discovered life was empty...it had no meaning. He wrote about this in a medical journal. Some 400 physicians responded telling him they had the same feeling! Then, this article was picked up and printed in a worldwide medical journal. Again, almost 500 physicians wrote and said they, too, had discovered life was empty!

Here were people with wealth, prestige and power
and with all their learning had not discovered the
secret of **what is LIFE!**   Have you?

Christ is the answer!

### Why Did God Create Man?

I am indebted to my good friend, Dr. Gary G. Cohen,
for his very valuable input into this chapter.  My
parents are of Arab heritage...born in Lebanon.
And Gary is of Jewish heritage.  But in Christ, we
are one...and I am grateful for his help.

1.  **God created man for Himself!**
    In Genesis 1:26,27 we read:

> God said,
> Let us make man in our image,
> in the image of God created He him;
> male and female created He them.

**God created man that man might glorify Him**
by living holy lives
    in obedience to God's revealed will,
by trusting God...in difficult times
and by living in blissful harmony
    with one another.

God also created man that man might enjoy Him
forever by living in happiness
    with his fellow man,
with the environment that God placed him in,
and in a loving-happy-faith relationship of
worship, obedience and trust with God.

God created man that man might share His own
happiness of life, love and dominion throughout
eternity.  Despite our present sinful state,
as redeemed believers, we will yet still share
an eternity with Jesus Christ!

2.  **If God's Purpose Was To Redeem Man...**
    **Why Does God Allow Man to Remain On Earth**
    **After Man Has Accepted Christ As His Saviour?**

    First, let us understand what the word
    <u>redemption</u> means.

    Redemption is the deliverance of the people of
        God from the bondage of sin
    by the perfect substitutionary sacrifice
        of Jesus Christ
    and their consequent restoration to God
        and His heavenly kingdom.

    Redemption is both a <u>remedy</u>
        to recover God's original purpose for man
            [since a sinful man could no longer
            glorify nor enjoy God forever]
    and the means used to <u>perfect</u>
        man's fallen character
        to that ideal state of holiness
    which an all-morally-righteous God
        desired from the beginning.

    <u>Upon redemption</u>
    [man's accepting Christ unto salvation]
    there is "initial sanctification." [Acts 20:32]
    God then,
        in the general course of most human lives,
    desires man to remain on earth to acquire
        "daily or progressive sanctification,"
    that is, to grow in spiritual maturity
        by struggling with the battles and
        temptations of life and Satan,
    through the power of faith and the Holy Spirit.

Sanctification means <u>set apart for God's use</u>. After
initial or <u>positional</u> sanctification, there is
<u>progressive</u> sanctification [John 17:17] and finally
<u>ultimate</u> sanctification when we are completely set
apart to God in Heaven [1 Thessalonians 5:23].

3. **If Through Foreknowledge**
   **God Knows Who Will Be Saved...Why Does He Allow**
   **The Unsaved To Continue To Live?**

God will not allow those who
   reject His saving mercy in Jesus Christ
  and His testimony
     in both nature and the Scriptures
     [general and special revelation]
to share His eternal Life [Revelation 20:11-15].

For now, during the course of this age, and
until the end of even the **1000** year Millennium,
God generally allows the wicked
   [those who have not accepted Jesus Christ
    as their personal Lord and Saviour]
to live out the course of their lives so that:

A. Their early removal, in some cases,
   might not injure the righteous who
   remain [Matthew 13:29,30]. (As an
   example, even "elect" or saved children
   need their unsaved parents, etc.)

B. Those who reject
   God's offer of salvation
   might have full opportunity in terms of
   length of life and testimony
   to believe unto redemption.

C. People are not forced or frightened into
   a false faith from seeing the ungodly
   swiftly drop over dead beside them.

D. Human history has a continuity and so
   that all do not think that God and life
   are so erratic that people die at a rate
   faster than they do already [at 70, 80
   or 90]. Life in itself would become
   more fearful than it already is with sin
   so powerfully dominant in the world.

4. **When God Created Man...**
   **Was Earth Designed as a Stepping Stone**
         **To Eternity?**
   **If So, Why Not Go Straight To Eternity?**

The present earth, good as it was [Genesis 2:1,2]
was to be replaced with a perfect New Earth
    which has no traces of sin.
    [Revelation 21:1 and 2 Peter 3:7-10]

The <u>process</u> of man being tempted,
    allowed to fall into sin,
    allowed to live in a life of suffering.
       of temptation, of struggle...
But with an opportunity for
    salvation,
    spiritual maturity
    growth in faith, and
    growth through self-sacrifice
was <u>apparently</u>
    deemed better in God's eternal eyesight
      [See Romans 8:28]
than that of God creating some type of
    pre-programmed no-free agency,
    non-free will,
    automaton robots
    in the moral sphere.

God apparently desires the majority of Christians
    [those who do not die in infancy or who
    are trusting in Christ just before dying]
to grow in maturity in the spiritual sense,
to overcome, and
to trust Him until death,
in the hope of the resurrection.

5. **If God's Purpose For Man Is To Win Souls...**
   **What About The Majority of Christians**
   **Who Live For Self?**

The Great Commission of Matthew 28:18-20 not
only commands Christians to win souls; that is
"make disciples"...but also to bring these into
the Church ("baptize") and "to teach them all
things which I have commanded."

Thus God's purpose for man goes far beyond only
winning souls. Jesus taught concerning all
phases of living. As an example, it is good
for man to eat, but life is more than eating.
So, too, winning souls is a Christian duty, but
only one part of the Christian life.

It is also a mistake for a verbally gifted
Pastor who is outgoing...to expect everyone
to possess gifts such as his own in equal
measure or zeal. The fruits of the Spirit of
Galatians 5 are not all nor only soul winning.

That so many Christians seem to live for self
only...shows that redemption is not complete
for the believer until "glorification," or
"ultimate sanctification" [Romans 8:30].

That a large number of Christians so live for
self...is certainly a sign of the Last Days!
We have witnessed a deceptive invasion of
worldly music into the Church, a watering down
of biblical standards, a transfer of emphasis
from the Bible to "Christian psychology," and
a growing trend away from dedication to Christ
towards an obsession with self-worth!

At the Judgment Seat of Christ, God will not
reward selfish Christians for acts, attitudes,
deeds, neglect, or for a life of selfishness.
See 1 Corinthians 3:11-15.

6. **What Then Is Life**
   **and**
   **What Is Its Purpose?**

God is the source of all life [John 1:3,4]!

On a previous page we have already discussed why God created man and the purpose of life.

Life is a combination of <u>two</u> parts:

   **Physical** or natural life
   **Spiritual** or eternal life

Man is <u>body</u>, <u>soul</u> and <u>spirit</u> [Genesis 2:7].

   the <u>body</u>...taken from the dust
   the <u>soul</u>...which he then becomes
   the <u>spirit</u>...of life that God gives him.

A. **The Body** [world-consciousness]
   is an instrument or vehicle of the life of
   the soul (Deuteronomy 12:23, Isaiah 53:12)
   Since Adam and Eve...the body seeks <u>evil</u>
   more easily than <u>good</u>.

B. **The Soul** [implies a self-conscious life]
   Plants, as an example, have no soul. Our
   soul is the seat of our affections, desires,
   emotions and active will (Psalm 42:1-6).

C. **The Spirit** [God-consciousness]
   is that part of man which "<u>knows</u>,"
   his mind (1 Corinthians 2:11). Because man
   is a "spirit' he is capable of communication
   with God (Job 32:8; Psalm 18:28). Man's
   spirit is the spring of his inmost thoughts
   and intents (Numbers 5:14, Proverbs 16:18
   and Psalm 34:18). It is the <u>spirit</u> which
   survives the death of the body and which
   goes to be with God.

## Where Are Your Priorities?

It is easy to understand what our **physical** or
natural life is all about. It is something we
can see and experience daily. But what we rarely
take time to consider is that physical life on this
earth is at the most...temporary. Yet, just about
all of our waking moments are devoted to this
aspect of our being!

If you are a Christian...having accepted
Jesus Christ as your personal Saviour and
Lord...just honestly ask yourself the question:

"How much time do I devote
to those things that are eternal?"

If you read the Bible diligently you will find that
the primary concern of the Scriptures is directed
towards spiritual or eternal life for man.

While both unsaved and saved have an endless
existence...the person who accepts Christ as
personal Saviour and Lord has a new nature, This
new birth is the beginning of spiritual life in him
[2 Peter 1:3,4]. This new nature becomes his
immediately upon his acceptance of Christ. This
act opens the door to sweet fellowship with God in
Christ. And most important, it is not interrupted
by physical death [1 Thessalonians 5:10]!

## Believers Receive a Heavenly Body

For the believer...even now he has eternal life!
Unless the Rapture occurs before he dies, his
earthly body will turn to dust.

But although he will be absent from his earthly
body...he will be present with the Lord. Be sure
to read 2 Corinthians 6:8. For an eternity...the
believer will then have a heavenly body.

## Our Temporary Housing

What happens to the believer who dies now?  Where does he go?

He goes <u>immediately</u> to be with the Lord!
[2 Corinthians 5:8]

In the King James Version of the Bible...
2 Corinthians 5:1 reads:

For we know
that if our earthly <u>house</u>
  of this tabernacle were dissolved,
we have a building of God
  a house not made with hands,
eternal in the heavens.

However, the correct translation should be:

For we know
that if **the earthly tent**...

A "tent" is a temporary housing.  Our <u>real self</u> is the <u>SPIRIT</u> within us...<u>not</u> our body!

Death is the "<u>loosing</u>"
    of the <u>temporary</u> tent [our body]
for the putting on of
    an <u>eternal</u> BUILDING [a building of God]!

Wouldn't you much rather have an eternal building made by God than a temporary tent?  We are reminded in Philippians 3:20 that our citizenship is <u>not</u> on earth but in Heaven!  God is not taking our present body and refurbishing it with cosmetic surgery, eye shadow, lipstick and Lady Clairol.  Christ's <u>first</u> body was made by woman [Galatians 4:4]...an **earth-compatible** body.  Christ's <u>second</u> body [and ours] is <u>not made with hands</u> [Hebrews 9:11]!  It is a **Heaven-compatible** body!

When you build a home...the architect first makes a
blueprint.  This plan is followed by the builder.
Because it will become your home, much time and
effort is devoted to this construction...even to
the smallest of details.

However, this earthly home at best will only last
50 to 100 years.  It is temporary.  And yet, you
devote so much time to the building, furnishing,
and maintaining of this home!

Should you not be more concerned about where you
and your family are going to spend an eternity!
Think about this...for a moment.  It may mean the
difference between Heaven and Hell!

### Even The Spice Racks Are Perfect!

She wears a pink lace dress.
She drives a big pink Cadillac.
She lives in a colossal pink mansion.

Her name is Ash...Mary Kay Ash...Queen of the
cosmetic industry.  [Incidentally, the Greek origin
of the word "cosmetic" means:
    "making order out of chaos"!

In 1986 Mary Kay Ash moved into her **19,000** square
foot dream house in Dallas, Texas.  It has:

    5 bedrooms
    11 bathrooms
    A host of other rooms plus 3 kitchens
    An olympic size swimming pool.

She furnished her home with antiques from France...
enough antiques to fill a boxcar!

    The entrance hall is 40 feet alone
    The ballroom has 28 foot high ceilings
        20 foot tall French mirrors
        3 balconies
    The toilets are handcrafted pink marble.

A **$5 Million** almost perfect home...

    Almost perfect
    because when she moved in
    and started to put in the spice racks...
        the spice racks
    are an inch too short
    for her spices to fit in!

How grateful we, as Christians, can be that
    Our citizenship is not on earth...
It is in Heaven...where everything is perfect...
**EVEN THE SPICE RACKS!**

## The Great Disappearance

One day millions of Christians from around the
world will suddenly disappear...being caught up to
be with Christ.  This is called the **Rapture.**

In 1 Thessalonians **4:13—18** we are given a preview
of what actually will occur.

1. The Dead in Christ shall rise **first** [vs. 16]
   We have a natural example of this in nature.
   Ever see how a caterpillar weaves a coffin
           and dies...
   Then, suddenly, emerges as a gorgeous butterfly!

   It was the same creature
           that went into the cocoon...
           but it has been changed...
               from an earthly crawler
           to a resurrected body...
           no longer limited to twigs and trees
               but with power of flight and freedom!

   It was sown in weakness...but raised in power!

2. The Living Believers will rise **next**!
   In 1 Thessalonians **4:17** God's Word tells us:

       Then we which are alive and remain
       shall be caught up
           together with them [those who were dead]
       in the clouds
       to meet the Lord in the air:
       and so shall we ever be
       with the Lord.

We are reminded that we have a **sure hope.**  We know
that believers who have died are rejoicing right
now in Christ.  And claiming these precious
promises we are "...to comfort [encourage] one
another with these words" [1 Thessalonians **4:18**].

## The Choice Is Yours

You have just read the most important challenge of
your life!

The decision you now make will last forever through
an endless eternity.

The decision to:

1. Be only concerned
       with this brief <u>natural</u> life
       will predetermine your future
       and you will spend an eternity
       in eternal punishment in the Lake of Fire
       [Revelation **14**:10,11; **20**:11-15]

            **or**

2. Accept Jesus Christ
       as your personal Saviour and Lord
       receiving <u>eternal</u> life
       and spend an eternity
       with Christ and your saved loved ones
       with **no more** sorrow
            **no more** crying
            **no more** pain
            **no more death!**        [Revelation 21:4]


There is a land of pure delight
   Where saints immortal reign
Infinite day excludes the night
   And pleasures banish pain.

The false and empty shadows
   The life of sin, are past...
God gives me mine inheritance
   THE LAND OF LIFE AT LAST!

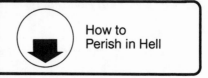
Many people, unfortunately, think life consists of earthly possessions. They spend all their lifetime collecting them... air conditioning, a swimming pool, two cars, a summer home at the shore or mountains...all possessions!

I have heard liberal clergymen scoff when you question them on Hell. They tell their congregations: "Hell is here on earth!" And by so deceiving them...they send their listeners straight to the pit of Hell!

Christ in Luke 12:16-21 reminds us about the rich fool. This man was so successful in his farming that his barns were overflowing. He couldn't get everything in. So, believing that money resolves all, he decided to tear down his barns and build bigger ones. Then he comforted himself by saying:

> ...Soul, you have many goods laid up for many years to come; take your ease, eat, drink and be merry.

But God told him:

> You fool! This very night your soul is required of you; and now who will own what you have prepared?
>
> *(Luke 12:19-20)*

The Lord tells us also about another rich man who was splendidly clothed and lived each day in mirth and luxury. One day a beggar, Lazarus, lay at his door and longed for a few scraps from the man's table. Eventually Lazarus died and he was carried by angels to be with Christ (Luke 16:22).

The rich man also died and was buried. But his soul went into Hell. There, in torment, he saw Lazarus in the far distance with Abraham. "Father Abraham," he shouted, "have some pity! Send Lazarus over here if only to dip the tip of his finger in water and cool my tongue, for I am in anguish in these flames" (Luke 16:24).

But Abraham reminded him that during his lifetime on earth he had everything he wanted; Lazarus had nothing...and it was too late to rectify the situation. Then the rich man pleaded with Abraham to at least warn his five brothers so they could avoid Hell. But Abraham reminded him that God's Word, our Bible, contains these warnings and they could read them anytime they want to.

But the rich man pleaded: "They won't bother to read them!" And Abraham made a very discerning reply: "...If they do not listen to Moses and the Prophets, neither will they be persuaded if someone rises from the dead" (Luke 16:31).

*Lazarus asking for a few scraps of bread finds that only the dogs are his friends. This account illustrates the facts that: (1) no purgatory awaits the righteous; (2) one's destiny is settled in death; and (3) man's opportunity for salvation is NOW!*

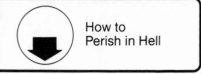
How to go to Hell?

It's easy!

Do NOTHING!   (John 3:18)

Just keep laughing along with the TV comedians who tell you "Well, if I go to Hell, I'll have a lot of company. All my friends will be there."

The closer I get to Christ the more revolting to me become the things of the world. I see how artificial they are. I have watched the late evening talk shows...watched the so-called stars parade in front of millions of viewers grasping for the height of popularity...and it's often like a re-run of Sodom and Gomorrah!

I have watched the TV giveaway programs, the soap operas and I have seen how they have warped the priorities of life in the hearts of men and women nationwide.

I have seen major networks devote one to three hours of prime time to bring to America rock concerts where drug-crazed youth spout out unintelligible ear-shattering sounds in the interest of "balanced programming." Those media personnel who are responsible for feeding this filth will have an eternity to answer for their error in judgment!

It is difficult to find many television programs anymore where sex does not ultimately become a major topic. It is not hard to predict that the X-rated motion pictures of the 1970's will be the accepted TV movies of the 1980's (or before)!

Most people don't want to talk about their future. Young people talk about getting an education. Those who have graduated from college talk about getting a job. Those who have jobs talk about getting ahead. Those who are ahead talk about retiring. And those who retire...are afraid to talk! Because the next step is DYING!

Suddenly all the years of scraping, stepping over other people, remodeling their home, building another home, buying two more cars, taking 3 more vacations to Miami, Acapulco or Tel Aviv...suddenly this does not mean anything anymore! They have come to the end of the road!

That's it! The glitter is gone. The glamour is gone! The jokes are gone! Their friends, for the most part are dead and gone! (As well as the comedians they watched). And there is nothing to laugh about. Hell becomes a reality! And by this time...so calloused they have become...that they fail to realize there **is an ANSWER** to eternal life. But they just can't believe it. So they do NOTHING. And by their inaction, they condemn themself to dying in their sins, in Hell...eternally!

*One day the sands of time will run out for your life. Then... suddenly...in a split moment...it will be forever too late for you to choose Christ and eternal life with Him!*

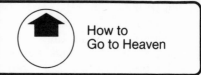
The solutions offered in this book are of no value to you...
until you first come face to face with life's greatest decision:

## WHAT WILL YOU DO WITH JESUS?

Will you state that He never existed?

Will you simply say that He was a good man who did good things...like many other good men?

Will you say His message is not relevant to our enlightened age?

Your decision should not be based on what your friends or relatives say or do not say...or on your own private concept of heaven or hell. These really, in the final analysis, *do not matter!*

What is important...and what will govern your tomorrow in ETERNITY...is WHAT DOES THE BIBLE SAY? In light of God's standards, set forth in the Bible, your final destiny will be determined.

You can, as many do, simply choose to ignore Christ and the Scriptures...go on living your life, doing the best you know how to meet your problems, work to provide an income for your family, set aside a nest egg for retirement...

But THEN WHAT?

What happens when it comes time for you to depart from this earth?

Then WHAT WILL YOU DO WITH JESUS?

It takes NO DECISION on your part to go to Hell!

It **does** take a DECISION on your part, however, to go to Heaven!

> *He that believeth on Him is not condemned:*
> *but he that believeth not is condemned already,*
> *because he hath not believed in the name of the*
> *only begotten Son of God.*
>
> *(John 3:18)*

Whether you are Jew or Gentile, here are five basic observations in the Bible of which you should be aware:

1. ALL SINNED

> For all have sinned, and come short of the glory of God.
>
> (Romans 3:23)

2. ALL LOVED

> For God so loved the world, that He gave His only begotten Son, that whosoever believeth in Him should not perish, but have everlasting life.
>
> (John 3:16)

3. ALL RAISED

> Marvel not at this: for the hour is coming, in which all that are in the graves shall hear his voice.
>
> And shall come forth; they that have done good, unto the resurrection of life; and they that have done evil, unto the resurrection of damnation.
>
> (John 5:28,29)

4. ALL JUDGED

> ...we shall all stand before the judgment seat of Christ.
>
> (Romans 14:10)
>
> And I saw the dead, small and great, stand before God; and the books were opened...
>
> (Revelation 20:12)

5. ALL SHALL BOW

> ...at the name of Jesus every knee should bow...
>
> (Philippians 2:10)

Right now, in simple faith, you can have the wonderful assurance of eternal life.

Ask yourself, honestly, the question...

## WHAT WILL I DO WITH JESUS?

Will you accept Jesus Christ as your personal Saviour and Lord or will you reject Him?

This you must decide yourself. No one else can decide that for you. The basis of your decision should be made on God's Word—the Bible.

Jesus tells us the following:

> "...him that cometh to me I will in no wise cast out...
>
> Verily, verily I say unto you, He that believeth on me hath everlasting life"
>
> (John 6:37,47)

He also is a righteous God and a God of indignation to those who reject Him....

> "...he that believeth not is condemned already, because he hath not believed in the name of the only begotten Son of God".
>
> (John 3:18)
>
> "And whosoever was not found written in the book of life was cast into the lake of fire".
>
> (Revelation 20:15)

## YOUR MOST IMPORTANT DECISION IN LIFE

Because sin entered the world and because God hates sin, God sent His Son Jesus Christ to die on the cross to pay the price for your sins and mine.

If you place your trust in Him, God will freely forgive you of your sins.

> "For by grace are ye saved through faith; and that not of yourselves: it is the gift of God:
>
> Not of works, lest any man should boast".
>
> (Ephesians 2:8,9)
>
> "...He that heareth my word, and believeth on Him that sent me, hath everlasting life, and shall not come into condemnation: but is passed from death unto life."
>
> (John 5:24)

What about you? Have you accepted Christ as your personal Saviour?

Do you realize that right now you can know the reality of this new life in Christ Jesus. Right now you can dispel the doubt that is in your mind concerning your future. Right now you can ask Christ to come into your heart. And right now you can be assured of eternal life in heaven.

All of your riches here on earth—all of your financial security—all of your material wealth, your houses, your land will crumble into nothingness in a few years.

And as God has told us:

> "As it is appointed unto men once to die, but after this the judgement:
>
> So Christ was once offered to bear the sins of many: and unto them that look for Him shall He appear the second time without sin unto salvation."
> (Hebrews 9:27,28)

## THE CHOICE

Are you willing to sacrifice an eternity with Christ in Heaven for a few years of questionable material gain that will lead to death and destruction? If you do not accept Christ as your personal Saviour, you have only yourself to blame for the consequences.

Or would you right now, as you are reading these very words of this book, like to know without a shadow of a doubt that you are on the road to Heaven—that death is not the end of life but actually the climactic beginning of the most wonderful existence that will ever be—a life with the Lord Jesus Christ and with your friends, your relatives, and your loved ones who have accepted Christ as their Saviour.

It's not a difficult thing to do. So many religions and so many people have tried to make the simple Gospel message of Christ complex. You cannot work your way into heaven —heaven is the gift of God for those who have their sins forgiven by trusting in Jesus Christ as the one who bore their sin.

No matter how great your works—no matter how kind you are—no matter how philanthropic you are—it means nothing in the sight of God, because in the sight of God, your riches are as filthy rags.

> "...all our righteousnesses are as filthy rags...."
> (Isaiah 64:6)

Christ expects you to come as you are, a sinner, recognizing your need of a Saviour, the Lord Jesus Christ.

## HOW TO GET TO HEAVEN

I have met many well-intentioned people who feel that "all roads lead to Heaven." This, unfortunately, is false. **All roads do NOT lead to Heaven.**

**67**

All roads lead to DEATH...except ONE ROAD and ONE WAY. Jesus Christ said:

> I am the door; by me if any man enter in, he shall be saved...
>
> *(John 10:9)*

> He that entereth not by the door into the sheep-fold, but climbeth up some other way, the same is a thief and a robber.
>
> *(John 10:1)*

> Thomas saith unto Him, Lord...how can we know the way?

> Jesus saith unto him, I am the way, the truth and the life: no man cometh unto the Father, but by me.
>
> *(John 14:5-6)*

> Take heed lest any man deceive you: For many shall come in my name, saying, I am Christ; and shall deceive many.
>
> *(Mark 13:5-6)*

> Neither is there salvation in any other; for there is no other name under Heaven given among men, whereby we must be saved.
>
> *(Acts 4:12)*

Many people feel they will get to Heaven through the teachings of Bahai, British-Israelism (Armstrong), Buddhism, Christian Science, Jehovah's Witnesses, Mormonism or some of the mystic cults of India or Japan. **But all these roads will lead you directly to Hell!**

There are not many Teachers. There is ONE Teacher, the Lord, Christ Jesus! There are not many roads. There is ONE ROAD...the Lord, Christ Jesus. The Bible warns us:

> But though we, or an angel from Heaven, preach any other gospel unto you than that which we have preached unto you, let him be accursed.

> As we said before, so say I now again, If any man preach any other gospel unto you than that ye have received, let him be accursed.
>
> *(Galatians 1:8-9)*

Understanding this, why not bow your head right now and give this simple prayer of faith to the Lord.

Say it in your own words. It does not have to be a beautiful oratorical prayer—simply a prayer of humble contrition.

## My Personal Decision for CHRIST

"Lord Jesus, I know that I'm a sinner and that I cannot save myself by good works.

I believe that you died for me and that you shed your blood for my sins.

I believe that you rose again from the dead.

And now I am receiving you as my personal Saviour, my Lord, my only hope of salvation.

I know that I'm a sinner and deserve to go to Hell.

I know that I cannot save myself.

Lord, be merciful to me, a sinner, and save me according to the promise of Your Word.

I want Christ to come into my heart now to be my Saviour, Lord and Master."

Signed . . . . . . . . . . . . . . . . . . . . . . . . . . . . . . . .

Date . . . . . . . . . . . . . . . . . . . . . . . . . . . . . . . .

If you have signed the above, having just taken Christ as your personal Saviour and Lord . . . I would like to rejoice with you in your new found faith.

Write to me . . . SALEM KIRBAN, **SECOND COMING, Inc.,** Box 278, Montrose, Pennsylvania 18801 . . . and I'll send you a little booklet to help you start living your new life in Christ.

NAME _____
(Please PRINT)

Address _____

City _____

State _____ Zip _____

# WHAT IS THE RAPTURE

## LIKE ? by Salem Kirban

One of these days MILLIONS will suddenly DISAPPEAR from this earth without any warning "*...in the twinkling of an eye.*" This is called **The RAPTURE!** The Bible, tells us that no one knows the day nor hour. However, God does give us clear indications of what to look for just before His coming for His saints! **We are now in that Time Period.** And this Report reveals how close we are to the Rapture.

*For the Lord Himself shall descend from heaven with a shout...and the dead in Christ shall rise first:*

*Then we which are alive and remain shall be caught up, together with them in the clouds, to meet the Lord in the air; and so shall we ever be with the Lord.*

[1 Thessalonians 4:16,17]

# WHAT IS THE *RAPTURE* LIKE ?

## Table of Contents

> This book is divided into five sections.
> This is the **Second** Section
> ## WHAT IS THE *RAPTURE* LIKE ?

# 1

## THE VANISHING CHRISTIANS

**When Millions Vanish**

One of these days, millions of people suddenly are going to vanish without any warning! And you are going to wonder why!

**Your First Step**

Now in order to understand the prophetic teachings of God's word—one must first believe that the Bible is the literal (true to fact) word of God.

One must also realize that it is necessary for one to accept Christ as his personal Saviour first if he expects to gain entrance into God's Heaven.

It is a false assumption to believe that there are many religions which all lead to the same place.

# Olivet Discourse ... An Overview

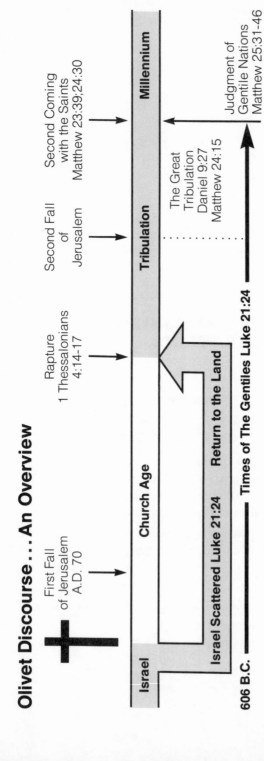

First Fall
of Jerusalem
A.D. 70

Rapture
1 Thessalonians
4:14-17

Second Fall
of
Jerusalem

Second Coming
with the Saints
Matthew 23:39;24:30

**Israel** **Church Age** **Tribulation** **Millennium**

Israel Scattered Luke 21:24    Return to the Land

**Times of The Gentiles Luke 21:24**

**606 B.C.**

The Great
Tribulation
Daniel 9:27
Matthew 24:15

Judgment of
Gentile Nations
Matthew 25:31-46

This is in direct contradiction to Christ's words found in John 14:6 in which He states:

*Jesus saith unto him, "I am the way, the truth, and the life: no man cometh unto the Father, but by me."*

**Deadly Unbelief**

Even the majority of church going people and the majority of clergymen in the world either do not understand God's teachings or simply want to create their own little religion. In so doing they mislead their congregations.

You will find many churches and clergymen who, for example, do not believe that the blood of Jesus Christ has any power to wash away sins. They do not believe in Heaven. They do not believe in the Second Coming of Christ.

They believe that heaven is here on earth and that the world will get better as people become more educated and more mature.

The Apostle Paul understood these conditions which would appear and wrote in 1 Corinthians 2:12:

*Now we have received, not the spirit of the world, but the spirit which is of God; that we might know the things that are freely given to us of God.*

**Education May Not Bring Wisdom**

Naturally, someone who has not accepted Christ as his personal Saviour cannot be expected to understand those things in God's Word which deal with the Second Coming of Christ.

Just because a man is well educated in this world does not mean that he is able to understand spiritual things.

In fact, quite often the opposite occurs. The Bible tells us that in these Last Days there will be people who will be

> *Ever learning, and never able to come to the knowledge of the truth*
>
> (2 Timothy 3:7)

The Bible also tells us in 1 Corinthians 2:14:

> *But the natural man receiveth not the things of the Spirit of God: for they are foolishness unto him: neither can he know them, because they are spiritually discerned.*

Let's assume you are a man of the world. You may be a friendly skeptic. Or you may simply feel that the only life that is going to exist for you is the life here on earth.

Blaise Pascal, one of the acknowledged masters of calculus in the 17th century, was asked why he believed in eternal salvation or eternal life.

In essence his remarks were as follows:

> *Let's assume that I am wrong and there is no life hereafter—then I have lost nothing. On the other hand, let's assume that I am right and there is life hereafter, then I have gained everything.*

**A Definite Blueprint**

God's plan for man is not a hit and miss plan based simply on ideas or theories. God's plan for man is a very definite blueprint which can be substantiated through previous scriptural events which have been fulfilled and can be followed with scriptural prophecies which have yet to be fulfilled.

However, God's plan requires faith on your part. And this is something that many people, although they practice it in their daily life—find it difficult to practice in their spiritual life.

Every year millions of people go on vacation and by faith follow the markings on the road maps when they are traveling in areas they have not previously traveled.

They believe in the road map because this map has been charted for them and shows them things to come such as detours, connecting roads, etc.

**Confirmed By History**

However, man in his finite mind, finds it difficult to read the Bible and discover that God has, in the Old Testament, charted things that have occurred—which have been historically confirmed. God has also charted events that have occurred in the New Testament. And both in the Old and New Testaments He charts things which *will* occur with the Second Coming of Christ, the Great Tribulation, and the Millennial Reign of God's people.

There are more than 300 Old and New Testament Scriptures which promise that Jesus will return to earth. *And these promises will be fulfilled just as literally as the 200 Old Testament prophecies of his virgin birth, death, burial and resurrection were fulfilled.*

# THE STAGES OF EARTH

**ETERNITY** | **THIS PRESENT EARTH** | **ETERNITY**

**ORIGINAL EARTH**

"In the beginning God created the Heaven and the earth." [Genesis 1:1]

**EARTH CURSED MAN SINS**

Genesis 3

**ANTEDELUVIAN**
*Before the Flood* **AGE WICKEDNESS INCREASES**

"And [God] spared not the old world, but saved Noah the eighth person, a preacher of righteousness, bringing in the flood upon the world of the ungodly." [2 Peter 2:5]

**FLOOD JUDGMENT**

"...I will cause it to rain upon the earth...and every living substance that I have made will I destroy from off the face of the earth." [Genesis 7:4]

**PRESENT EVIL AGE**

"[Christ] Who gave Himself for our sins, that He might deliver us from this present evil world..." [Galatians 1:4]

**TRIBULATION PERIOD JUDGMENT**

"Then shall the Lord go forth and fight against those nations...and His feet shall stand...upon the Mount of Olives." [Zechariah 14:3,4]

**1000 YEAR MILLENNIAL AGE**

"...and they lived and reigned with Christ a thousand years." [Revelation 20:4]

**EARTH DESTROYED BY FIRE**

"...the elements shall melt with fervent heat, the earth also and the works that are therein shall be burned up." [2 Peter 3:10]

**THE NEW HEAVENS AND NEW EARTH**

"And I saw a new Heaven and a new earth for the first heaven and the first earth were passed away, and there was no more sea." [Revelation 21:1]

---

## CHRIST'S SECOND COMING

---

**The
Rapture
Explained**

It is not our desire to become theologically deep in our explanation of God's prophecies. The purpose of this book is to very simply outline to you what will occur beginning with the vanishing of millions of people suddenly from this earth. This vanishing is termed the Rapture. Briefly this means the calling up (or translation) of born-again believers to meet Christ in the air at the Second Coming.

> *The first step in God's future plan for man is the Rapture, this is when the dead in Christ will be raised and the living Christians will be caught up. You can read this in 1 Thessalonians 4:16, 17.*
>
> Rapture is not a Bible word. It is an Old English word which means *"to be caught up"* such as 1 Thessalonians 4:17 declares will happen to the believer at Christ's Second Coming. He will be *"caught up"* (raptured) to be with Christ forever.
>
> Christ tells us that when we see certain signs that we can be sure that the end will soon be coming to pass.

Let's look for a minute at God's blueprint on the next few pages and after the blueprint is explained to you, we will go into detail on each facet of God's blueprint.

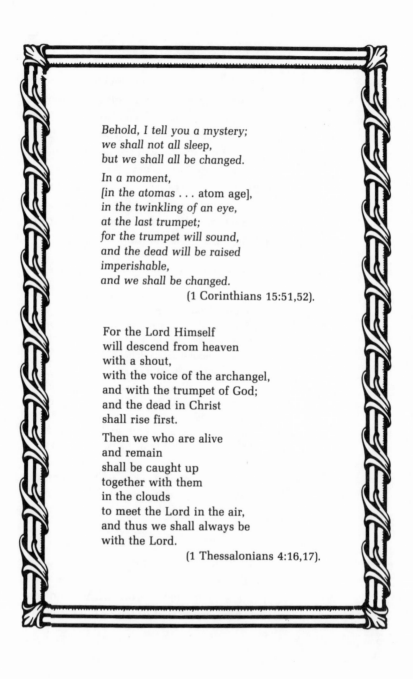

*Behold, I tell you a mystery;*
*we shall not all sleep,*
*but we shall all be changed.*

*In a moment,*
*[in the atomas . . . atom age],*
*in the twinkling of an eye,*
*at the last trumpet;*
*for the trumpet will sound,*
*and the dead will be raised*
*imperishable,*
*and we shall be changed.*

(1 Corinthians 15:51,52).


For the Lord Himself
will descend from heaven
with a shout,
with the voice of the archangel,
and with the trumpet of God;
and the dead in Christ
shall rise first.

Then we who are alive
and remain
shall be caught up
together with them
in the clouds
to meet the Lord in the air,
and thus we shall always be
with the Lord.

(1 Thessalonians 4:16,17).

## AS IN THE DAYS OF NOAH . . .

**History**
**Repeated**

Concerning the Last Days, look what Christ said.

> *But as the days of Noah were, so shall also the coming of the Son of man be.*
>
> *For as in the days*
> *that were before the flood*
> *they were eating and drinking,*
> *marrying and giving in marriage, until*
> *the day that Noah entered into the ark,*
>
> *And knew not*
> *until the flood came,*
> *and took them all away; so shall*
> *also the coming of the Son of man be.*
> [Matthew 24:37-39]

**A**
**Look**
**Back**

Just for a moment, let's look back to the days of Noah as found in Genesis, Chapter 6.

In Genesis: we read:

> *And God saw that the wickedness of man was great in the earth, and that every imagination of the thoughts of his heart was only evil continually.*

God was so disturbed by the situation of the day that He told Noah:

> *And God said unto Noah, The end of all flesh is come before me; for the earth is filled with violence through them; and, behold I will destroy them with the earth.*
>
> (Genesis 6:13)

Are we again living "... in the days of Noah"?

**Ridicule Begins**

One can imagine the ridicule that Noah received when he was buiding an ark in the middle of dry land. You can imagine what the townspeople thought when they came up and questioned Noah and asked him what he was doing. Noah, of course, replied that the Lord had promised to destroy the earth by a flood and that he was building an ark so that he and his family could be saved.

**An Age Of Prosperity**

This apparently was an age of great prosperity and also great wickedness and it was inconceivable among these people of affluence that such a thing as a world flood could occur.

And yet the flood did occur and Noah and his family were saved, and this is the first and last time that God's wrath was poured out upon the world through the means of a flood.

In fact, God promised to Noah in Genesis 9:12-15 that he would make a covenant with him and with every living creature that this would be the last time the world would be destroyed by flood. And the sign of this covenant would be that He would set a rainbow in the cloud and this would remind His people of this promise.

However, God goes on further to relate in other portions of Scripture that there will be destruction on the earth, but it will be destruction caused by other elements and not by another great flood.

In fact, let us look at the comparison between Noah's days and our days.

**Spiritual
Desires
Declining**

There are more and more evidences that we are living in a materialistic world where people are more concerned about worldly pleasures and their own financial gains—than about the spiritual welfare of others or for that matter, the spiritual welfare of themselves and their own families.

# 2

## TRAGEDY AND TRIUMPH

### WARS, EARTHQUAKES AND FAMINES

**Tragedies
To
Increase**

Signs of the Coming of Christ include wars, earthquakes and famines. Christ says in Luke 21:9 that you will hear of wars and rumors of wars. He tells us not to be terrified for these things must come to pass before the Lord comes. He then goes on to say in verses 10 and 11 the following:

*Then said He unto them,
Nation shall rise against nation,
and kingdom against kingdom.* [10]

*And great earthquakes
shall be in divers* [various] *places,
and famines, and pestilences* [plagues];
*and fearful sights and great signs
shall there be from Heaven.* [11]

All we have to do is read our daily newspaper to witness the fact of increasing and more complex wars. We read daily the evidences of famines, the tragedy of great earthquakes . . . man's inhumanity to man and the results of an exploding population.

# The Philadelphia Inquirer

Vol. 320, No. 291 ★    © 1989, Philadelphia Newspapers Inc.    Wednesday, October 18, 1989    Thirty-Five Cents
Call (215) 665-1234 for lower home delivery rate

# Scores Die as Calif. Quake Collapses Roads, Buildings

## Tremor sparks Bay Area fires, postpones Series

By Michael E. Ruane
Inquirer Staff Writer

A powerful earthquake struck northern California last night, buckling bridges and highways, igniting ruptured gas mains and killing scores of people in Oakland, San Francisco and Santa Cruz.

The quake collapsed a section of the San Francisco-Oakland Bay Bridge and rattled Candlestick Park as fans and players assembled there for the third game of the World Se-... The game had to be postponed.

the field and could be seen bein comforted by their husbands. Som were crying.

"It was a bizarre scene with player and fans milling around looking u at the structure," said Inquire sports writer Jayson Stark, who wa in the stadium.

After the first shock wave, the sign for Section 52 of the ballpark wa wrenched so that the 5 was high u and the 2 down low, and some peopl reported chunks of concrete falling from...

On Tuesday, October 17, 1989, a powerful earthquake struck northern California buckling bridges and highways, igniting ruptured gas mains and killing over 60 people. The quake also collapsed a section of the San Francisco-Oakland Bay Bridge. The quake struck at 5:04 PM and measured 6.9 on the Richter scale.

If an earthquake struck New York City thousands would be killed instantly by the collapse of skyscrapers!

The recent devastating earthquakes here once again called to attention how deadly these events are and how helpless we are to combat them.

In this century alone ONE MILLION PEOPLE have died in earthquakes and their attendant floods, fires and famines. And more than 50,000 of the deaths have occurred in this decade with Iran the victim three times. Man has often strived to prevent this holocaust but without success.

In February, 1971 an earthquake struck the Los Angeles area resulting in the death of 64 people. Yet Californians ignore the fact that they live on top of the San Andreas fault that could at any time bring death and disaster.

---

### EARTHQUAKES To Increase

---

Scientists have two theories on the causes of earthquakes. One is that the earth is still cooling down from a molten state . . . the other is that it is expanding. But both seem to agree that there is about 1000 tons per square inch—280 miles below the surface—which is constantly bearing on the earth's thin crust.

**May
Hit
California**

Most earthquakes have been confined to two main zones. One zone runs from New Zealand up through the Philippines and Japan to Alaska then down the Pacific coast of America. Some who have studied

HELP ME, MY GOD! Looking up in the sky, an Iranian girl cries out, "Oh, my God, what happened?" This girl lost her family as a powerful earthquake ruined her village in Iran on June 26, 1990.

the movements of the San Andreas fault in California believe it is entirely possible that part of California could break away in a major earthquake and slip into the sea.

God brought judgment on Sodom and Gomorrah with earth upheavals that produced fire and brimstone. See Genesis 13:10. And it could happen again!

The other zone stretches from Morrocco through Greece and Iran along the Indian side of the Himalayas and south to Java.

The worst known earthquake happened in China in January, 1556 when an estimated 830,000 people died. Other big-killer quakes this century: Japan, 1923, 150,000 dead and $2400 MILLION worth of damage. Chile, 1930, 20,000 dead. Turkey, 1940 30,000 dead.

**Earthquakes Can Be A Sign**

*What does this mean:* One of the first recorded earthquakes is described in 1 Kings 19:11,12. And one of the most remarkable is spoken about in Zechariah 14:5. Another memorable one occurred at the time of our Saviour's crucifixion (Matthew 27:51). Earthquakes are revealed with the introduction of the seven trumpets in Revelation.

Earthquakes serve to remind us that God is still on the throne. They also reveal man's utter helplessness and should awaken him to his need of the Saviour.

This is very clearly outlined in Luke 21:25-28 which reads as follows:

## *Bitter Cold Disrupts Power, Travel, and Life in General*

*Deep Freeze in
the East Goes
Deeper Still*

In February, 1994...those living on the East Coast experienced
the most frigid blizzard weather of the century.   ● Meanwhile,
Californians, having lived through riots, floods, wildfires and
drought, came in for another shock.   It was 4:30 AM Monday
morning, January 17, 1994 when a major earthquake hit the
Los Angeles area...the worst in over 25 years!

# Major Earthquake Hits L.A. Area;
# Dozens Killed, Freeways Collapse

### Power, water out
### in much of region;
### disaster declared

In July, 1993, torrential rains drenched the Midwest. Iowa was declared a disaster area as floods also reached Illinois and Missouri. The West Coast was suffering from forest fires. Drought hit other parts of the country as erratic climate changes created havoc worldwide.

MORE RAIN SLOWS
DES MOINES BATTLE
AGAINST THE FLOOD

IOWA RULED DISASTER AREA
--------------------
Clinton Is Cutting Short A Visit
To Hawaii So He Can T our
the Ravaged Midwest

Des Moines Is Victim to
Flooding That Has Put
30,000 Out of Homes

As flood waters rise in Des Moines, an exhausted volunteer rests.

**Crippled Sewage Plants Empty Into Flood Waters**

**Floods Leave 250,000 Without Water To Drink**

*And there shall be signs in the sun,*
*and in the moon, and in the stars;*
*and upon the earth distress of nations,*
*with perplexity; the sea and the waves*
*roaring;* [25]

*Men's hearts failing them for fear, and*
*for looking after those things which are*
*coming on the earth: for the powers of*
*heaven shall be shaken.* [26]

*And then shall they see the Son of man*
*coming in a cloud*
*with power and great glory.* [27]

*And when these things begin to come to*
*pass, then look up,*
*and lift up your heads;*
*for your redemption draweth nigh.* [28]

**Awesome Power!**

Never before has man had the power to utterly destroy the human race! And this is quite prophetically spoken about in Matthew 24:21, 22 which reads.

*For then shall be great tribulation,*
*such as was not*
*since the beginning of the world*
*to this time,*
*no, nor ever shall be.* [21]
*And except those days be shortened,*
*there should no flesh be saved:*
*but for the elect's sake*
*those days shall be shortened.* [22]

Here Christ is telling us that unless these days be shortened—then man, chiefly through his own destructive creative powers, will kill off all civilization.

And this is all summed up in Luke 21:28 which tells us:

> *And when these things*
> *begin to come to pass,*
> *then look up,*
> *and lift up your heads;*
> *for your redemption draweth nigh.* [28]

## GROWING SIGNS

**With Greater Intensity!**

While these signs have occurred in other days at other times, and while there have always been wars, rumors of wars, famines, pestilences, earthquakes and wickedness . . . it is important to note that all of these signs have never been present before at the same time with such intensity.

In the days in which we live, all these signs are now present simultaneously.

That's why these words in Luke 21-28 are so significant for our day and age for the Lord tells us that when these things begin to come to pass, we are to look up for the day of redemption draws nigh.

## ORDER OF EVENTS

In 1 Thessalonians 4:15-17 we are given the order in which the events at the Coming of Christ for His church will occur.

1. *The Lord Himself will descend from heaven.*
2. *The Lord will shout.*
3. *The Lord will allow the archangel to speak.*
4. *He will blow a trumpet.*
5. *The dead in Christ will rise first.*
6. *The living believers will join the raised ones.*
7. *They will be reunited.*
8. *Then they will rise into the air.*
9. *They will meet the Lord.*
10. *They will remain ever with Him.*

When this event does occur, every unbeliever will be left behind. Those unsaved dead (non-believers) will remain in the unseen world and they will not be raised until 1,000 years later. In the meantime, they will be in constant torment. See Revelation 20:5.

And the living unbelievers will reamin on the earth to face the wrath of God. We will discuss this portion of Scripture in a succeeding chapter.

It might be difficult for some to believe that the Lord will come again and take away the believers.

**A**
**Promise**

But in Acts 1:11 we read:

> ...*Ye men of Galilee, why*
> *stand ye gazing up into Heaven?*
> *this same Jesus,*
> *which is taken up from you*
> *into Heaven,*
> *shall so come in like manner*
> *as ye have seen Him go*
> *into Heaven.* [11]

As you may recall, as Jesus' disciples stood on Mount Olivet with Him that He was taken away from them into heaven.

This was partial fulfillment of John 14:2 & 3 which reads:

> *In my Father's house*
> *are many mansions:*
> *if it were not so,*
> *I would have told you.*
> *I go to prepare a place for you.* [2]

> *And if I go*
> *and prepare a place for you,*
> *I will come again,*
> *and receive you unto myself;*
> *that where I am,*
> *there ye may be also.* [3]

---

## THE SECOND COMING . . .
### How It Will Occur

---

**A**
**Joyous**
**Event**

The Rapture, which will occur when the saints of God are taken up into heaven to be with Christ, is a joyous event. It is termed the Second Coming of Christ.

However, this should not be confused with the latter phase of His Second Coming,

# JUDGMENT DAYS

**JUDGMENT OF UNBELIEVERS**

**BOOK of LIFE**

THE BOOKS OPENED

"And whosoever was not found written in the book of life was cast into the Lake of Fire." (Rev. 20:15)

LAKE OF FIRE

"... the tares are the children of the wicked one; The enemy that sowed them is the devil; the harvest is the end of the world; and the reapers are the angels. As therefore the tares are gathered and burned in the fire; so shall it be in the end of this world."
(Matthew 13:38-40)

1000 YEAR MILLENNIUM

GOLD | PRECIOUS STONES
SILVER

"and I will dwell in the house of the Lord forever." (Psalm 23:6)

**REWARD JUDGMENTS FOR BELIEVERS**

**INCORRUPTIBLE CROWN** (Victor's Crown)
"... every man that striveth for the mastery is temperate in all things ... they do it to obtain a corruptible crown; we an INCORRUPTIBLE." (1 Corinthians 9:25)

**CROWN OF REJOICING** (Soul Winner's Crown)
"... what is our hope ... or crown of rejoicing? Are not even ye in the presence of our Lord Jesus Christ at His coming? For ye are our glory and joy." (II Thessalonians 2:19, 20)

**CROWN OF RIGHTEOUSNESS**
"Henceforth there is laid up for me a crown of righteousness, which the Lord, the righteous judge, shall give me at that day; and not to me only, but unto all them also that love His appearing." (II Timothy 4:8)

**CROWN OF GLORY** (Crown for Service)
"Feed the flock of God which is among you ... (be) examples to the flock. ... And when the chief Shepherd shall appear, ye shall receive a crown of glory that fadeth not away." (1 Peter 5:2-4)

**CROWN OF LIFE** (Martyr's Crown)
"... the devil shall cast some of you into prison, that ye may be tried ... be thou faithful unto death, and I will give thee a crown of life." (Revelation 2:10)

WOOD HAY STUBBLE

"Every man's work shall be made manifest ... because it shall be revealed by fire ... if any man's work abide ... he shall receive a reward ... if any man's work shall be burned, he shall suffer loss: but he himself shall be saved; yet so as by fire." (1 Corinthians 3:13-15)

**RAPTURE**
**BELIEVERS meet CHRIST in the air**

which will be after the Tribulation Period.

There are actually two chief phases of the Second Coming of Christ. The primary phase of the Second Coming occurs before the Tribulation and is the lifting of the saints to Christ in which they will disappear or vanish from the earth in "the twinkling of an eye."

The latter phase of the Second Coming when Christ appears to destroy the Antichrist, occurs *after* the seven year Tribulation Period which will be discussed in another chapter.

**A
Time
For
Judgment**

And while we stated that the Rapture is a joyous event—this latter phase of the Second Coming will be a terrible event when the Lord takes vengeance upon the ungodly and destroys the wicked.

> If you happen to be on earth after the Rapture occurs, then this book will become very important to you. For it will be a blueprint of the events that will take place in the coming days and will reveal the trials and tribulations that you will face.

It will also show you how to rise above these trials triumphantly and be assured of eternal life.

Naturally, your first step should be to read the Bible and put it in a safe place where it will not be stolen or burned for this will become your most important possession and will be your key to eternal life.

## AN IMMEDIATE PARTING

**A Time
Of
Separation**

For when the Rapture (or Second Coming of Christ) does come it will not only separate believers from unbelievers but it will separate husbands from wives, brothers from sisters, and friends from friends.

In just the twinkling of an eye you might discover that your wife is no longer there in the kitchen or you might call your husband's office and discover that he has suddenly disappeared.

You might be on a picnic with your children and in just an instant realize that they have simply vanished.

You might be driving down the road on a turnpike at 55 miles an hour and suddenly see some cars erratically hurtling down the highway, driverless.

You might be flying in an airplane when suddenly the pilot vanishes and the co-pilot has to take over the controls.

You might be sitting in church on a Sunday morning and in a congregation of 500 people, suddenly 30, 44 or 50 people simply disappear from the audience and yet you and hundreds of others are left on earth including the minister!

**Two
Phases**

This is the scene that will occur when Christ first comes back to earth to receive His saints unto Himself. This is commonly known as the Rapture or the Second Coming of Christ.

So that you understand it more clearly, the First Coming of Christ occurred when Christ was born in Bethlehem some 1900 years ago.

**First Phase**

The first phase of the Second Coming of Christ will occur at what is termed the Rapture, when Christ comes to meet born again believers in the air.

**Second Phase**

The latter phase of the Second Coming of Christ will actually occur AFTER the seven year Tribulation Period (i.e., seven years after the Rapture) in which Christ will come to reign on earth for a thousand years with His saints. From Revelation chapter 20 we do know that the length of the Millennium is 1000 years. As previously explained, Millennium is the time after the return of Christ when the saints reign with Christ. This Millennium period will occur immediately after the seven year Tribulation period.

**No place in God's Words does He tell us the exact date in which He will return for the Rapture. In fact, He assures us that no mortal knows nor can any calculate this date (Matthew 24:36, 42)!**

He does give us signs which we have discussed previously in this chapter. In any event, Christ could come in 1985 or 1989 or 2010 **or some other date.** This we do not know.

All we know is that the return of the Lord is imminent! And that we should live as if we

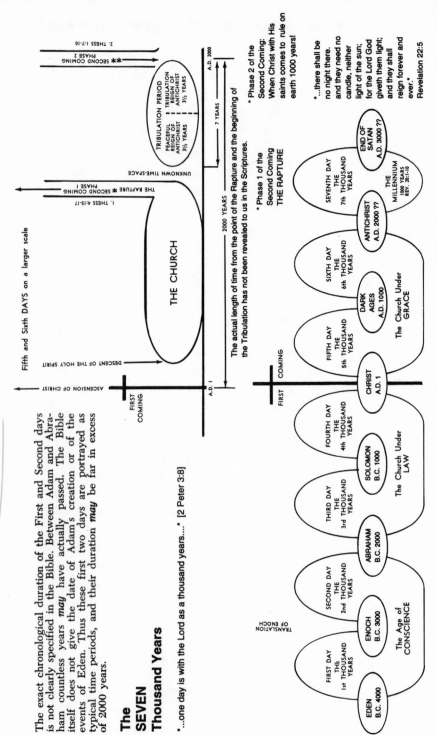

The exact chronological duration of the First and Second days is not clearly specified in the Bible. Between Adam and Abraham countless years *may* have actually passed. The Bible itself does not give the date of Adam's creation or of the events of Eden. Thus these first two days are portrayed as typical time periods, and their duration *may* be far in excess of 2000 years.

# The SEVEN Thousand Years

"...one day is with the Lord as a thousand years...." [2 Peter 3:8]

Fifth and Sixth DAYS on a larger scale

ASCENSION OF CHRIST

DESCENT OF THE HOLY SPIRIT

THE CHURCH

FIRST COMING

A.D. 1

1. THESS 4:15-17

THE RAPTURE ★ SECOND COMING PHASE 1

2. THESS 1:7-10

** SECOND COMING PHASE 2

TRIBULATION PERIOD
PEACEFUL REIGN OF ANTICHRIST 3½ YEARS
TRIBULATION REIGN OF ANTICHRIST 3½ YEARS

A.D. 2000

7 YEARS

UNKNOWN TIME-SPACE

2000 YEARS

The actual length of time from the point of the Rapture and the beginning of the Tribulation has not been revealed to us in the Scriptures.

* Phase 1 of the Second Coming: THE RAPTURE

* Phase 2 of the Second Coming: When Christ with His saints comes to rule on earth 1000 years!

"...there shall be no night there, and they need no light of the sun; neither light of the Lord God giveth them light; and they shall reign forever and ever." Revelation 22:5

EDEN B.C. 4000

FIRST DAY THE 1st THOUSAND YEARS

ENOCH B.C. 3000

SECOND DAY THE 2nd THOUSAND YEARS

TRANSLATION OF ENOCH

The Age of CONSCIENCE

ABRAHAM B.C. 2000

THIRD DAY THE 3rd THOUSAND YEARS

SOLOMON B.C. 1000

FOURTH DAY THE 4th THOUSAND YEARS

The Church Under LAW

CHRIST A.D. 1

FIRST COMING

FIFTH DAY THE 5th THOUSAND YEARS

DARK AGES A.D. 1000

SIXTH DAY THE 6th THOUSAND YEARS

The Church Under GRACE

ANTICHRIST A.D. 2000 ??

SEVENTH DAY THE 7th THOUSAND YEARS

END OF SATAN A.D. 3000 ??

THE MILLENNIUM 1000 YEARS REV. 20:1-10

expected the return of the Lord at any moment—living expectantly.

Realizing this, how much more important it is for one to make sure that he has accepted Christ as his personal Saviour and to make sure that he knows he is saved from death unto life.

**Quicker Than A Wink!**

One of these days the people of the world will be shocked by the sudden vanishing of millions in the twinkling of an eye. The dictionary has defined a twinkle as: *"a split second action; quicker than a wink."*

Just that quick, those who have accepted Christ and are alive will be caught up to meet Christ; but the dead who have accepted Christ will rise first and take part in this glorious Rapture.

In   1 Thessalonians 4:18   the Lord says:

> *Wherefore comfort one another*
> *with these words.*

These words indeed, are a great comfort to those who are believers in Christ. However, they spell the beginning of great terror and tragedy for those who at this point are unbelievers and find themselves still remaining on earth.

It is to you that this book and this chapter are primarily written.

For it is my hope that you will come to know Jesus Christ as your personal Saviour and in knowing Him, will be assured of eternal life.

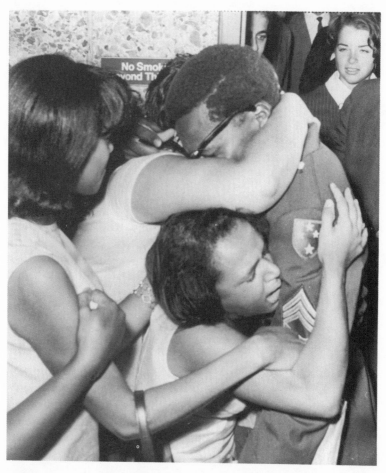

Soldier returns from dead. S/Sgt. James O. Williams is greeted by relatives as he arrived at airport in Detroit. Michigan on a 30-day leave. Williams' widowed mother had been notified by Army officers that her son had died in Vietnam. A telegram confirmed his death. But the next day Army authorities again called to report the Army had made a mistake.

What a wonderful reunion those who have accepted Christ as personal Saviour will have with their loved ones who have "gone ahead" from this earth. And what tragic sorrow and inexpressible grief awaits those who reject Christ. *And whosoever was not found written in the book of life was cast into the lake of fire* (Revelation 20:15).

John 5:24 tells us:

> *Verily, verily, I say unto you,*
> *He that heareth my Word,*
> *and believeth on Him that sent me,*
> *hath everlasting life,*
> *and shall not come into condemnation;*
> *but is passed*
> *from death unto life.* [24]

**The**
**Choice**
**Is**
**Yours!**

The gospel of Christ is as simple as that. Those that believe in Him and accept Him as their personal Saviour will not come into condemnation but will pass from death unto life.

But to those who do not believe, their inheritance will be death and destruction into an everlasting hell.

It is sometimes difficult for one to imagine what will happen when the actual Rapture occurs when Christ brings His saints up from earth to meet Him in the air—prior to the seven years of tribulation for the nonbelievers.

Therefore, I have written the next chapter in novel form simply to show you how these things may occur to one individual. Perhaps, in this novel form it can more graphically describe to you the vivid reality of these events.

# 3

## I SAW THE SAINTS RISE

Bill and I had just finished covering the Presidential conventions. And it was with a sigh of relief that we boarded our flight in Chicago bound for the West Coast.

It seemed as though not a day passed without a major news event and my job as a reporter on the Los Angeles Times kept me running in circles.

There was always some cleric spouting words of peace and some *"funny people"* sitting on top of mountains waiting for the destruction of the world.

One thing I hoped for and that was that my wife would leave me alone and quit pestering me to attend church on Sunday. It was my only day of peace ... and I needed a rest after those two political conventions.

As my eyes closed in a half sleep I could hear her saying, *"George, come on, get up out of bed and come to church with the children and me."* And I would just turn over and say," *"Helen, leave me alone in peace, I see enough hypocrites throughout the week."*

And she would always reply,

*All right, George,*
*I'll leave you alone.*
*There's a Bible by your bed*
  *and the book mark's at*
  *I Corinthians, chapter 15.*

*Please read it and*
  *I'll see you at the Rapture.*

That Helen could be a comic sometimes . . . I thought . . . half asleep . . . why is it every Sunday she had to hand me that same line . . . *"I'll see you at the Rapture?"* Did she really believe that stuff?

As our plane soared into the heavens and the sunlight came breaking through I glanced out over the fluffy white clouds below, stretched out in my seat, and while I slowly sipped a cocktail I mused to myself . . . Rapture . . . what a fairy tale. Why, as a reporter I knew the world was getting better and better . . . new advances in technology . . . heart transplants an everyday occurrence . . . our first rocket ships had landed on the moon and there was talk of a regular commuter service. It looked like Pan American would get the first sheduled airline flights. Why, people were even living longer. At the medical convention I covered just a few days ago they had unveiled their first replacement bank of human parts. I remember viewing long cases of arms, legs, hearts, livers and kidneys. Doctors were talking about the success of their cancer replacement program . . . a program that made it possible to remove cancer ridden limbs and replace them with new ones from accident victims. And for the first time a serum for arresting cancer had proved 100% effective!

In my mind . . . there was no doubt about it. This old world was on the upswing. Why, even people were living longer. And there was talk of discarding old bodies and having brain transplants. This was the 21st century—not the Middle Ages. That's why I couldn't understand Helen's old fashioned concepts about God. She was one of the few I knew and her type of church was on the way out. Most churches had kept up with the times. But Helen's old church keeps singing, *"The Old Rugged Cross"* as though they really believed it.

I remember someone once saying ... *"in unity there is strength."* And this country was sure getting unified. Helen was horrified but I was happy when I covered the United Church Fellowship. It was an historic occasion. Two very important things happened. The Protestants finally acquiesced on some silly old notions they had held on to and united with the Catholic church. And that's the way it should be. They now call it the CHURCH OF THE WORLD. Their theme was *"Heaven on Earth for the World."* It was a marvelous banner and a real thrill to see all the Protestant denomination leaders and all the Catholic leaders join hands on the platform singing their newly written hymn as the congregation of over 5000 clergy joined in ...

> I know thy works, that thou art neither cold nor hot: I would thou wert cold or hot. So then because thou art lukewarm, and neither cold nor hot, I will spue thee out of my mouth. (Revelation 3:15,16).

*Praise God from whom all blessings flow*
*God's in His heaven on earth below*
*Let men unite, cast out all fears*
*For heaven is earth for endless years!*

It was a catchy tune and set the pace for the entire convention ... and that tune spread like wildfire all over the world. Even the President adopted it as the official United States hymn in the interest of world-wide harmony. It was a brilliant gesture on his part!

### New World Leader Elected

The second great thing that happened at the United Church Fellowship in Rome was the election of a new world leader. And in one of the major news events of the year ... a prominent statesman in the United States was elected honorary leader of the CHURCH OF THE WORLD. Brother Bartholomew was a dark horse. He seemed to rise up from nowhere . . . and I can't describe it . . . it was like magnetism. He had resolved the Arab-Israeli conflict and gave the Jews peace. And it was he who had almost single handedly stopped the war in China. The United States had been fighting them for 5 years and it seemed like another Vietnam.

Russia was just about ready to step in on the side of China. Brother Bartholomew secretly flew into China . . . and from what I heard miraculously cured Leader Chou from almost certain death. He walked unharmed through Shanghai. Some even said that he had given sight to the blind, hearing to the deaf and made crippled men walk straight. China had never seen anything like it. And when he returned to the United States with a peace proposal in his hand—the Americans loved him—he could have asked for anything and got it!

> And in the latter time of their Kingdom, when the transgressors are come to the full, a King of Fierce countenance, and understanding dark sentences, shall stand up. And his power shall be mighty, but not by his own power: and he shall destroy wonderfully, and shall prosper . . . (Daniel 8:23,24).

And he did ask . . . and he did get it!

That's the only thing that bothers me. He seems so powerful . . . and yet as I've interviewed him . . . he seems so kind . . . so considerate . . . so dedicated to world peace which he says can only come about through a one world government.

Perhaps he may be right. Anyway he was kind enough to give me the exclusive story about his part in forming the Federated States of Europe and how he convinced our President to join the organization.

With that, the stewardess asked if I wanted another cocktail. I said no . . . which reminded me of dear old Helen again. To her, drinking was a sin. How can it be a sin . . . I reminded her . . . when the cocktail lounge at the United Church Fellowship Building was filled with high clerics all drinking. And all she would say was . . . *"You'll see, George . . . just you wait . . . they're tools of the Devil."*

How ridiculous I thought . . . but why argue with my wife.

It was then . . . as I was half daydreaming . . . that Bill asked me a funny question . . .

"George, do you believe in fly-ing saucers?"

"In this modern day and age, Bill, do you still believe those fairy tales?"

> Then we which are alive and remain shall be caught up to-gether with them in the clouds, to meet the Lord in the air: and so shall we ever be with the Lord.
> (1 Thessalonians 4:17).

"Well, not really, but I've never seen the heavens look so fun-ny. Look way over there at that unusual formation of clouds."

With that I left him to his cloud watching and I went back to my half-dozing day dreaming.

Brother Bartholomew was a man of action. And the people loved him. Our war with China, which he stopped, had seen over 250,000 of our prime young men killed in action. Oh . . . we killed over 2 million Chinese . . . but that seemed like a drop in the bucket.

So it was a real tribute to him and the United States when he was elected Honorary Leader of the CHURCH OF THE WORLD. The people were grateful. And the President in deference to his abilities had summoned us to the White House to make an announcement "of great import to the peace of the world."

I'll never forget that announcement as over 1000 reporters stood on the White House lawn on a warm, sunny day. The President was all smiles. Next to him was Brother Bar-tholomew. TV cameras were everywhere. This was the first time the WORLD NETWORK OF TELEVISION was telecasting. This was a new network that Brother Bar-tholomew had brought about. It was his belief that if all news media could be controlled to send out GOOD, then evil would not prevail and the world would understand each other and get better and better.

Now, why hadn't I thought of that idea? So far the Federated States of Europe had joined the WORLD NET-WORK as well as the United States, Canada and South America.

## A Startling Announcement

And now the President was speaking:

*Ladies and Gentlemen . . .*
  *all of you know how hard*
  *I have worked for world peace.*
*But there comes one far better than I*
  *who has achieved that which I thought*
  *would never be possible.*
*The Bible tells us that*
  *faith can remove mountains.*
*And with us today*
  *is one who I firmly believe*
  *is God's man for this hour—*
  *a Saint on earth—*
  *Brother Bartholomew.*

*Through his good works*
  *he has demonstrated*
  *that he truly can*
  *remove mountains.*
*I am happy to announce to you today*
  *that Brother Bartholomew*
  *has convinced both Russia and China*
  *to join the WORLD NETWORK of television*
  *and to work for mutual understanding*
  *of all nations.*

*Because of his work in China*
  *in ending their war,*
  *and because I feel that the leaders*
  *of the world tomorrow*
  *will be leaders in God's church,*
  *I am directing to be built*
  *within the year*
  *a new 50 story*
  ***World Church Headquarters** building*
  *in the heart of Washington, D.C.*
  *on the Capitol grounds.*

This was the most sensational news of the year! And the reporters scampered to their phones! This convinced me that the world was getting better and better everyday.

I was going to really give it to Helen . . . tell her all about this fantastic new development . . . about world leaders finally recognizing God and asking a holy man to be the leader of the country . . . for the world. This was really heaven on earth . . . and I was witnessing it.

> And for this cause God shall send them strong delusion, that they should believe a lie.
> (2 Thessalonians 2:11).

## A Strange Reaction

But I knew it—that day I rushed home to tell Helen the news first hand—you would think she would have been thrilled. Instead she just sat down on the couch and cried and kept repeating to me,

> George, you just don't understand,
>   you just don't understand.
>   This is the beginning of
>   the END

And I must confess, I didn't understand. How could anyone understand her and her Bible . . . especially Revelation with its trumpets and seals and horsemen . . . what a fairy tale!

How glad I was to be in on all this momentous news as it was happening—great advances in medicine, a cure for cancer, a united world church, a world leader appointed right from the United States and now a world church headquarters right in Washington, D.C.

Brother Bartholomew had confided to a few of us what his next project was and it seemed unbelievable . . . for no one thought that the Jews in Israel would ever find peace. They were constantly harrassed by enemies all around them. Russia threatened to bring their massive armies down and even their horsemen and swallow them up. It was like the perils of Egypt all over again. But over the doorway to

Brother Bartholomew's office was something that was symbolic of his whole leadership.

WORLD PEACE IS HEAVEN . . .
WHERE PEACE ABIDES
HEAVEN IS THERE ALSO

The turmoil of Israel was threatening world peace. And the Presidential conventions conveyed this element of unrest. It seemed that there was no suitable candidate in either party. Both parties appeared deadlocked.

Vote after vote was taken but no standard bearer was chosen. And then I remembered that grand old white haired man stand up at the Republican convention and given a standing ovation. He was one of the former leaders of the Presbyterian Church who was instrumental in bringing his church into the CHURCH OF THE WORLD at the Rome meetings.

Gentlemen,
    It is evident that when man proposes,
    God disposes.
I have watched man after man
    propose a leader for your party
    and for the Democratic party
    . . . and man has not succeeded.
May I be so bold to suggest
    that now God should have his way.
Let's have a new
    UNITED CONVENTION
    of Democrats and Republicans
    and let's give God a chance.
I move that we so do,
    and elect Brother Bartholomew
    as our DUAL representative
    as PRESIDENT of the United States
    and HONORARY HEAD
    of THE CHURCH OF THE WORLD!

I'll never forget that day. The delegates went wild with excitement. And I was amazed as I watched them join hands and circle the auditorium singing "... *let men unite, cast out all fears ... for heaven is earth for endless years.*" And now that convention was over. Brother Bartholomew was elected unanimously. And I was going home. I almost missed the plane. These new supersonic jets carry 1000 people but I was the last one to get a seat. I was happy I had made the late afternoon flight. I would be home shortly. And I had a lot to tell Helen!

### A Sudden Disappearance

Just then Bill shouted excitedly, "*George, look out that window ... I tell you that's not just a cloud. I've never seen the sky so funny looking. It's as though it was opening up ... George, IT IS OPENING UP ... PEELING BACK LIKE A SCROLL ... George, what's happening?*"

And there shall be signs in the sun, and in the moon, and in the stars; and upon the earth distress of nations, with perplexity; the sea and the waves roaring. (Luke 21:25).

He was shouting now ... and I felt embarrassed. But I looked around and everyone in the plane was standing up and pointing with excitement.

And then it happened ... Almost like a twinkling of an eye.

It seemed like the plane got much lighter ... turned abruptly and went into a dive from 80,000 feet high.

I lost consciousness ... I don't remember exactly what happened. There had been two stewardesses standing next to me; but when I awoke only one was there!

I picked her up off the floor and she rushed to the pilot's cabin. When she came out she was ashen white ... and put her hand to her mouth to hold a scream.

Just then the intercom came on and we heard a voice ...

*Ladies and Gentlemen . . .*
*something rather unusual has happened.*
*We are not sure what . . .*
*but please be calm . . .*
*everything is under control.*
*Our pilot has vanished . . .*
*perhaps some mysterious*
*celestial illness.*
*This caused the abrupt dive . . .*
*but your co-pilot now has*
*full control of the aircraft.*
*Please keep your seatbelts fastened.*

Why should that make the stewardess shout with fear . . . I wondered . . . and then I looked around me and she pointed with trembling hands . . .

*"LOOK . . ."*
*she screamed,*
*"HALF OF THE PASSENGERS ARE MISSING!"*

I'll never forget the chills that ran up and down my spine. **HALF OF THE PASSENGERS ARE MISSING.** It wasn't half . . . but it looked as though 100 or so just disappeared. And I turned to tell Bill.

**BUT BILL WASN'T THERE!**

And suddenly it came to me.

**I WAS HERE!**

When we landed, I rushed to my car. Crowds were collecting at the airport because many flights had been cancelled due to crew members not reporting for duty. I got on to the clogged highway . . . clogged with driverless cars . . . was the world going crazy? It seemed as if a multitude of sleepy drivers had all at once decided to stop no matter where they were. Most had pulled to the side of the road; but no-where were any of these drivers to be seen. A train was halfway across a highway!

### Surprise at Home

I just had to get home. Tears poured down my cheeks . . . and a cold sweat engulfed me.

I drove up the drive. Thank God, Helen's car was still there. She was home.

I rushed in the door and shouted, *"Honey I'm home . . . are you all right?"*

No answer.

Again I shouted, *"Helen, where are you? I'm home! Where are the children?"*

No answer.

Frantically, I ran through every room shouting, **"Helen, Helen!"**

And my own voice came echoing back through the empty halls!

And then a voice of the past seemed to echo in my mind . . . "All right, George, I'll leave you alone. There's a Bible by your bed and the bookmark's at I Corinthians, chapter 15. Please read it and I'll see you at the Rapture."

**For the Lord Himself shall descend from heaven with a shout, with the voice of the archangel, and with the trump of God: and the dead in Christ shall rise first: Then we which are alive and remain shall be caught up together with them in the clouds, to meet the Lord in the air: and so shall we ever be with the Lord.**
**(1 Thessalonians 4:16,17).**

"THE RAPTURE! That's it! This is the RAPTURE! And my Helen and my children are gone!"

Quickly I ran into the bedroom and there it was—the Bible was still on the bedstand. I hurriedly opened it at the place of the bookmark.

Hurry, read, hurry, read. I must hurry. Why can't I read? The tears were flowing down my face. My eyes were so filled that the print seemed blurred . . . but I had to read what it said. Time was so precious. Why didn't I read this book before . . . when there was so much time. Why? Why?

Finally my eyes focused through the tears . . . and I read
. . . 1 Corinthians 15:52,53.

*Behold, I show you a mystery;*
*We shall not all sleep,*
*but we shall be changed.*

*In a moment,*
*in the twinkling of an eye,*
*at the last trump;*
*for the trumpet shall sound,*
*and the dead shall be raised*
*incorruptible,*
*and we shall be changed . . .*

It must be true! It must be true! **Everything Helen said
must be true!** That Bible . . . that talk about accepting Jesus
Christ as personal Saviour . . . that talk of Christ dying on the
cross for our sins . . . to give us eternal life . . . that talk of the
Tribulation period. **ALL OF IT MUST BE TRUE!** I was
hysterical, sobbing, kissing the picture of Helen. Then the
phone rang!

That jangled, harsh ring jarred me from my hysteria. With
a crying voice I answered it . . .

"Hello," I said.

"Hello, is this George?"

"Yes."

"George, this is Tom Malone at WORLD NETWORK
TELEVISION. Brother Bartholomew has called a news conference for tomorrow in CHURCH OF THE WORLD Headquarters in Washington. He has some important peace moves
to discuss and also will explain this weird disappearance of
some heretics. I want you to be there to cover the story for us."

"OK, Tom, I'll be there. Goodbye."

And with a sigh of relief, I hung up.

The world was getting better and better. This so called
Rapture must be a hoax. Why did I let myself get excited?
This was God's way of punishing those who did not unite in

a world church—that's why Helen disappeared and her following.

*WHERE PEACE ABIDES . . .*
*HEAVEN IS THERE ALSO!*          **Revelation Chapter 17**

World peace was just around the corner.

I had many questions to ask Brother Bartholomew tomorrow.

But Brother Bartholomew would have the answers!

And that's all that mattered!          **2 Thessalonians 2:1-12**

Unrestrained joy! What better photograph can depict the happiness of reunion with loved ones! Held captive in North Vietnam for **5 1/2** years...Lt. Col. Robert L. Stirm [then 41] is finally free.

In Heaven there will only be triumph forevermore!

# 4

## WILL WE VIEW ALL OF PAST HISTORY WHEN WE TRAVEL *FASTER THAN THE SPEED OF LIGHT* AT THE RAPTURE...

## ?

It is hard to imagine how fast we will travel when we go to be with Christ at the Rapture.   Let us try to set the scene. God tells believers in 1 Corinthians 15:51, 52:

> ...*we shall all be changed,*  [made different]
> *in a moment* [instant]
> *in the twinkling of an eye....*
> [the blink of an eye takes 1/10th of a second
> the nerve impulse causing the blink reflex
> travels at approximately 30 miles per hour.
> In that short a time, **all believers** will leave
> earth to be with Christ!]

You may not realize this but modern technology has advanced so far that in **1/10th** of a second [a twinkle] a microcomputer can process millions of programmed instructions!   If man can do this, should you doubt that God [who created man] can raise [*rapture*] **all** believers both living and in the grave in **1/10th** of a second.

Some refuse to believe the body can rise again because it is contrary to their experience.  Yet someone living in the heart of Africa has never experienced a snow storm but that does not mean there is no snow.  Neither does it follow because we never saw a person raised from the dead, that the apostles did not see it.    [Acts 9:36-43]

Another reason some do not believe in the resurrection [*a coming to life again*] is that it is contrary to the seeming immutability [*never changing*] of the laws of nature. However, one thing these doubters forget is this: The resurrection and Rapture is not to be brought about by the regular action of the laws of nature, but by supernatural powers!

Those who die in Christ, *in a split second,* will be raised, clothed in incorruption and immortality. Then, those believers who are alive at that time, will rise to meet them and Christ in the air! We shall not all sleep but we shall **all** be changed!

For the Lord Himself shall descend from heaven with a shout...and the dead in Christ shall rise first:

Then we which are alive and remain shall be caught up, together with them in the clouds, to meet the Lord in the air; and so shall we ever be with the Lord.

[1 Thessalonians 4:16,17]

**Where fore, comfort one another with these words.**

[1 Thessalonians 4:18]

---

## The RAPTURE...
## An Exhilarating Journey Through Space!

---

Many years ago, Dr. Emil Gaverluk, whose specialty was in science and communications, observed the below possible scenario on the event of the Rapture.

Basically, he suggests that when we are raptured, we will travel so fast, we will catch up with light that has been transmitted through 6000 years of history...and we will be able to view these events on our way to Heaven.

Dr. Gaverluk's suggests that in our raptured state, our sense of sight will be enhanced. We will be able to see in three dimension as we do on earth. However, we will have 360 degree vision. We will be able to see all around us viewing everything at one time.

Light is still a mystery to us. The speed of light is about **186,000** miles per <u>second</u>! It was Albert Einstein who concluded that time would pass <u>more slowly</u> in a space ship travelling at **near** the speed of light. To prove this theory, in July, 1977, extremely accurate atomic clocks were placed aboard a U.S. satellite and sent into orbit. On their return, the clocks were compared with a similar clock at the Naval Research Laboratory in Washington, D.C.. It was discovered that the clocks aboard the satellite had s-l-o-w-e-d down at that speed.

Scientists express distances in space in terms of the fastest thing in the Universe...the speed of light! A beam of light travels 5878 million million miles in a year...almost **6 Trillion miles**! So we describe a <u>distance</u>

as the time it takes light
from a star or some other body in space
to reach us.

This distance is expressed in **LIGHT YEARS.**

## AS WE ARE RAPTURED...
## WILL WE GET A
## BIRD'S EYE VIEW OF <u>PAST</u> HISTORY

**FROM ADAM and EVE,
ABRAM'S FLIGHT FROM HARAN,
MOSES' VICTORY OVER PHARAOH,
THE WALLS OF JERICHO FALLING DOWN,
DAVID'S VICTORY OVER GOLIATH,
DANIEL IN THE LION'S DEN,
JOHN BAPTIZING JESUS,
CHRIST FEEDING THE 5000,
PETER WALKING ON WATER,
CHRIST IN THE GARDEN OF GETHSEMANE,
THE CRUCIFIXION,
PAUL ON THE ROAD TO DAMASCUS and
JOHN ON THE ISLE OF PATMOS**

**?**

## The Moment We Are Raptured
## WE WILL NEVER AGE...
## TIME WILL ACTUALLY STAND STILL!

We have established the fact that **distance** is measured by
**Light Years** and that the time it takes for light to travel in
**one year** is a **Light Year**
[and that Light travels
5878 million million miles in one year].

Now the furthest galaxy we can see is the **Andromeda
Galaxy**. The Andromeda Galaxy, a spiral galaxy like our
own Milky Way, can be seen with the naked eye as a faint
patch in the sky...yet is it **2.2 million light years away.**
Einstein concluded that the speed of light was the
universe's only <u>constant</u> [never changing].

Accepting this as truth, an astronaut traveling at 90% of
the speed of light...would not feel any different than a
person on earth. But, because at that speed, time would
slow down...a clock on the space ship
would take **one hour**
to record **what on earth is 26 minutes**...
because time would have slowed down.

**Therefore, the man in the space ship would be aging <u>at
less than half</u> the rate of earthbound individuals!**

Whether you realize it or not...we are living in a very high
speed world. Our earth is rushing headlong into space.
Every point on the equator is moving at about 1000 miles
per hour as the earth spins on its own axis. On its annual
journey around the sun, the earth as a whole moves at
about **67,000** miles per hour! As our galaxy, the **Milky
Way Galaxy**, spins around its own center, the whole solar
system moves with it, traveling about 492,000 miles per
hour! And the most distant galaxies are rushing away
from our own Milky Way at about **186,000** miles per
**second!**

# 3 DECISIVE WARS

| War | Participants | Occurs | Reason for War | Outcome | Scripture References |
|---|---|---|---|---|---|
| **1** | Russia and Allies (Arab nations, Iran, Germany) vs. Israel | Before or during first 3½ years of Tribulation Period (This could happen at any time!) | Russia desires Israel's vast mineral wealth. | God will intervene and through an earthquake in Israel plus rain and hail, the Russian army will be wiped out. It will take the Israelites 7 years to collect the debris. It will also take them 7 months to bury the dead! | Ezekiel 38:1-39:16 |
| **2** Battle of Armageddon | Armies from All Nations vs. God at Jerusalem | At End of 7 year Tribulation Period | Flushed with power Antichrist will defy God, seek to destroy the 144,000 witnessing Jews and Jerusalem. | The Lord Jesus Christ comes down from heaven and wipes out the combined armies of more than 200 million men. The blood bath covers over 185 miles of Israel and is "even unto the horse bridles." (Revelation 14:20) Antichrist and the False Prophet are cast alive into the Lake of Fire. (Revelation 19:20) Satan is bound in the bottomless pit for 1000 years. (Revelation 20:1-3) | Joel 3:9, 12 Zechariah 14:1-4 Revelation 16:13-16 Revelation 19:11-21 Ezekiel 39:17-29 |
| **3** The Final Rebellion | Satan vs. God | At End of 1000 year Millennium Period | God allows Satan one more opportunity on earth to preach his deceiving message. | Satan will be successful in deceiving vast multitudes (out of those born during the millennial period) to turn away from Christ. This horde of perhaps millions of people will completely circle the Believers in Jerusalem in a state of siege. When this occurs, God brings FIRE down from Heaven killing the millions in Satan's army. Satan is then cast into the Lake of Fire, where the False Prophet and Antichrist are, and they will be tormented day and night for ever and ever. | Revelation 20:7-10 |

---

### WE SHALL BE LIKE HIM...
[1 John 3:2]

---

The Universe is defined as the *totality of everything that exists.*   Yet, being finite *[having measurable limits]* it is very difficult for us to understand the vastness of the Universe and the awesome power of God who created the entire Universe and is <u>in</u>finite *[without beginning or end and without any limits to His power]*

Understanding the above, we can better understand that verse in 1 John 3:2 which promises:

> *Beloved,* **now** *are we the sons of God,*
> *and it doth not yet appear*
> > **what we shall be:**
> *but we* **know**
> that, when He shall appear,
> > **we shall be like Him**;
> for we shall see Him as He is.

This verse refers to the Rapture.   As believers we are <u>already</u> the sons of God.   And when we meet Jesus Christ at the Rapture...our bodies will be transformed to be **like Him**.   We shall have a purified and changed body, with the material elements so transformed as to make them fit for eternal life and immortality.

Realizing the above...that *we shall be like Him*...means that with our **new bodies** we would have **new eyes** with far greater power than our present eyesight.

Therefore, imagine at the Rapture, traveling at faster than the speed of light,  being able to see light reflections that occurred through 6000 years of history and <u>actually being able to view these events</u>!   This may be difficult for you to grasp.   But, remember, the moment you are raptured, your body is **instantly** transformed with **infinite** powers! And 6000 years of history will be but a moment of time!

## WE MAY BE ABLE TO LOOK BACK IN TIME!

Dr. Emil Gaverluk suggests that:

> with our new bodies, our new eyes,
> and traveling at faster than the speed of light
> [186,000 miles per **second**]
> at the time of the Rapture...
> we will actually see the very images
> [on the wave front of light]
> which were recorded <u>at the time</u>
> that particular light bounced off that object.

To explain further, we will reach the first year wave front and see the exact images in 3-dimensional form, that actually occurred last year.   If a loved one died six months ago, you will see that one as you actually saw him six months ago.   Every light image reflected off this earth is out there in space!   Dr. Gaverluk suggests that as we fly upward towards Heaven...we will go backward into history as we move through these wave fronts.

What is a wave front?   Right now, during the day, you are witnessing LIGHT which, in actuality are **light waves**. As we experience each moment of these light waves...the light waves then hurtle through space stretching into longer wavelengths.   The natural invisible waves of radiant energy, such as light, come basically from the sun. Television light waves are 10 thousand million cycles per second.  While the sun's light rays are 100 million million million cycles per second!

As an example, when you listen to a live concert on the radio [100 million cycles **per second**],  you hear the music **sooner** than someone listening in the concert hall!   This astonishing fact is because radio waves carry the sound to your home <u>at the speed of light</u>.   Whereas, sound waves [the vibrations of voices or instruments] take longer to travel through the concert hall on their own.

# VIEWING THE PAST WITH A FORWARD JOY

Do you realize that every light image reflected off this earth is right now out there in space!

Therefore, it will become quite possible that at the **2000 year wave front of light** you will be able to see everything that happened in all the earth at that time including the entire ministry of Jesus, His crucifixion and His awesome resurrection!

Dr. Gaverluk suggests it will be fantastic to go back through Old Testament times and see the prophets, each of them performing before us <u>exactly</u> what they did at the actual time of their life! During the **7** years we will be away from earth [after the Rapture and during the Tribulation Period] the events will come at us *faster* than the speed of light. The reason: our perfect bodies will be capable of receiving all of these new experiences and will become part of our own personal experience.

Imagine seeing the widow gathering a few sticks to make a fire when Elijah comes on the scene...or witnessing Christ at Pilate's hall !

## WILL CHRIST Use NATURAL Laws
## or a SUPERNATURAL Miracle
## To RAPTURE US?

I don't know the answer. However, if Natural Laws were used...quite possibly it may be through the power of the **magnet**. If you had a box filled with 10 nails that were hopelessly mixed in with 1000 plastic toothpicks...it would be quite a job to find the nails. However, if you held a magnet over that box...the 10 nails would instantly [*in the twinkling of an eye*] **jump** to the magnet.

Now our bodies are made up of **CELLS**. Cells are so small they must be viewed through a microscope. Your body is made up of Trillions of cells...which are the basic unit of life! Cells vary in life span. Cells in the lining of the intestine die after a day and a half...white blood cells after **13** days and red blood cells after **120** days. Nerve cells can live for **100** years. Cells, of course, reproduce themselves...some every **10** to **30** hours.

A chemical compound within the cell, called **ATP** [*adenosine triphosphate*], is the electricity that powers your body. This energy is called **electrons**.

*Mitochondria* are rod-like structures that are the powerhouses that produce energy to keep the cell going. This chain of energy may carry **30** electrons per **second**.

When you consider there are **15,000** chains in a **single** Mitochondria...and **50 to 5000** mitochondria in a **cell** and Trillions of cells in your body...your body is fueled with an enormous power of electrical energy!

**IF** Christ chooses to use Natural Laws to call up believers at the Rapture...then here follows my theory.

Since cells are magnetic energy...He could cause the cells of Christians to be magnetically-responsive to His magnetic powers from on high. And instantly we would be drawn up to meet Him in the air! Non-Christians would have a biological reversal so that their bodies would not be drawn by this magnetic force.

If you question whether your body is an electrical force...rub your feet back and forth on a rug and then quickly touch someone. Both you and they will be shocked. Well, this is food for thought.

Man's scientific accomplishments sometimes causes him to boast of his own abilities, drawing him away from God. But all knowledge is God-given and the universe is evidence of His creation.

You can imagine the surprise when one day...perhaps soon...suddenly..."...*in the twinkling of an eye...*" millions of people disappear!   Yet those left on earth will still not believe.  In fact their hearts will be even more hardened against God.

But for believers...it will the ultimate thrill as we leave this earth and soar at unbelievable speeds to be with Christ in Heaven!

## OCCUR?

E

R

U

T

P

A

## WHEN WILL THE R

We are living in an age of change...*rapid* change. Perhaps the very fact that changes are occurring so quickly dulls one's senses to the realization of what is actually happening to this world!  Most of the changes are **not** for the better. They are changes that are preparing us for the soon coming Rapture and the awesome judgments during the **7**-year Tribulation Period.

The word **RAPTURE** refers to the time, just before the 7-year Tribulation Period, when believing Christians [both dead and alive] will *"...in the twinkling of an eye..."* rise up to meet Christ in the air.  See 1 Corinthians 15:52 and 1 Thessalonians 4:14-17 in the New Testament portion of the Bible.

Often I am asked when I think the Rapture will occur. God's Word is very clear that we should not set dates.  In Matthew 24:36 we are told **no** man knows the day nor the hour.   And furthermore...even the angels in Heaven have no idea when the Rapture will occur.  The only one who knows is God the Father!  It is sad that some Christian leaders have attempted to set dates.    This is unscriptural and gives rise to sensationalism.

---

### *As In The Days of Noah...*

---

Our Lord does give us a clue as to the conditions that will be present just prior to the Rapture. You remember Christ said: *"But as the days of Noah were, so shall the coming of the Son of man be"* [Matthew 24:37]. He then allows Paul in about 64 A.D. to tell through his letter to Timothy **what these Last Days will be like.** In 2 Timothy 3:1-7 the world conditions are listed that will indicate the soon coming of the Lord. **And here is the key to knowing the season when the Rapture will occur!**

---

2 Timothy 3:2    *Men shall be lovers of their own selves, covetous*
        **[lovers of money]**
        *boasters, proud, blasphemers*
        **[TV and motion pictures abound in this]**
        *disobedient to parents* **[so evident today]**
        *unthankful, unholy* **[our materialistic world]**

2 Timothy 3:3    *Without natural affection, trucebreakers, false accusers...despisers of those that are good.*
        **[Immorality is accepted as normal behavior today...even among many so-called evangelical churches]**

2 Timothy 3:4    *...lovers of pleasure more than lovers of God.*
        **[It is sad to see so many believers compromising the Word of God so they can enjoy pleasure for a season]**

---

**In giving us these clues...our Lord warns us to:**

---

*Therefore be ye also ready;*
*for in such an hour as ye think **not***
*the Son of man cometh!"*
[Matthew 24:44]

---

---

**What Are Two Of The Most Important Signs
That Occur Just Prior To The Rapture?**

---

## ① AN APPEARANCE OF PEACE IN THE MIDDLE EAST

You may not realize it...but on Thursday, September 9, 1993...you saw Bible prophecy in action.

- The **P.L.O.** recognized the right of the State of Israel to exist in peace and security.

- The Government of **Israel** recognized the **P.L.O.** as the representative of the Palestinian people.

This has great prophetic significance. This agreement... from a Biblical viewpoint...is of <u>far greater importance</u> than the Carter agreement between Israel and Egypt.

While this peace will not hold...it is a pattern of peace attempts between Arab and Jew that will reach its final achievement in the Tribulation Period. Antichrist will be able to make a firm peace between Arab and Jew. He will be hailed as a hero...accomplishing what no other world leader could accomplish. That peace will last 3 1/2 years before Antichrist shows his true colors towards Israel... desecrating their Temple in Jerusalem. Israel will not know true peace until the Prince of Peace, Jesus Christ, returns at the Battle of Armageddon. And the Battle of Armageddon will not take place until the end of the 7-year Tribulation Period!

However, this current Israeli-Palestinian Peace Treaty is setting the stage for what will occur with Antichrist. As believers we should rejoice. For this pattern of peace reveals to us that we are <u>very near</u> to the day when Christ will rapture His saints to be with Him.

# 50 SLAIN IN WEST BANK MOSQUE AS ISRAELI MILITANT OPENS FIRE; CLINTON MOVES TO RESCUE TALKS

On Thursday, September 9, 1993...

- the **P.L.O.** recognized the right of the State of Israel to exist in peace and security.

- the nation of Israel recognized the **P.L.O.** as the representatives of Palestinian people.

This path to peace was suddenly shattered on February 15, 1994 when an American-born Jewish militant walked into the Hebron mosque and killed some **50** men, women and children who were praying.

Eventually, Israel and the Arab nations may achieve an appearance of peace. While this peace will not hold...it is a pattern of peace between Arab and Jew that will reach its final achievement in the Tribulation Period. As believers we should rejoice! For these peace attempts reveal to us that we are <u>very near</u> to the day when Christ will rapture His saints to be with Him!

---

### Suddenly The Pieces of the Puzzle Are Coming Together

---

There is a passage of Scripture in Ezekiel 38:11 that often escapes our attention:

> *...I will go up*
> *to the land of unwalled villages;*
> *I will go to them at rest,*
> > *that dwell safely,*
> > *all of them dwelling without walls,*
> *and having neither bars nor gates.*

Who is making this boast? Russia and the nations in its confederacy! At some future time, the Northern alliance will realize that Israel is dwelling at rest...feeling secure because the world is at peace. Israel relaxes under a series of hypnotizing promises.

Israel today with its highly mobilized army and tight security...how could it ever come to a point where it would be *'unwalled"* without bars nor gates. Arab nations, however, are presently not breathing down her neck. Instead the **P.L.O.**, Egypt, Syria and Jordan are sending signals of peace. Even Russia has mellowed in its contacts with Israel.

Eventually, this will cause Israel to let down her guard... live in unwalled cities. Does this seem impossible? Who would have thought that the Berlin Wall erected in **1961** would suddenly fall **28** years later in November, **1989**! Then there was the birth of Communism that originated in **1917** dominating the Eastern bloc of nations! Who would have thought that overnight...**72** years later...the Berlin Wall would fall down and countries like Poland, Hungary, Czechoslovakia, Romania and Lithuania would gain their freedom! But it happened!

Perhaps at present it would seem to you impossible that Israel will one day *"...dwell safely...in unwalled villages..."*, but that day will come...**maybe sooner than we think!**

---

### Peace Highway Planned

---

The headline was startling!    The *Jerusalem Post* in its
October 15, 1993 edition headlined:

---

**PEACE HIGHWAY WOULD STRETCH FROM EGYPT TO TURKEY**
A highway linking Alexandria in Egypt with Turkey's
Iskenderun near Aleppo, Syria, via the Trans-Israel
highway [Route Six] is being planned by the Housing
Ministry as part of preparations for the peace era.

---

Imagine a highway that will run up the Mediterranean
coast from Egypt...through Israel...through Lebanon...
through Syria and up to Turkey!!!   Is there any Scripture
for this?    Of course!   Read Isaiah 19:23-25:

> *In that day there shall be a highway*
> *out of Egypt to Assyria* [Iraq],
> *And the Assyrian shall come into Egypt,*
> *and the Egyptian into Assyria* [Iraq],
> *And the Egyptians shall serve with the Assyrians.*
>
> *In that day shall Israel be the third*
> *with Egypt and with Assyria* [Iraq],
> *even a blessing in the midst of the land:*
>
> *Whom the Lord of hosts shall bless, saying,*
> *Blessed be Egypt my people,*
> *and Assyria* [Iraq] *the work of my hands,*
> *And Israel mine inheritance.*

This prophecy was written by God through the prophet
Isaiah about **2800** years ago **[800 B.C.]**!   And in **1993**,
the fulfillment of this prophecy is beginning to come true.
Israeli officials are already planning a real highway made
of asphalt with gas stations, restaurants and hotels along
the way!   Its final fulfillment will be in the **1000** year
Millennium!   **But if this is <u>already being planned</u>... can
the Rapture be far off ?**

| **Egypt Will Be In Constant Turmoil** |
| --- |

Another indication of the soon coming Rapture is the ever constant strife that Egypt is now experiencing.

[By the way, when I say *soon coming Rapture*, I am not setting dates. **Soon** could be next week, next month, next year or many years from now. Only God knows!]

Look at Isaiah 19:20:

> *And it shall be a sign...in the land of Egypt:*
> *for they shall cry unto the Lord*
> *because of the oppressors,*
> *And He shall send them a Saviour...*

Could these *"oppressors"* be the Muslim Fundamentalists that are now terrorizing Egypt's population as well as tourists who visit this land?     Muslim militants have as their goal the creating of an Islamic state in Egypt.

Tourist cruise boats along the Nile are escorted by troops manning heavy machine guns in patrol boats.    In the last two years over **300** people have been killed...including **100** police officers.  Egypt's tourism industry once brought in **$2.2** Billion a year but has now been wrecked. Southern Egypt's farmers now carry AK-47 assault rifles with them and rarely stray from house and fields.   The government has offered rewards of from **$8000** to **$12,000** to those who will volunteer information on these militants.  The average monthly salary is only **$50** a month...but few take advantage of this reward money offer...for fear of their life.

Egypt, a moderate Muslim nation, is now fighting for its life against militant Islamic leaders.   By having the **P.L.O.** and Israel sign a peace agreement right in Cairo in February, 1994...they have increased the anger of Muslim militants against President Hosni Mubarkak's government.

The *Hamas* Islam fundamentalists have stated in their covenant:   *"The land of Palestine* [modern-day Israel] *is an 'Islamic waaf'* [holy possession] *consecrated for future Moslem generations until judgment day.  No one can renounce it or any part of it, or abandon it or any part of it."*

*Chief Rabbi Lau with Pope John Paul II.*

**Pope Meets Israeli Rabbi Amid Talk of Diplomatic Relations**
Pope John Paul II met near Rome with Yisrael Meir Lau, Chief
Rabbi of Israel's Ashkenazi Jews on September 21, 1993.   The
Pope endorsed peace moves that could signal progress toward
Vatican-Israeli relations.   Rabbi Shlomo Goren, a predecessor of
Rabbi Lau, denounced this meeting as *"blasphemy beyond
expression."*   The Vatican is one of the very few countries that
does not recognize Israel.   Even the Eastern Communist bloc of
nations has recognized Israel.

## ② ISRAELI and the VATICAN LEADERS TALK OF DIPLOMATIC RELATIONS

Thus far...rapidly accelerating our countdown to the rapture...we see:

- The P.L.O. and Israel signing a Peace Treaty
- A highway planned between Israel and Arab nations
- Egypt in a struggle to survive a militant overthrow and now
- Israel and Vatican leaders having serious talks that will eventually lead to diplomatic recognition.

The *Jerusalem Post*, on the last day of 1993 headlined:

### ISRAEL-VATICAN AGREEMENT SEEN AS DAWN OF NEW ERA

Deputy Foreign Minister Yossi Beillin, who signed the accord for Israel, said that the agreement with the Vatican was difficult psychologically, just as was the agreement with the P.L.O....but he described both as historic breakthroughs.

For over 1700 years, Catholic theology taught that the Jewish people would be perpetually punished for having rejected the Messiah. Catholic leadership encouraged persecution against the Jews from 500 A.D. on. Jewish bankers bore the brunt of the hostility by the world because they charged such high interest rates. Everything Jewish became distasteful to many Christians. Jewish features, language, manners, diet and ritual seemed to the Christian eye offensive. Jews were accused of kidnapping Christian children to sacrifice them to their God and to poisoning the wells. In France, about 1200 A.D. bishops preached anti-semetic sermons.

## Jews Forced To Wear Identifying Badges

Jews were forced to send a representative to the Cathedral at Toulouse each Good Friday. He would publicly receive a box on the ears as a mild reminder of everlasting guilt. In the Middle Ages many Popes forbade transactions between Christians and Jews. Christians were not allowed to associate with Jews, to serve them or to use them as physicians. Catholic hierarchy insisted that secular authorities confine the Jews to separate quarters, compel them to wear a distinguishing badge and compel them to attend churches and hear sermons aimed to convert them. In 1775 A.D. Pope Pius VI added new restrictions on the Jews including the edict that they must not ride in carriages, nor sing dirges at funerals, nor erect tombstones over their dead.

The anti-Semitism of the Catholic church carried over into the 20th Century. An historian reports that "...*in most cases, Pope Pius XII actively collaborated with the Nazis in the destruction of Jews and in most cases turned a blind eye, an unfeeling heart and a silent tongue to their annihilation.*" The Vatican's actions during the Holocaust was only a continuation of its long history of animosity towards Jewish people.

Ari and Shira Sorko-Ram report that in 1904 Theodore Herzl, father of modern Israel, asked Pope Pius X to press Turkey to allow the Jews to have their own homeland. Pope Pius X explained that he would have no part in it because "...*as the Jews did not recognize our Lord, we cannot recognize the Jewish people.*" In fact, in June, 1954, the word *"Israel"* was still taboo inside the Vatican. And in 1964, Pope Paul refused to enter the western Jewish part of Jerusalem.

It was not until 1984 when Pope John Paul II spoke of "...*the state of Israel...a desired security and just tranquillity for the Jewish people, who in that land preserve such precious witness of their history and their faith.*"

## Vatican's Ultimate Goal
## Internationalization of Jerusalem!

Suddenly, on September 21, 1993, the Pope met with Israeli Rabbi Amid.   They talked of establishing diplomatic relations.   Up to this time, the Vatican has been one of the very few countries that does not recognize Israel.

By recognizing Israel, the Vatican hopes it will lead to the internationalization of Jerusalem, rather than it being known solely as the capital of Israel.  Thus, by recognizing Israel, the Vatican would hope to have some influence in this direction concerning Jerusalem's future.   Many orthodox Jews see this as a threat that there will be massive conversion of Jews to Catholicism.

What is surprising is that not a single Protestant denomination [Baptist, Assembly of God, Lutheran, etc.] has officially acknowledged the State of Israel as the homeland for the Jewish people.

The historic moment came on December 30, 1993 when the Vatican's Holy See established diplomatic ties with the Jewish state of Israel.   This agreement suggests that Jews and Catholics are bound in a way that is separate and distinct from any other relationship between Judaism and the rest of Christendom.   The Vatican said its embassy would not be in Jerusalem but in Jaffa.

By special agreement with the Vatican, the status of Jerusalem is to be finally decided by 1999.   The Vatican is seeking to make Jerusalem an international city.

We are presently witnessing a growing ecumenical movement in which major denominational churches seek to compromise their foundational beliefs in order to merge together into one World Church.   This World Church will eventually have its headquarters most likely in Jerusalem. The head of this World Church will be the **False Prophet**.

## After Almost 2000 Years...
## IS THIS THE BEGINNING OF THE WORLD CHURCH?

Very shortly you will be seeing more ecumenical services between Protestant, Jews and Catholics as well as other religions such as Buddhism. The word "ecumenical" means *"universal"*. **The False Prophet** will take advantage of this universal church and act as its leader. He will encourage everyone to direct their worship to the World Leader who eventually will be known as **Antichrist**.

For two years the European nations and the United States took no action when 50,000 women were raped in Bosnia and concentration camps abounded. They took no action when multiple thousands were killed in the war between Serbs, Croats and Muslims. They, and the **UN**, made threats of reprisal but never took action. The problem... they had no forceful leader. This is setting the stage for a powerful world leader. He will be Antichrist.

Two important verses are found in Revelation 17:12,13:

> *"And the ten horns which thou sawest are ten kings,*
> *which have received no kingdom as yet;*
> *but receive power as kings*
> *one hour with the beast* [Antichrist]
> ***These have one mind, and shall***
> ***give their power and strength***
> ***unto the beast."*** [Antichrist]

With the Vatican now recognizing Israel...the last link to the puzzle has been solved. This will lead the way to a World Church that will cooperate with a World Leader. The religious world leader will be able to perform what appear to be miracles even making fire come down out of the heavens to earth in the presence of witnesses. Read Revelation 13:13. In this particular instance, he imitates Elijah [2 Kings 1:10].

Can you now see how world events are starting this fulfillment? Can the Rapture be far off?

# 6

## IN SUCH AN HOUR AS YOU THINK NOT...

In Matthew 24:42,44, Christ warns us:

> *Watch therefore:*
> *for ye know not what hour your Lord doth come...*
>
> *Therefore be ye also ready:*
> *for in such an hour as **ye think not***
> *the Son of man cometh.*

Christ could come in the year 2000. He could come in the year 1995. He could come <u>at any time</u>...even tomorrow! Christ does not expect us to be sitting around waiting for His coming. He expects us to be winning souls and also strengthening saints. Don't listen to those who set dates. It simply is not Scriptural!

For many reasons, we do know that this world is in the same situation as it was during the days of Noah. Think about it for a moment. That was some 4500 years ago! And here we are...4500 years later following the same pattern. What was the pattern of living in the days of Noah?

## We Are Now Living In Days
## That Are Comparable To the Days of Noah!

We find out in Genesis **6**!  Here was the lifestyle:

**1.** Sexual promiscuousness
> [indiscriminately engaging in sexual intercourse]

**2.** Much of the population had evil hearts

**3.** Crime rate was rapidly rising

**4.** Mankind was vicious, degenerate and depraved,
> perverted and morally bad

Think of it!  After over **1600** years of human history [from Adam to the Flood] people were so utterly morally corrupt that God decided they were not fit to live.  Of all mankind during Noah's time, only **four men** and **four women** were spared!  This was an age when men became fathers when they were 65 years up to 500 years of age. **In fact, Noah was 500 years old when his first son was born.**  The Flood came 100 years later!

Now through calculations it is estimated that at the time Noah was building his ark...the human population was over 1 Billion people.  [See page 26 of *The Genesis Flood*] For at least **100** years, while Noah was building this ark, all but **8** people ignored God's warning.

Compare the sad state of the world in Noah's time to the even greater chaos in the world today.  Just look back ten years ago and compare the value system of that day to the so called *"liberated"* value system of today.  It's not hard to determine that we are duplicating the sins of Sodom to a more intense degree.  And while doing so, these so-called world leaders laugh at God.  But their time will come and they will have plenty of time to reflect on their leadership...in Hell!

---

**1.
There Is A Treacherous War To Undermine The Family**

---

In many so-called civilized countries such as the United
States...government programs are designed to tear down
the family unit.

Violent crime has increased **560%**
Illegitimate birth rates increased by more than **400%**
The divorce rate has increased four fold
Teen suicides increased by **200%**
Abortion is legal, condoned by the U.S. government

[In the U.S. alone we have slaughtered
over **30** million babies. To put this in perspective,
that is like killing every man, woman and child
in the **combined** states of Alaska, Delaware,
District of Columbia, Hawaii, Idaho, Iowa, Kansas,
Kentucky, Louisiana, Massachusetts, Nebraska,
North Carolina and North Dakota!]

We have successfully and legally killed them in the
**WOMB**. Now we are quickly drifting to pass Euthanasia
laws to kill them as they near the **TOMB**. And we thought
Hitler was bad. He only killed **12** Million people. Through
abortion alone we have already exceeded that death toll...
killing **30** Million in the name of *an enlightened State*.

And what tragedies has this lack of moral standards
reaped? Currently the annual number firearm deaths
among children ages 5-19 in the U.S. is over **5000**! And
look at this: **270,000** children take guns to school every
day while **160,000** children stay home from school
because of fear.

Today, if you teach your children the Biblical stand
against abortion and homosexuality...this can be judged
as a *"hate crime"* because you are "poisoning" the mind of
your child against the merits of *"alternative lifestyles"*.
This would be considered child abuse.

## 2.
## Heading Towards A One World Godless Government

The United States, which should be the world's leader in morality and spiritual ideals...has sunk to a new low. And much of this occurred **in just one year**...1993. Executive orders were issued to:

1. Lift the ban on homosexuals in the military

2. Lift the ban on fetal tissue research

3. Lift the ban on abortion counseling in federally funded clinics

4. Provide funds for the first time for abortions in military hospitals overseas.

5. Include in a national health plan government-paid abortions...paid for by our taxes.

6. Appoint a Surgeon General who encourages girls when they go out on a date to "...*put a condom in her purse*".

7. Appoint a ACLU activist on the Supreme Court who expressed the opinion that

    A. The traditional family concept of the husband as a breadwinner and wife as a homemaker must be eliminated.
    B. The Homestead Law must give twice as much benefit to couples who live apart as to a husband and wife who live together.
    C. The age of consent for sexual acts must be lowered to 12 years of age.
    D. Prostitution must be legalized.

8. Government plans call for spending up to $7 Billion to reach the nation's 10-19-year-olds to get teenagers to use condoms and accept the *"safe sex"* ideology.

> **3.**
> **We Have Become Obsessed**
> **With The Lusts Of The Flesh**

A study of a current year's television season shows that children's programming actually features **more violence than prime time**:

|  | CHILDREN'S PROGRAMS | PRIME TIME |
|---|---|---|
| Violent acts per hour | 32 | 4 |
| Violent characters | 56% | 34% |
| Characters who are victims of violence | 74% | 34% |
| Characters involved in violence as perpetrators or victims | 79% | 47% |

Finally, after 40 years of denial, despite more than **3000** studies, the TV industry has <u>at last conceded</u> that violence on television **does** encourage violence in real life.
**NEWSWEEK**, in its July 12th, 1993 issue listed
**ONE DAY'S BODY COUNT**
between the hours of **6 am** and **midnight** on April 2, 1993 as seen on ABC, CBS, NBC, PBS, Fox, WDCA-Wash., Turner, USA, MTV and HBO combined:

| ACT | NUMBER OF SCENES | PERCENT OF TOTAL |
|---|---|---|
| Serious assaults [without guns] | 389 | 20% |
| Gunplay | 362 | 18% |
| Isolated punches | 273 | 14% |
| Pushing, dragging | 272 | 14% |
| Menacing threat with a weapon | 226 | 11% |
| Slaps | 128 | 6% |

---

**4.**
**Satan's Final Fling...**
**A WORLD OUT OF CONTROL!**

---

According to a study by the American Psychological Association, the average child will witness **8000** made-for-TV murders before finishing elementary school!   The networks and motion picture producers will tell you that *"violence SELLS!"*.   And, unfortunately...it does.   We have taken God out of our schools and are now attempting to remove God from our homes.   Therefore, that which we are sowing, we are now going to reap!   And our present leadership is not a shining example of biblical standards.   Is it any wonder that God is going to exercise judgment on America...*SOON*!

Throughout the world there is a growing trend towards **HUMANISM**.   Humanism is the theology of the **New Age Movement**.   The New Age Movement boasts of **five** basic beliefs in their doctrine:

1.  **The Irrelevance of Deity**
    Man's cooperative efforts towards social well-being are of prime importance.   God has nothing to do with man's progress.

2.  **The Supremacy of "Human Reason"**
    Man alone can think out the answers to the great questions that confront mankind.

3.  **The Inevitability of Progress**
    Evolution is the answer to man's salvation.   The State is the guardian angel that will control the environment and look after the best interests of man.   [This leads, of course, to dictatorship and Antichrist]

4.  **Science, the Guide to Progress**
    Science itself will be the ultimate provider for mankind.   Science will come up with genetic answers to provide a more uniform, manageable population.

## 5. The Self-Sufficiency of Man

Man is inherently good and is in no need of salvation. Man is autonomous [can function independently] without help from God.

Humanism basically began in Renaissance Italy [about 1400 A.D.] when the principal writers of the Middle Ages made a cult of man's human powers. They revived the works of Plato, Homer, Cicero and also Dante's *Divine Comedy* which he wrote in 1300 A.D.

Humanists have gained control of the educational system in the United States and most of the world.. And we are seeing now what a wild harvest it is reaping! Humanism is a sinister, subtle seduction that comes in the back door while you are at the front door keeping alert for the enemy! Satan has many tricks up his sleeve! Humanism is one of his most effective.

Humanism has infiltrated and captured most of the world's school systems. Humanism is a theology that **deifies** man and **dethrones** God. From Lucifer's fall, to the tower of Babel, the sensual Sumerians, the degenerate Druids, the rebellious people of Israel, the Chinese and Indian cults of confusion, the paradox of Islam...Satan's thin line of conspiracy is centered on one major theme... **HUMANISM!**

Humanism is a system of thought or action that holds that man is capable of self-fulfillment, peace on earth, and right ethical conduct <u>without</u> recourse to God. The fruits of Humanism include **[1]** acceptance of abortion as a free choice, **[2]** encouragement of euthanasia **[3]** abolition of prayer in schools or any public place and **[4]** approval of unrestricted free speech including distribution of pornography both in printed form and on the screen.

Humanism is a doctrine which centers solely on human interests and values. Humanists do not believe in God nor in salvation through Jesus Christ.

**TWO MORE SIGNS THAT BRING US CLOSER TO THE RAPTURE!**

① In the United States and in many parts of the world there is an intense effort to introduce an Identification Card. The President of the U.S. revealed a **Health Security** card that would mark everyone in the U.S. This health program would require that even Christians would be forced to pay *"their share"* to cover abortion costs in hospitals and clinics...giving **HIV** education and counseling on how to use a condom...plus pay for condom distribution in middle and high schools.

② Another sign is the rapid movement of nations to change their money sign towards a One World global currency. Already most countries have a similar blank space in their currency. This space is reserved for the **One World Bank code number**.

## 5
## Seeking The Death of CHRISTIANITY

There is a growing trend to blame the world's ills on Christianity. Because Christians believe in the sanctity of life...humanists consider Christians as a *"risk factor"* to be controlled by government. One clinical psychiatrist wrote in *The Humanist* magazine that Christianity *"is incompatible with the principles of sound mental health..."*

Events that are preparing the way for the entrance of Antichrist and bring us close to the Rapture include:

1. Placing a special spy computer chip in every telephone and computer allowing the Government to intrude on your privacy.

2. Making home schooling illegal.

3. Passing laws that will make Christian activities a criminal act subject to persecution.

4. No holds barred TV where sex acts will not simply be simulated [as it is now] but shown as it actually takes place...including lesbian and homosexual acts.

5. Developing a One World Numbering System which will be hailed as a great move to combat crime.

6. Increasing the police force worldwide saying such a move is the answer to crime. It will become a tool for Antichrist to effectively use. Who will define "crime"? Eventually holding a prayer meeting in your home will be a crime...just as protesting in front of an abortion clinic is now a "racketeering" crime!

7. World leaders who will profess to be Christians but, by their actions, deny both God's power and His very clear commandments, and instead become unwitting tools of Satan.

**6
Because of Man's Sin...
THIS EARTH IS BEING DESTROYED**

Man has not been a wise steward of earth's resources.
And Scriptures tell us that **after**
        the 7-year Tribulation Period,
        the Battle of Armageddon
        and the 1000 year Millennium...
this earth will be purified through a burning process.

Earth depends on **ozone** for its own survival. When
scientists tell you there are holes in the ozone layer...this
has nothing to do with components in shaving cream or
hair spray. What it has to do with is a **lack of oxygen** in
our atmosphere. According to some scientists, **4000**
years ago the oxygen level on this earth was at **38%**.
Today it is less than **18%**...and some cities are down to
less than **7%**.

We need at least **15%** of oxygen in the atmosphere to
survive. This means at levels lower than **15%** a large
portion of the population will be sick. Without oxygen
you get no oxygenization. Without oxygenization you get
cells that cannot be removed from the body and you will
die in your own waste. Ozone is a powerful oxidizer and
removes waste.

Today with **18%** oxygen there is just not enough oxygen
to produce the ozone that we need to protect this earth.

Based on this premise, some scientists believe we will
not be able to survive on this planet in another **40** years
just because of the loss of oxygen. Some **4000** years
ago, the entire continent of Europe was a deciduous
forest. Today there is only a small fraction of forest
remaining. **Unless there are dramatic changes...
that 40 year date would end about the year 2033.**

# 7

## WE ARE LIVING IN A
# CRAZY
## MIXED UP WORLD!

Never before have so many outrageous events occurred that are a clear indication that we are living in the Last Days...just prior to the Rapture. We seem to forget how life used to be. Through Satan's successful tool of **gradualism** we suddenly find ourselves engulfed in an inferno of evil. And the amazing and tragic fact is that our leaders call **EVIL**...GOOD!!!! In the last 20 years our value system has been completely reversed.

### What was once RIGHT

Bible reading in Schools ● Chastity before Marriage
TV programs suitable for all ● Preserving of the Family Unit
Laws that protected the baby in the womb

### ➔ Is now WRONG

### And what was once WRONG

Not allowing Bible Reading in Schools ● Sex before Marriage
Violence and Sex on Television ● One Parent families
Anti-life Abortion Clinics

### ➔ Is now RIGHT

The Tragedy is that these trends have happened so gradually that even Christians are fooled by Satan. Just how many Christians do you know who first lived together **before** getting married months later? Do you grasp the significance of this?

## Satan's Time Is Very Short

Satan realizes that his time is <u>very short</u>. He knows the Rapture is near. And at the end of the **7-Year** Tribulation Period he will be thrown into the Lake of Fire where he must remain for 1000 years! Therefore he is pulling out all stops...making his demons work overtime to *"make hay while the sun shines."* And you are witnessing the effects of Satan's <u>*accelerated*</u> activities right now.

## Is The CHURCH Part of the PROBLEM?

In the last few years, I have spoken in some 400 Churches nationwide. It has given me good insight into how Churches are run. And it leaves much to be desired! In many churches I have been I have witnessed faithful Pastors doing an excellent job and they are to be commended! But in many churches I have found an unbalanced emphasis on fringe programs such as Christian "*psychology*" and the "**I, *Myself and Me*"** theology.

Too many Churches substitute
        **singing** for **substance**.
        **emotion** for **education**.

## Most Church Members Have No Idea of Future Events!

I am appalled at how many faithful members of church congregations are unaware of future events and God's plan **from the Rapture to the New Heavens and New Earth.** In four special messages I give on Bible Prophecy...I provide the congregation with a Worksheet Folder. As I give these four message...they fill in the blanks. By the dual presentation of hearing and writing...<u>it leaves a permanent imprint</u>. I am surprised how many come up to me and say they never heard this before and never knew God's Plan for their future during the Tribulation Period [when they are in Heaven], in the Millennium and in the New Heavens and New Earth.

## Emphasis In The Wrong Direction

Why am I taking the time to give this background?
Because most born-again Church members have no idea what
is going on. Unfortunately, many believers are looking for the
immediate: prosperity...healing and what God can do for
**THEM**. But they are missing the greater and more important
picture...**that Satan is very much alive** and well and becoming
increasingly bolder in these Last Days. It is time for Christians
to be aware of the critical situation we now face. ➤ We are
now the prime **TARGETS** for persecution.

---

## GROWING WORLD CRISIS...
## A SURE SIGN
## WE ARE LIVING IN THE LAST DAYS
## AND SETTING THE STAGE FOR
## THE BATTLE OF ARMAGEDDON!

---

Let's look at the world scene around us at events that are
happening right now. God's Word tells us in Matthew 24:33
that: "*,,,when ye shall see all these* **things**, *know that it* [the
Tribulation Period] *is near, even at the doors!*"

What *things* is Christ warning us about? Just go back to
Matthew 24 starting at verse **5**: He tells us there will be:

1. False Christs [Matthew 24, verse 5]
2. Many wars [verse 6]
3. Nations and kingdoms fighting [verse 7]
4. Famines, pestilences, earthquakes [verse 7]
5. Ye [Christians] shall be hated [verse 9]
6. Iniquity [sin] shall abound [verse 12]
7. The love of many shall wax cold [verse 12]

Now all of the above refer to the chaos that will occur in the
Tribulation Period. But the sad fact is that these signs are
occurring **NOW**! But God's Word tells us in Matthew 24:21
that [and this is the key word] the **INTENSITY or force** of
these judgments will be far greater. How great?

> *"...such as was not since the beginning of the world, to this time, no, nor ever shall be!"*

## Look At These Signs of IMPENDING DOOM FOUR WORLD POWER BLOCS NOW FORMING

If you understand Bible prophecy...you will realize that there are **4 POWER BLOCS** that take part in the Tribulation Period.

**1.** The Asian Bloc
   [principally China and Japan]
**2.** The Russian Bloc
**3.** The Arab Bloc
**4.** The European Common Market Bloc

## 1.   The ASIAN Bloc

What about the Asian bloc?  The vast country of China is now suffering a severe water shortage!  Heaven River in China dried up **20** years ago.  Canals no longer bring water from Beijing's reservoirs.  And it has been longer than **10** years since anyone could afford to fill a rice paddy!

### A Threatening Imbalance

You must remember that China has   **22%**  of the population of the world but just **8%** of its resources and only **7%** of productive land.  In the 1950's farmers in China could secure water in their wells just **16 feet** below the surface.  Now they must go at least **160 feet**!  And now, even the Middle East and Africa as well as the U.S. are experiencing vanishing water supplies!  ■ As we reach the end of our resources the **China/ Japan alliance** will grow stronger.  And their powers of world aggression will again rear their ugly head. ■ This Asian Bloc is now setting the stage for its final formation in the **Battle of Armageddon**.  At that time this Chinese/Japanese bloc will cross the dried up Euphrates River and kill **1/3rd** of the armies on that battlefield [Revelation 9:14-16; 16:12]

## 2. The RUSSIAN Bloc

**The Russian Bear is WAKING UP!** With the fall of Gorbachev many people thought the threat from Russia was dead. But they were mistaken. The Russian bear was only taking a nap. President Boris Yeltsin gave the world a false sense of security. Now we are seeing the real Boris Yeltsin and communism in action. New laws are now being formulated that deny the right of the **21** ethnically different regions to be independent. It would force them to be controlled by Russia..

### What does this mean?

It means the Russian block powers will again be unified. And to control the **21** ethnic regions, force will be used to keep them in line. Already riot police are taking training lessons in a central Moscow stadium while a Yeltsin rival is gaining popularity and seeks to crush the West and the Jews! The Russian bear is waking up. And part of that Russian bloc is **Germany**.

> How soon we forget that Germany was the headquarters for Mayer Amschel Bauer who later changed his name to Mayer Amschel **Rothschild**!

### GERMANY Will Become An Ally of RUSSIA!

There have been **3 Reichs** in Germany thus far. The word **REICH** means empire. ① The **1st Reich** was when the Pope appointed **Otto The Great** as head of the Holy Roman Empire. ② The **2nd Reich** was led by **Otto von Bismarck** [1871-1917]. ③ The **3rd Reich** or empire began in 1934 and lasted until 1945. It was led by an obscure paperhanger, **Adolf Hitler**. With the fall of the Berlin Wall...you saw the emergence of the **4th REICH**.

It is my belief that this **4th REICH** in Germany will finally unite with Russia in her attempt to invade Israel. This could occur before the Rapture.

---

### 3.   The ARAB Bloc

---

In Daniel 11:40 we find a third power in conflict with the
European Federation of States.  This is known as the **King of
the SOUTH**.  This power advances on Israel and sets off a
movement of nations that brings about its destruction.  It
would appear that the King of the South is Egypt aligned with
other Arab nations and, together, allied with Russia and her
allies [King of the North].

---

### 4.   The EUROPEAN Bloc

---

The three alliances...**ASIAN, ARAB** and **RUSSIAN** bloc powers
will challenge the ever growing power of Antichrist.
Antichrist will be the head of the **10** nation **United States of
EUROPE**.  We already are seeing this federation in its final
formation.  And by 1996 they should have a unified currency.

This prophecy is revealed in Revelation 17:12-13, which shows
that these nations that were once a part of the Roman Empire
will gather together and are going to enter into an agreement
to give their authority to one man as their head.  **That one man
will be ANTICHRIST!**   Of course that will not occur until the
beginning of the 7-year Tribulation Period...which comes **after**
the Rapture.   [See Daniel 7:7-8, 23-26 and Revelation 13]

How does **Rothschild** secret meetings in **1773** affect the plans
of the New World Order today?   You will be surprised that
what happened **221** years ago has a <u>direct bearing</u> on events
occurring **right now**!   These events bring us to the brink of the
Tribulation Period.  We can already see the initial forming of
these 4-bloc coalitions as chaotic world events demand a
world leader!

Understanding this...

### Can the  RAPTURE  be far off?

# 8

## HOW YOU CAN TELL
## WHEN THE RAPTURE IS NEAR ?

# WHEN THE SALT LOSES ITS FLAVOR !

In Matthew 5:13,14
Christ tells us that we as Christians are the **salt of the earth** and we are the **light of the world**!   When the salt has lost its flavor *"...it is thenceforth good for nothing..."*

Christians are therefore both **Salt** and **Light**.   **SALT** is essential to life as a <u>preservative</u>.   **LIGHT** is also essential to life as a <u>guide</u>.   Scripturally, when this world deteriorates near a point where it is <u>without salt</u> [Christians] and <u>without light</u>, life on this earth, in God's Plan, cannot continue.   God's judgment will follow.

**What is happening to the Salt [Christians] ?**   In the world's most powerful country, the United States...they are suffering a growing persecution.   Satan is using as his tools godless people who promote abortion, unbridled sex, pornography and abolition of home schooling and the promotion of a humanistic education system.   This is watering down salt's effectiveness in today's world.

**What is happening to the Light [Christians] ?**   We are witnessing churches that once were strong in the faith... wavering towards a social, entertaining Gospel where the major emphasis is on psychology and counseling with only a sprinkling of the Word.   Our light is diminishing from a floodlight to a 15 watt bulb!

| The Most Dangerous Counterfeit |
| --- |

As we near the soon coming Rapture we will witness more and more counterfeit Christians...those that *"...profess that they know God; but in works they deny Him, being abominable, and disobedient, and unto every good work reprobate"* [unfit to do anything good].    [Titus 1:16]

All around us we are surrounded by counterfeit theologies and programs that claim to be Christian.   And too many believers are fooled...thus their value as salt is watered down and ineffective.   Look at the music of the Church. Hymns that spoke of the redeeming blood of Christ are now replaced with religious *rock* and non-memorable tunes.  Most Christians today have never sung such Scriptural hymns as

**The Solid Rock**
*My Hope is Built on Nothing Less,*
*Than Jesus' Blood and Righteousness*

**Blessed Assurance**
*Blessed Assurance, Jesus is Mine!*
*O what a Foretaste of Glory Divine!*

**Since I Have Been Redeemed**
*I have a Song I Love To Sing.*
  *Since I have been Redeemed.*
*Of my Redeemer, Savior King,*
  *Since I have been Redeemed*

**The Old Rugged Cross**
*On a hill far away stood an old Rugged Cross*
*The Emblem of Suffering and Shame*
*And I love that Old Cross where the dearest and best*
*For a world of lost Sinners was slain!*

**I *Will Sing Of My Redeemer***
*I will sing of My Redeemer*
  *And His wondrous love to me;*
*On the cruel cross He suffered,*
  *From the curse to set me free.*

## 4  Reasons The Church Is Losing Its SALT

### 1   THE CHURCH BU$INE$$

Many churches today become obsessed with building programs.  I have spoken in many churches in America, but I have felt more warmth, more moving of the Holy Spirit in a plain, simple church in Macon, Missouri...in a country church on a dirt road in Gypsum, Kansas, in a small rustic church in Fairhope, Alabama and in a very small church in Alford, Pennsylvania.

We recognize, of course, that every congregation needs an <u>adequate</u> church building in which to hold worship services.   And the key word is: <u>ADEQUATE</u>!  But, too often, to meet the expenses of vast overhead both in the buildings and salaries...programs begin to change from a Biblical emphasis to an amusement arcade.  Tickets are sold for assigned seating for musical concerts.  Anything goes from light displays to living Christmas trees.  If it weren't so tragic it would be a circus!

### Even The Words Change

In many churches we no longer even ask people to accept Christ and be **SAVED** [Acts 16:31].   Nor do we dare to tell them if they reject Christ as their personal Saviour and Lord, they will be **LOST** and go to **HELL** eternally!

Instead, we camouflage the Gospel and ask people to make a *"commitment"* to Christ...to *"share your life with Him"*...or *"...have a personal relationship with Jesus Christ."*  Now the word *"commitment"* is a *"safe"* 3-syllable word.  Hardly anyone knows how to spell it...let alone what it means! Is it any wonder that many once solid churches are now filled with *"surface"* Christians...with no depth nor any desire to serve Christ.   Too many churches are becoming social centers...sort of religious country clubs.

And the *"SALT"* is quickly eroding away!

## 2   THE BIBLE BU$INE$$

In the last 30 years we have seen about 50 different versions of the Bible come to market.   In my opinion, this is one of Satan's most clever deceptions.

In 1 Corinthians 14:33 we are told that   *"...God is not the author of confusion."*   But we are now in the midst of confusion.  It began by publishers saying that people could not understand the King James Version.   Then, invariably, they would point out a few pet passages where the English meaning of the word has changed.   However, marginal references could easily have explained such archaic words.

Let me say this:   I don't believe the King James Version was used by the apostle Paul...but I do believe it is the most acceptable...if for no other reason, then for this:

It provides a          **Constancy**
         and a          **Consistency**

in Bible memorization
and in Bible reading.

### And in <u>uniformity</u> there is strength!

Satan detests uniformity in a Christian's life.  To weaken this link of <u>uniformity</u> Satan delights in seeing scores of new translations of the Bible.   Such a "Babel of Bible Versions" spawns an inconsistent, erratic and confused Christian public.  And in such disunity, the witness of the Christian church is further weakened. Some may compare it to Samson losing his hair to Delilah.

**Why all these versions?**   Could it be that the Bible is the world's best seller.  And from a purely business standpoint, publishing another version of the Bible can bring **BIG PROFIT$**.   One thing may be accomplished...it can be Satan's strategy to water down the Salt!

## 3   THE MUSIC BU$INE$$

The superficial church has spawned a superficial salvation and superficial songs. This is the age of Christian *"artists"*. They come complete with staff and back-up musicians and booking agents. And, for a price, they will come to your church.   But most Gospel singers and singing groups carry a big price tag. It is not unusual for a church to shell out **$5000** to a Christian *"artist"* to sing **45** minutes! And you can be assured the church will be packed!

But when the Pastor gives a down-to-earth solid biblical message...those *"music-oriented"* Christians are far off attending another musicale.   Talk about dedication and sacrificial living and this group thinks you are talking in a foreign language.   And do you notice how people clap after every musical number!

St. John Chrysostom, a Greek bishop, in the year **350 A.D.** had been preaching on the need to receive God's truth in the heart, rather than merely agreeing superficially.   It was recorded that:

While he thus spoke, the vain, frivolous multitude broke out in loud applause.

**"For what,"** exclaimed the bishop, **"is this noise?**

I uttered plainly the law which ought to be observed by us, and you cannot endure for a single moment to hear me quietly!

If you will applaud, do it in the market, or when you hear the harpers and actors;  the Church is no theater!"

Next we will be applauding when the ushers come down the aisle to take up the offering!

## 4  THE PROPHET$  FOR  PROFIT

In the last 25 years, coinciding with the growth of religious television, we have seen a growth of self-appointed *"prophet$"*.  They are busy building monuments to themselves and raking in the evangelical dollar.

Their message is usually not one of sin and salvation. Rather it is of self and self-preservation.  Their emphasis is too often not on God but on greed.  They know all the right words to say to give their message a *"Bible flavor"* and prepare the sheep for shearing.

Because they are man-centered instead of God-centered they usually draw very large crowds and are financially successful.   Too many Christians think that big-time success is evidence of God's blessing on a ministry. **This simply is not true!**

Neither Paul's ministry or John the Baptist's could be considered "successful" according to today's guidelines. Both ended up in jail and were beheaded.   The prophet**$** for PROFIT use many approaches to increase both their importance and bankroll.   [And usually, when I expose their unbiblical approach I get letters from donors vowing not to send **Second Coming/*Missions*** another cent]. This is evidence to me how successful Satan is in capturing their minds.   Remember the prince of this world is Satan!  See John  16:11.

Satan would have us detour our dedication and our dollars to self-centered interests...groups that promise *"miracles"* if you come to their meeting and give them your *"first-fruits and pay your vow"*.

**SECOND COMING/*Missions*** is dedicated to getting out the Gospel by way of the printed Word...around the world *"...to the Jew first and also to the Greek* [Romans 1:16]. Your faithful monthly Gift will help us obey this Great Commission and hasten His coming.

# The SALT Is Losing Its FLAVOR!

Salt is extremely essential to life. In the past, men have been willing to die for salt! Wars have been waged over salt! Ancient people were controlled by the use of salt. When Julius Caesar went to war in northern Europe, he took with him not only his armies but also men who would make salt for him!

The Roman Emperors Vespasian and Titus waged endless wars in the Holy Land. Their primary reason was not for religious reasons, but to maintain control of the salt mines near the Dead Sea. Cassiodorus, a Goth administrator of the 5th century [now Germany] said *"It may well be that some seek not gold, but there lives not a man who does not need salt!"*

In Medieval France, salt was so highly taxed that men would risk **15** years of slavery on the King's ships...or even life imprisonment...to try to get some tax-free salt for their families. This salt tax was one of the main reasons for the start of the French Revolution!

In Africa, families often sold children into slavery just to get a handful of salt. Through the beginning of time salt has been a **PRESERVATIVE**! Salt is essential to life! Did it ever occur to you that a baby in a mother's womb is surrounded by a salty fluid. Our blood is salty. Even our tears are salty!

It is not difficult, therefore, to know that we are now living in the End Times **just prior to the Rapture**! Just look at the world around you! Compare it to even 10 years ago. We have polluted our earth. We are murdering babies in the womb by the millions! We have polluted the minds of our youth! We have a leadership who knows the Bible but does exactly the opposite of what it stands for! Wars are on the increase.

## The Next Event...The RAPTURE!

The New Age leaders are having their day. The humanists are having their day. The Planned Parenthood directors are having their day. The Hitlers of today are having their day. The compromising Theologians are having their day. And they are successful in eroding away the very living support or sustenance of their life...**SALT!** Their time is *rapidly* running down. **Their destiny: an eternity in Hell!**

My friend, the late Jim Duffecy, former head of Open Air Campaigners, used to tell this story of an Australian co-worker who was a great soul-winner. This man was originally from Scotland and spoke with a Scottish burr, making a whirring sound with his r's. One day he picked up a hitchhiker and asked him:

*"Sir, do you like to smoke?"* The man replied: *"Yes!"*
*"Do you like to drink, sir?"* Again he replied: *"Yes!"*

*"Well, sir,"* the evangelist replied...rolling his r's, *"I would suggest you smoke as much as you can...3 or 4 packs a day...and drink as much as you can every day! For you are headed for a place where you will no longer be able to smoke or drink...so take advantage of it now!"*

The man was so stunned he quickly accepted Jesus Christ as His personal Saviour.

Do you want to know when the Rapture will occur? God, in His Word, gives us a very definite clue. It is found in 1 Thessalonians 4: 16. Just keep your eyes on the cemeteries of this world. When you see the dead rise...if you are a believer, you know **YOU ARE NEXT !**

*Even so, come, Lord Jesus*

HE THE PEARLY GATES
WILL OPEN
SO THAT I
MAY ENTER IN...
FOR HE PURCHASED
MY REDEMPTION
AND FORGAVE ME
ALL MY SIN !

# WHAT IS
# HELL
# LIKE?

How sad that many people spend their entire life preparing for a few years of retirement. We are alloted about **70** years on earth, yet most of our waking hours are concerned with this small unit of time. We rarely give thought to eternity!

When asked about one's future, many put off making a decision to accept Christ as personal Saviour and Lord of their life. **This Report details exactly what Hell is like.** *It also clearly explains how to get to Heaven!*

# SALEM KIRBAN

# WHAT IS HELL LIKE ?

## Table of Contents

This book is divided into five sections.
This is the **Third** Section
## WHAT IS HELL LIKE ?

# 1

## THE NIGHT THAT NEVER ENDS
### Hell Is The Place Of Eternal Suffering!

**The
Final
Revolt**

At the end of the Millennial Period of 1000 years, many people, as numerous as the sands of the sea, will join with Satan in a final revolt against God and His people.

This vast, extremely vast, army will represent the dregs of civilization still determined that they can achieve a world far better than God in His infinite wisdom.

How often in the past has man sought to take things in his own hands and boast of his accomplishments . . . accomplishments that in reality were possible only because God permitted them.

Not even the abundance of the 1000 year Millennium Period will be good enough for them.

And, unfortunately, these people will not learn their lesson from the events at the end of the Tribulation Period when Antichrist and the False Prophet seek to wipe out Israel. For it is at that time that God intervenes and wipes out a combined army whose size seems to approach some 200 million men . . . leaving a blood bath that will cover 185 miles of Israel! (Revelation 14:20).

Satan on three different occasions attempted to tempt Jesus Christ
and make Christ subservient to himself (Matthew 4:1-11)!

## SATAN BOUND FOR 1000 YEARS

**Antichrist and False Prophet Cast Into Lake of Fire!**

It is at this time that Antichrist and the False Prophet are cast into the Lake of Fire. An angel casts Satan into the Bottomless Pit for 1000 years!

Now Satan is on the march again. Apparently the 1000 years in the Bottomless Pit will not reform him . . . but make him more sinister in character.

Then, for a brief season, the divine restraint will be relaxed. One purpose of this is to provide one last and supreme demonstration of the appalling wickedness of the non-believing human heart!

**The Final War**

With all his men, more numerous than the sands of the sea, one would think Satan would make some dent in his invasion of the area around Jerusalem.

And, were it not for God . . . he could and would. But something unusual occurs!

God causes a spectacular phenomenon to take place.

Here's how the Bible describes it:

> . . . fire came down from God out of Heaven, and devoured them!
>
> (Revelation 20:9)

Think of it! Multiple thousands, in fact millions of people, in a flashing moment, are suddenly consumed by fire that came thundering down from Heaven.

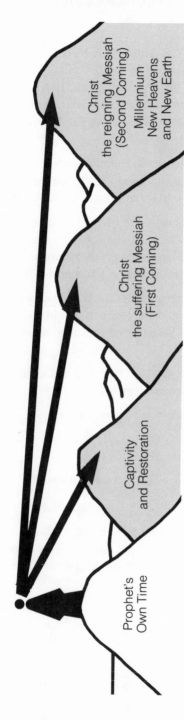

Christ
the reigning Messiah
(Second Coming)

Millennium
New Heavens
and New Earth

Christ
the suffering Messiah
(First Coming)

Captivity
and Restoration

Prophet's
Own Time

## Time Period Views of The Prophets
The prophets had a twofold ministry. They exposed the sins of their own time. They also revealed the future (as God revealed it to them).

When reading the Books written by the 16 prophets (Isaiah through Malachi) this Chart will help you understand the scope of time periods referred to by the prophet.

## SATAN BROUGHT SIN INTO THE WORLD

**The
Final
Defeat**

Where did it all begin? It began after Genesis 1:31 which reads:

> And God saw every thing that he had made, and behold, it was very good. . . .
> (Genesis 1:31)

It was after this that the fall of Satan must have taken place. It was Satan who caused the fall of the human race.

Read Genesis 3. And God predicted His judgment in Eden in Genesis 3:15 and this was accomplished on the cross (John 12:31-33).

**Satan's
Inheritance**

Satan's power was second only to God. What was Satan's inheritance? God tells us in Ezekiel 28:11-19 when He here speaks to the wicked King of Tyre who is indwelt by Satan as was Judas (John 13:27). Hence God's words here are aimed directly at Satan.

> You were in Eden, the garden of God; every precious stone was your covering . . .
>
> You were the annointed cherub . . .
>
> You were blameless in your ways from the day you were created, until iniquity and guilt were found in you. . . .
>
> . . . you were filled with lawlessness and violence . . . your heart was very proud . . . you corrupted your wisdom for the sake of your splendor. I cast you to the ground; I lay you before kings that they might gaze at you.
>
> You have profaned your sanctuaries by the multitude of your iniquities . . . Therefore I have brought forth a fire from your midst; it has consumed you, and I have reduced you to ashes upon the earth in the sight of all who looked at you. . . .
>
> . . . you have come to a horrible end and shall never return to being . . .
> (Ezekiel 28:13-19)

# Two Different "Gog and Magogs"

## Final Rebellion

In Ezekiel 38:1–39:16 we read of Gog and Magog (38:2) coming out of the **north** to invade Israel. God intervenes and miraculously saves Israel from the Russian invasion. The Gog and Magog war of Ezekiel 38:1–39:16 is an **anti-Israel** invasion from the **north**.

The Gog and Magog of Revelation 20:7-10 is an **anti-Christ** onslaught by people gathered **from all over the earth**. They are not the same events.

Thus the names "Gog and Magog" come to represent any large assemblage of people who wickedly war against God and who are suddenly destroyed by Him. Compare Isaiah 1:10.

## SATAN'S CRUSHED HOPES

**Satan
Never
Satisfied!**

Ezekiel 28:16 is quite prophetic of today's world . . . especially the phrase that says, "you were filled with lawlessness and violence . . ." Isn't this a picture of our condition right now!

Now that we have examined the exalted position Satan once had . . . we can now go further into his judgment by God. This is the end of the line for Satan . . . and for his followers. For God's judgment in the form of fire from above consumes them. And as related in Ezekiel 28:19 . . . "you have come to a horrible end. . . ."

With Satan, the originator of sin, not satisfied to be second to Christ in majesty and glory . . . but seeking to rebel against God and "exalt my throne *above* the stars of God . . . is it any wonder the world today defies and denies God?

And can you now see why that God, through Solomon, wrote:

> . . . there is no new thing under the sun.
> (Ecclesiastes 1:9)

So Satan's ambitions, generated early in the earth's beginnings and nurtured through all time until the end of the 1000 year Millennial Period . . . are finally once and for all CRUSHED by God. In one swift judgment—related in just 12 short words—God, in effect, says to Satan's ambitions, "Satan, THIS IS THE END!" Just 12 words crush Satan's hopes:

> . . . and fire came down from God out of Heaven, and devoured them.
> (Revelation 20:9)

# THE RESURRECTIONS

**Heaven**

Resurrection and Ascension of Christ into Heaven
(Matthew 27:52-53 tells of others who were resurrected after Christ—these were the wave-sheaf of the harvest to come. Leviticus 23:10-11.)

Acts 1:1-11
Matthew 27:50-53

**Paradise**

Believers who have died before the Rapture. Present in a celestial, spiritual body.*

"And Jesus said unto him, Verily I say unto thee, Today shalt thou be with me in paradise."
Luke 23:43

"We are confident, I say, and willing rather to be absent from the body, and to be present with the Lord."
2 Corinthians 5:8

Believers meet with Christ in the air
1 Thessalonians 4:16

"...the dead in Christ shall rise First..."

"Then we which are alive and remain shall be caught up together with them in the clouds to meet the Lord in the air...." 1 Thessalonians 4:16-17

**Judgment Seat of Christ**

"For we must all appear before the judgment seat of Christ...."
2 Corinthians 5:10
Believers now in New Bodies
Philippians 3:20-21

Resurrection of Tribulation Saints
Daniel 12:1-2

Marriage of the Lamb
Revelation 19:7-9

Christ Returns to Earth with His Saints
1 Thessalonians 3:13; Zechariah 14:4

"And I saw the dead, small and great, stand before God; and the books were opened: and another book was opened, which is the book of life: and the dead were judged out of those things which were written in the books, according to their works.
And the sea gave up the dead which were in it; and death and hell delivered up the dead which were in them: and they were judged every man according to their works."
Revelation 20:12-13

**Great White Throne**

"And whosoever was not found written in the Book of Life was cast into the Lake of Fire."
Revelation 20:15

Unbelievers cast into Lake of Fire eternally

Resurrection of the Dead Unbelievers
Revelation 20:11-13; Jude 6

| About A.D. 30 | This Present Age | A.D.? | Rapture | Seven Year Tribulation Period | Mount of Olives Armageddon | 1000 Year Millennial Age | With Satan Antichrist and False Prophet |

*Physical body remains in grave awaiting Rapture

# 2

## THE MOST TRAGIC MOMENT
## OF TOMORROW
### The Saddest Roll Call In History

**Even
The Devils
Believe!**

What happens next?

Is Satan dead? Are his millions of followers dead and forgotten? No. Their harvest of sin has been sown. Now is the time they will reap their "rewards."

**First** God takes care of Satan whose deception caused millions to abandon Christ.

> And the devil (Satan) that deceived them was cast into the Lake of Fire and Brimstone, where the beast (Antichrist) and the false prophet are, and shall be tormented day and night for ever and ever.
> (Revelation 20:10)

There are some who will read this passage and laugh. "Thrown into the Lake of Fire . . . what a fairy tale . . . an allegory . . . surely a God of love could not do this . . . and how can one be tormented day and night forever and ever?"

Perhaps you, as mere man, don't believe. But think about this for a moment, Satan and his angels believe! Turn to James 2:19

> . . . the devils also believe and tremble.
> (James 2:19)

If Satan and his angels believe . . . and in believing . . . tremble . . . should you any less believe that when God says something . . . He means it!

Satan is thus judged and cast into the Lake of Fire with Antichrist and the False Prophet who have already been there a 1000 years.

**179**

## LIFE'S MOST TRAGIC MOMENT!

**The
Great
White Throne**

Now comes the most tragic moment of this world.

> Then I saw a great white throne and the One Who was seated upon it, from Whose presence and from the sight of Whose face earth and sky fled away and no place was found for them.
>
> (Revelation 20:11)

Apparently the awesomeness of this occasion is so tragic it is hard for anyone to fully comprehend . . . "the earth and sky" even flee from it.

In your study of the Scripture you may recall that at the start of the Tribulation Period a throne of judgment was set in Heaven. Of this throne we read,

> . . . and there was a rainbow round about the throne. . . .
>
> (Revelation 4:3)

The significance of the **rainbow** about this throne is that in the midst of the seven years of Tribulation judgments, God will show mercy and many will be saved (Revelation 7 shows this to be so). This is the **Judgment Seat of Christ** for **believers.** So Genesis 9:11-13 shows the bow to be the sign of God's covenant that He will not again destroy all flesh.

But to the **unbelievers** . . . when their time of judgment comes before God, God sits on his **Great White Throne** and *no rainbow* encircles the Throne! It will be a most frightening occasion —far more frightening than anything man could conjure.

The throne is pure WHITE representing God's absolute Holiness! Its glistening whiteness cries out in judgment against all sin and sinners.

## NEITHER MONEY NOR GOOD WORKS
## WILL BUY YOUR WAY INTO HEAVEN!

**The
Saddest
Roll Call
In
History!**

Sin needs to be put away! Sinners must be punished. The WHITE THRONE cries out with Holiness and Justice against sinful mankind. Oh, the stark terror of those who are here before this Throne, for they would not turn to God so that in mercy Christ's sacrificial blood could have washed their sins away. Now it is too late! And the Throne is all White and **there is no rainbow.** The time for judgment has arrived!

> *And I saw the dead, small and great, stand before God; and the books were opened: and another book was opened, which is the book of life: and the dead were judged out of those things which were written in the books according to their works.*
>
> *And the sea give up the dead which were in it; and death and hell delivered up the dead which were in them: and they were judged every man according to their works.*
> (Revelation 20:12, 13)

**Here is the saddest roll call in history!** No matter how poor or how rich you are in today's world . . . money does *not* buy your way into Heaven . . . no more so than good works!

And both small and great now have to give an accounting of themselves—the small and the great who did not accept Jesus Christ as personal Saviour and Lord in their heart!

## THE RESURRECTION OF JUDGMENT

**Resurrection Of The Lost!**

This resurrection after the 1000 year Millennial Period is called the **Resurrection of the LOST.** The Christians—those who have accepted Christ—are NOT dead at this time. They were raised at the Rapture prior to the 7 year Tribulation Period. That was called the **First Resurrection.** This Resurrection of the Lost is called the **Second Resurrection.**

That is why Christ says:

> Blessed and holy is he that hath part in the first resurrection: on such the second death hath no power. . . .
>
> (Revelation 20:6)

Thus the unsaved DEAD (and these are the only people who are dead at this time) are raised up from the dead! This includes the millions who were consumed by fire in their rebellion against God immediately after the 1000 year Millennial Period!

It does not include Satan, however, who was immediately after this Period, thrown into the Lake of Fire.

## ALL UNBELIEVERS WILL GO TO HELL

**Judged
By
God**

This **Great White Throne Judgment** seals the eternal separation of the unsaved wicked from God. Note that in Revelation 20:13 we are told that every man was judged according to his works.

**First, keep this in mind, all the unbelievers will go to Hell! None will go to Heaven!**

But all unbelievers will not receive the same punishment. Their punishment will be eternal, forever and forever, but the degree of punishment will vary with each individual . . . according to his works! Christ relates this truth through Luke in the form of a parable when He says:

> The Master . . . will come on a day when he does not expect him and at an hour of which he does not know, and will punish him and cut him off and assign his lot with the unfaithful.
>
> And that servant who knew his master's will, but did not get ready . . . shall be beaten with many lashes.
>
> But he who did not know and did things worthy of a beating shall be beaten with few lashes. . . .
>
> (Luke 12:46-48)

So now it is finished . . . or rather just beginning . . . for the dead—the unbelievers. Now comes a judgment in only 18 words that will condemn them forever to a real, everlasting Hell:

> AND WHOSOEVER WAS NOT FOUND WRITTEN IN THE BOOK OF LIFE WAS CAST INTO THE LAKE OF FIRE.
>
> (Revelation 20:15)

## WHAT IS THE LAKE OF FIRE?

It is of interest to note that C. T. Schwarze, formerly of New York University, wrote in a thesis that such a place as a Lake of Fire is actually known to science today.

The word *lake* must connote a body of matter having liquid form. Therefore, if Scripture is truth, this eternal fire must be in liquid form or in some form in the spirit world that has qualities or characteristics resembling a liquid.

. . . the very simple example of the portions of Scripture we are discussing *lies in the existence of the singular phenomena of the skies known as midget or white dwarf stars!* . . . a midget star is one which, because of some things which have happened to it (not quite clear at this time), should be roughly 5,000 or more *times* as big as it really is! Applying this idea for illustration to such a planet as the earth, you must conceive the earth as having shrunk to such an extent that its diameter would be about 400 miles . . . instead of being 8,000 miles in diameter as it really is.

### Temperature Inside Stars Extremely Hot

This enormous density . . . has a great deal to do with our subject. . . . Most people know the sun, our nearest star is rather hot . . . there is general agreement that the temperature at or near the center of stars is between 25 million and 30 million degrees Fahrenheit! . . . At such temperatures much can happen, like the bursting of atoms, which helps to explain the phenomenon of the white dwarf.

At such a temperature, 30,000,000 degrees Fahrenheit, atoms would explode and lose their electrons even though the attraction between nucleus and electrons is thought to be an octillion . . . times the attraction of gravity. The separated parts could then be better packed in, particularly under such great pressure.

## WHAT IS THE LAKE OF FIRE?

With the constant activity of X-rays, atom walls could not be reformed; therefore enormous densities, such as are found in the midgets, can be attained. Now, please note, at such high temperatures all matter would be in the form of gas . . . in a white dwarf the pressure is so great that gasses become compressed to the consistency of a liquid although they may still respond to the characteristics of a gas. . . .

### Midget Stars Can Never Cool Off!

Before such a star could cool off and gradually become dark it would have to expand to normal proportions. That is, it would have to get to be more than 5,000 times its present size. Here is the difficulty. Such expansion would cause enormous heat which, in turn, would absolutely keep the star compressed, so that, *insofar as astronomers and physicists know, the midget stars can never cool off!* . . . The white dwarf, to all intents, can *never* burn out.

### An Eternal Liquid Fire!

May I summarize to show that here the claims of the Bible, God's Word, are scientifically plausible? We find, first, an eternal fire which cannot burn out. Being of a liquid consistency it is, secondly, a Lake of Fire. In the third place, it cannot be quenched, for any quenching material, such as water, would immediately have its atoms stripped of electrons and be packed in with the rest. In the fourth place, since astronomers have been, and still are, studying this strange phenomenon, it is only too evident that the Lake of Fire *has been prepared* and is now ready. Although we cannot say that God will actually use these lakes of fire in fulfilling His Word, the answer to the skeptic is in the heavens where there *are* lakes of fire.

The final judgment of Hell is certainly an awesome one. Yet many make light of Hell . . . saying, "If there is a Hell, I'll be so busy shaking hands with my friends I won't have time for anything else."

## YOUR DECISION
## MUST BE MADE WHILE YOU ARE ALIVE!

**There
Is
NO
Second Chance!**

There is an English proverb which says

*Hell is paved with good intentions.*

And here at last, many will wish they had put their good intentions into action . . . but it will be too late! **There is no second chance.** The opportunity for you who are living today is NOW! If you do not accept Christ NOW while you are living . . . then your destination is Hell.

Remember this one important fact:

IT DOES **NOT**
REQUIRE A DECISION TO GO TO HELL
                              but
IT *DOES*
REQUIRE A DECISION TO GO TO HEAVEN

Thus ends . . . and begins . . . the most tragic moment in history . . . a moment that for the unbeliever will be an eternity in constant torment in Hell.

# 3

## WHAT IS HELL LIKE?
### Hell Is Already In Existence!

**Hell
Is A
Prepared Place!**

Is there a real Hell? YES! Is there real torment? YES! Is it everlasting? YES! Look at Matthew 25:41 where the Lord, who neither lied nor exaggerated, says to the unbelievers:

> . . . Depart from me, ye cursed, into everlasting fire, prepared for the devil and his angels:
>
> (for) these shall go away into everlasting punishment: but the righteous into life eternal.
> (Matthew 25:41, 46)

Dr. J. Dwight Pentecost in his book Things To Come points out that in the phrase in Matthew 25:41 which says "prepared for the devil and his angels . . ."

The word "prepared" literally is "having been prepared," suggesting that the Lake of Fire is *already* in existence and awaiting its occupants. But what will be occuring in Hell?

**Hell's
Fury!**

All the non-believers, with Satan, with Antichrist and with the False Prophet and Satan's angels will be together in Hell. It will *not* be a time for grand reunions. It *will* be a time for eternal torment!

187

## 1. A PLACE OF CONSCIOUSNESS

**In
Agony!**

You will recall in a previous chapter we related the Scriptures concerning a certain rich man and Lazarus, a beggar. The rich man was conscious in Hell and he was in torment:

> And in Hades (the realm of the dead, Hell),
> being in torment, he lifted up his eyes . . .
> and cried out. . . .
>
> (Luke 16:23, 24)

This Scripture indicates that the unsaved dead are CONSCIOUS.

## 2. A PLACE OF TORMENT

**In
Torment!**

Both in the above verse just quoted and in verse 28 of Luke 16:

> . . . warn them (the rich man's 5 bothers) . . .
> lest they too come into this place of torment.

we have an indication from God that Hell is a real place of torment . . . Also Hell, from these Scriptures, is shown as a hot place for the rich man asks that Lazarus (the beggar who went to Heaven) "dip the tip of his finger in water and cool my tongue; for I am in anguish in this flame" (Luke 16:24 Amplified Bible).

Can you imagine the intense suffering from an unbearable heat? Anyone who has been to Vietnam or other hot climates where the suffocating humidity envelops you along with the intense heat can appreciate this scene.

Also picture the desperateness of the occasion when the rich man would welcome the beggar Lazarus to get water on his finger to alleviate the suffering!

Hell is truly a place of real torment!

## 3. A PLACE OF DARKNESS

**Constant
Gloom!**

We are told in Matthew that the unsaved

> . . . *will be driven out into the darkness
> outside, where there will be weeping and
> grinding of teeth.*
>
> (Matthew 8:12)

Also

> . . . *throw him (the unsaved) into the darkness
> outside (of Heaven); there will be weeping
> and grinding of teeth.*
>
> (Matthew 22:13)

And in Jude 13 we are told that the "gloom of darkness" has been "reserved forever" for those outside of Christ. What a picture of hopelessness!

## 4. ETERNAL SEPARATION
## FROM LOVED ONES

**No
Hope Of
Communication!**

Think about this for a moment. If you are an unbeliever and some of your best friends and loved relatives . . . perhaps even a husband or wife are BELIEVERS . . . they will go to Heaven . . . and you will be eternally separated from them!

> *There shall be weeping and gnashing of teeth,
> when ye shall see Abraham, and Isaac, and
> Jacob, and all the prophets, in the kingdom
> of God, and you yourselves thrust out.*
>
> (Luke 13:28)

What a tragedy to enter Hell and then to realize that you are now eternally separated from those whom you loved so much on this earth!

## 5. NOT THE SLIGHTEST HOPE OF RELEASE

No
Reprieve!

Many places in Scripture tell of Hell being a place of eternal judgment from which there is no turning back. In Hebrews 6:2 we learn that Hell is a place of "eternal judgment." In Matthew 25:46 it is revealed that the unbeliever will "go away into everlasting punishment . . ."

No wonder Jesus said in the Sermon on the Mount (this is for those who say, The Sermon on the Mount is my only creed),

> . . . if thy right eye offend thee, pluck it out, and cast it from thee: for it is profitable for thee that one of thy members should perish, and not that thy whole body should be cast into hell.

> And if thy right hand offend thee, cut it off, and cast it from thee: for it is profitable for thee that one of thy members should perish, and not that thy whole body should be cast into hell.

> (Matthew 5:29, 30)

## 6. THE TORMENT OF UNSATISFIED LUSTFUL CRAVINGS

**No
Fulfilment!**

In Hell the unbeliever will *never gain satisfaction.*
Sin will continue in Hell but it will be a constant
craving . . . without fulfilling. Thus we read,

> He who is unrighteous (unjust, wicked) let
> him be unrighteous still, and he that is filthy
> (vile, impure) let him be filthy still . . .
> (Daniel 12:10, Revelation 22:11)

These words here are referring to the activity in
Hell. Can you imagine the surprise that awaits
the filth peddlers who on this earth are having a
heyday distributing pornographic films and literature.

At least, here on earth this activity brings them
barrels of cash while they influence negatively
the lives of others.

But in Hell, these filth peddlers will have their
cravings and lusts . . . but these will be unfulfilled
cravings. Can you imagine the intensity of suffering this will cause!

Perhaps there may even be unfulfilled love in
sex, unfulfilled forever in Hell.

Someone has said Hell is a place where:

the Belshazzars will not have their wine
the Ahabs will not have their Naboth's vineyards
the Felixes will not have their Drusillas
Herods will not have their sensuous dances
the Judases will not have their cankered gold!

This will give you some insight on Hell's anguish-
ing fury!

## 7. THE TORMENT OF MEMORY IN HELL

**A Terrible Anguish!**

This, perhaps, could be the most agonizing aspect of those in Hell . . . the torment of a memory . . . a memory that will evoke continual anguish. This is brought out so clearly in Luke 16:27, 28 where the rich man implores Abraham to:

> . . . send him (Lazarus, who is in Heaven) to my father's house:
>
> For I have five brethren; that he may testify unto them, lest they also come into this place of torment.
>
> (Luke 16:27, 28)

What an insight into Hell! Imagine if those unsaved dead right now could speak to us for just a moment . . . what a warning they would give . . . and yet, sad to say, would anyone pay attention?

How pointedly Abraham replied . . . and how prophetically when he said,

> . . . If they hear not Moses and the prophets, neither will they be persuaded. THOUGH ONE ROSE FROM THE DEAD.
>
> (Luke 16:31)

Thus, the unbeliever in Hell must go through an eternity in torment with a searing, ever-present memory!

# 4

## WHERE ARE THE UNSAVED DEAD NOW?
### Scriptures Reveal A Surprising Answer!

**Before**
**The**
**Judgment Day!**

What happens to those unbelievers who have already died, who will die today, tomorrow or anytime in the future before the beginning of the 1000 year Millennium?

Dr. J. Dwight Pentecost, in his book Things to Come points out that there are **four** different words used in Scriptures to describe the place of the dead until their resurrection at the **Great White Throne Judgment** at the close of the Millennium.

These four words do NOT always refer to the eternal state of Hell (which begins after the 1000 year Millennium) but rather often to the temporary place in which the dead await their resurrection. Here are those words:

## What Manner of Persons Ought Ye To Be!

There shall come in the Last Days
    scoffers,
    walking after their own lusts,
    and saying,
*Where is the promise of His coming? . . .*

But, beloved,
be not ignorant of this one thing,
that one day is with the Lord
    as a thousand years,
and a thousand years
    as one day.

The Lord is not slack concerning His promise . . .
    but is longsuffering toward us,
    not willing
    that any should perish,
    but that all
        should come to repentance.

But the day of the Lord
    will come as a thief in the night . . .
in which the heavens shall pass away . . .
the earth also . . .

Seeing then,
that all these things shall be dissolved
    what manner of persons
    ought ye to be
in all holy living and godliness,
Looking for and hasting unto
    the coming
    of the day of God . . .

(2 Peter 3:3,4,8,9-12)

## 4 WORDS DESCRIBE
## THE PLACE OF THE UNSAVED DEAD

**Picture
Of
Eternal
Doom!**

1. SHEOL
   This is used 65 times in the Old Testament of which 31 times it is translated "grave."
2. HADES (literally, the "unseen world.)
   This is used generally to describe the unsaved dead who are awaiting the resurrection unto the Great White Throne. In every instance but one it is translated as "hell."
3. TARTAROS
   This word is only used once in Scripture (2 Peter 2:4) and refers to the judgment on the wicked angels.
4. GEHENNA
   This is used 12 times in the New Testament.
   *(Matthew 5:22, 29-30, Mark 9:43, etc)*

(In the Hebrew this word literally means "Valley" *[Ge]* "of Hennon" *[Henna]*. Its fires burning the garbage of Jerusalem provided Christ with the perfect picture of the eternal doom of those who are lost.)

## WE REAP AS WE HAVE SOWN

**Even
In Torment
NOW!**

Therefore the unbelieving dead are right now in torment and in misery in their temporary place of punishment—Hades or Hell, awaiting their final resurrection after the 1000 year Millennial reign of Christ which will then be immediately followed by the Great White Throne judgment and their eternal condemnation to the Lake of Fire (Revelation 20:11-15).

It was Charles H. Spurgeon who told a group of seminary students, "When you speak of heaven, let your face light up and be irradiated with a heavenly gleam. Let your eyes shine with reflected glory."

It was Walt Whitman who wrote:

Roaming in thought over the Universe, I saw the
little that is Good steadily hastening towards
immortality,
And the vast that is Evil I saw hastening to merge
itself and become lost and dead.

The fabric of our life today will determine whether we wear a cloak of righteousness tomorrow. John Greenleaf Whittier penned these words:

The tissue of the Life to be
We weave with colors all our own.
And in the field of Destiny
We reap as we have sown.

## YOUR DECISION
## DETERMINES YOUR DESTINY

**The
Awesome
Tragedy!**

The story has been told of a picture painted by an artist who set the scene in a night background. Across the dark waters of a lonely lake a solitary man could be seen rowing a small boat. A high wind churned the waters of the lake into white-crested billows which raged around the little skiff.

Above was a dark and angry sky. But through the blackness there shone one lone star. Upon this the rower fixed his gaze—and on through the storm he rowed.

He was undismayed by the midnight blackness! Beneath the picture the artist had written: "If I lose that, I am lost!"

How true of life. If one does not follow the Star of our hope—the Lord Jesus Christ . . . he is lost.

In this life the "tissue" of our future life is woven.

We reap as we have sown.

If we sow in unbelief . . . we destine ourself to an eternal, real Hell forever.

On the other hand, if we sow in belief, through the acceptance of Jesus Christ as our Saviour and Lord . . . our harvest is an ETERNITY in Heaven!

**How
Long
Is
Eternity?**

Try to imagine that this earth upon which we dwell is nothing but sand. Now try to imagine that a little bird could fly from a faraway planet to ours and carry back with him a tiny grain of sand, and the round trip would take a thousand years.

Now try to imagine how long it would take for that little bird to carry away this entire earth, a grain of sand each thousand years.

The time required for this would be but a moment in comparison to eternity.

*And whosoever was not found written in the book of life was cast into the Lake of Fire.*
(Revelation 20:15)

Is this where you want to spend ETERNITY, in the Night that NEVER Ends?

# 5

## THE TWO JUDGMENTS
### One For Believers . . . One For Unbelievers!

A question frequently asked is:

Must *believers*
face the Judgment Seat
as well as those that are *lost?*

Yes and no.

While both the **believer** and the **lost** must each face a judgment seat . . . in the divine purpose . . . there is a vital difference between the type of judgment which each experiences. The **believer** has **already** been cleansed from sin by the blood of Christ and so will not come under condemnation for sin.

**FOR THE BELIEVER** Judgment Seat of Christ

## 1. JUDGMENT SEAT OF CHRIST
### For the Believer
### (A Judgment of the Believer's Stewardship)

A. This will take place after the Rapture.

B. All believers will appear.
2 Corinthians 5:10 states:
*We must all appear before the judgment seat of Christ; that every one may receive the things done in his body.*

C. There will be personal confession.
*Every knee shall bow, and every tongue shall confess. . . .*
(Romans 14:11)

D. Each shall give an accounting of himself.
*So then everyone of us shall give account of himself to God.*
(Romans 14:12)

## JUDGMENTS and their DISTINCTION

**1. Judgment of the Church** *The Judgment Seat of Christ*
   (2 Corinthians 5:10-11)

Here we have the judgment of the believer's works . . . not his sins. Hebrews 10:17 tells us that the Christian's sins and iniquities will be remembered no more. But Matthew 12:36, Romans 14:10, Colossians 3:24-25 remind us that every work must come to judgment. This judgment **occurs at the return of Christ for His church** (Rapture) . . . immediately after the Rapture but before the marriage supper of the Lamb.

**2. Judgment of individual Gentiles**
   (Matthew 25:32)

This event is fully anticipated in the Old Testament. See Psalm 2:1-10, Isaiah 63:1-6, Joel 3:2-16; Zephaniah 3:8 and Zechariah 14:1-3.

Here the sheep (believers) are separated from the goats (unbelievers). This **occurs after the Tribulation Period** when those Gentiles who have come to Christ during this perilous period will be ushered into the kingdom and eternal life. The goats (unbelievers) will be cast into everlasting fire for their sins.

**3. Judgment of Israel**
   (Ezekiel 20:33-38)

When Christ returns **after the Tribulation Period** He will regather the Jews and purge those who rebelled. This will be accomplished after He first delivers the whole nation from its persecutors. Those who, like the sheep among the Gentiles, are believers in Jesus Christ will be ushered into the kingdom.

**4. Judgment of the Wicked** *The Great White Throne Judgment*
   (Revelation 20:11-15)

For this judgment we look to the time **after the Millennium** (1000 years). This last judgment comes to all unbelievers of all ages at the Great White Throne. The Holy God, the Sovereign Judge, will be seated on the throne. These unbelievers will be judged according to their sinful works. And because not one of them has his name written in the Lamb's book of life . . . they will be cast into the lake of fire.

There will be no escape forever!

## 1. JUDGMENT SEAT OF CHRIST
**For the Believer**
**(A Judgment of the Believer's Stewardship) (continued)**

E.  The Basis of this judgment—
Since it will be an accounting of our stewardship it will necessarily concern
- (1) privileges enjoyed
- (2) faithfulness displayed

    *Since "it is required of a steward that he be faithful," this judgment seat will reveal the <u>extent</u> of each believer's steadfastness* (1 Corinthians 4:2).

    *For unto whomsoever much is given, of him shall be much required* (Luke 12:48).

F.  The Rewards
- (1) Classification

    1 Corinthians 3:11, 12 tells us there will be a test by fire to distinguish between the durable and the perishable . . . the precious and the worthless.

- (2) Durability

    The works
    symbolized by gold, silver and precious stones will be rewarded worthily, and the reward will be "according as his work shall be" (Revelation 22:12).

- (3) Eternal loss

    *"If any man's works shall be burned, he shall suffer loss"* (1 Corinthians 3:15).

G.  Eternal Distinctions
"There is one glory of the sun, and another glory of the moon, and another glory of the stars: for one star differeth from another star in glory. So also is the resurrection of the [saved] dead" (1 Corinthians 15:41).

Wood, hay and stubble do not shine. But gold, silver and precious stone do. Gold, as the richest symbol, would shine as the sun and would signify the ultimate in Heavenly rewards. Daniel 12:3 tell us *"And they that be wise shall shine as the brightness of the firmament; and they that turn many to righteousness as the stars for ever and ever."*

# Sequence of Coming Judgments

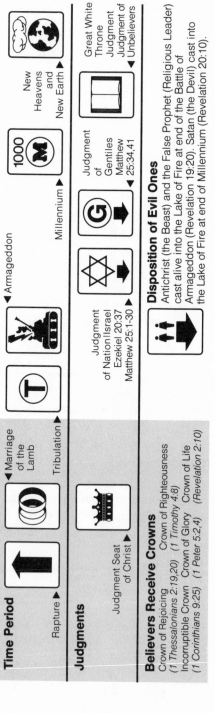

**Time Period**

Rapture ▶ | Marriage of the Lamb ▶ | Tribulation ▶ | ▼ Armageddon | Millennium ▶ | New Heavens and New Earth

**Judgments**

Judgment Seat of Christ ▶ | Judgment of Nation Israel Ezekiel 20:37 Matthew 25:1-30 ▲ | Judgment of Gentiles Matthew 25:34,41 ▼ | Great White Throne Judgment Judgment of Unbelievers ▼

**Believers Receive Crowns**

Crown of Rejoicing    Crown of Righteousness
(1 Thessalonians 2:19,20)  (1 Timothy 4:8)
Incorruptible Crown  Crown of Glory   Crown of Life
(1 Corinthians 9:25)  (1 Peter 5:2,4)   (Revelation 2:10)

**Disposition of Evil Ones**

Antichrist (the Beast) and the False Prophet (Religious Leader) cast alive into the Lake of Fire at end of the Battle of Armageddon (Revelation 19:20). Satan (the Devil) cast into the Lake of Fire at end of Millennium (Revelation 20:10).

## 2. THE GREAT WHITE THRONE, JUDGMENT

**Judgment for the Lost**

A. Will take place after the Millennium (Revelation 20:5, 11-15).

B. All the lost will appear.

*And I saw the [lost] dead, small and great, stand before God
. . . and the sea gave up the dead which were in it, and death
and hell delivered up the dead which were in them . . .*

(Revelation 20:12-13)

"Death" refers to what happens to the body when it dies.
"Hell" (*hades*, the "unseen" world) refers to the place where
the soul and spirit of unbelievers go at death.

Hell is the place where the unbelieving dead experience torment until the time they are resurrected to stand before the
Great White Throne (Luke 16:19-31).

C. Unbeliever's body, soul and spirit will be reunited.

At the **Great White Throne Judgment**, the unbeliever will be
resurrected (this is known as the *Second Resurrection*; the
*First Resurrection* referring to the resurrection of the believers
at and after the Rapture).

At the resurrection of the unbelievers,

death (where his body has gone)

and hell (where his soul and spirit have gone)

will give up the dead. The unbeliever's body, soul and spirit
will be reunited for this judgment.

D. The awesome face of God will cause terrible fear.

*And I saw a great white throne, and Him that sat on
it, from whose face the earth and the heaven fled
away; and there was found no place for them (Revelation 20:11).*

This judgment takes place, not in Heaven, nor on earth, but
somewhere in between the two . . . as indicated by the above
verse.

## 2. THE GREAT WHITE THRONE, JUDGMENT
### Judgment for the Lost (Continued)

E.  The Basis of this judgment—

This judgment is <u>not</u> to determine whether those who stand before this judgment bar are saved or not. All those that were to be saved have already been saved and are in Heaven, enjoying eternal blessing.

> This is rather a judgment on the evil works of the unsaved (called the *lost*).

F.  The result of the judgment—

Revelation 20:15 makes the result of this judgment very clear:

> **"And whosoever was not found written in the book of life was cast into the Lake of Fire."**
>> Eternal separation from God
>> is the eternal destiny of the unsaved.

G.  The destiny of the lost—

The destiny of the lost is a place in the Lake of Fire.
(Revelation 19:20; 20:10, 14-15; 21:8)

The Lake of Fire is portrayed as a *place,* not just a state.

The Lake of Fire is described as

> (1) Everlasting fire
>> . . . *depart from me, ye cursed, into everlasting fire"* (Matthew 25:41).

> (2) Unquenchable fire
>> . . . *it is better for thee to enter into life maimed, than having two hands to go into hell, into the fire that never shall be quenched"* (Mark 9:43).

> (3) Black and dark
>> . . . *to whom is reserved the blackness of darkness for ever"* (Jude 1:13).

> (4) Constant torment for ever. *No* annihilation.
>> *the smoke of their torment ascendeth up for ever and ever: and they have no rest day or night."*
>>> (Revelation 14:11)

# 6

## THE AWESOME REALITY OF HELL
### How Hell May Be Experienced Eternally!

---

### AS ONE MAN IMAGINES IT!

The below, although written in semi-fiction style, gives some Scriptural concepts of what it may be like to be forever banished to an eternity in Hell. It is an excerpt from the book **666/1000** by Salem Kirban. If you wish a copy of this 480-page book, send a Gift of $25 to **SECOND COMING/*Missions*,** Box 278, Montrose, Pennsylvania 18801. Postpaid.

---

## SORROW at SINAI

Abel Epstein was both bewildered and furious. Where had Brother Bartholomew disappeared? And what a time to leave!

Every phone in the control center was ringing. And each one he answered brought messages of utter confusion and calamity.

"Get us help, get us help. Mayday! Mayday! Some unseen force is wiping out our entire army!"

Abel Epstein, in an attempt to remain calm replied, "Pull back your forces 3 miles and let's reappraise the situation. Brother Bartholomew is not here. He's probably on his way out to the front."

"Negative, sir, he is not here...and we have no forces to pull back. Just the Lieutenant and I remain from our entire regiment."

Epstein angrily slammed down the phone.

For the first time in his life fear suddenly gripped him. Cold sweat poured out over his massive body. He jerked the Jerusalem contact phone from the wall and bellowed, "Get me Dr. Curter."

Dr. Curter was beginning to have doubts about the whole Megiddo expedition as he sat in his laboratory atop Mt. Herzl. From here looking northeast he could see the Mount of Olives.

Picking up his binoculars he scanned the horizon as suddenly the whole area was flooded with brilliant sunlight. Unusual, he thought. Something is happening.

It was only when he spotted Bill Sanders embracing his wife Faye that Dr. Curter lost his composure. His face turned ashen white. How could this be. He had personally witnessed the guillotine execution of Sanders. Could it be a dream?

The jangling phone brought him to his senses.

"Hello, this is Dr. Curter."

"Curter, this is Epstein at Megiddo Control Center. Everyone's gone mad here. Utter chaos. I'm boarding a helicopter. Will be there in 10 minutes. Stay where you are. I have a plan."

"A plan for what?" Dr. Curter was about to ask. But before he could, Epstein had hung up.

As Epstein boarded Brother Bartholomew's helicopter he instructed the pilot to circle the Megiddo plains.

What he saw was unbelievable.

What was once a plain now seemed like a quagmire. Here in the heat of the desert...the dry 105° heat...where in the world did the water come from?

He picked up the radio phone and after several tries finally reached a ground commander.

"What's happening down there? Where's the red mud coming from?"

"It's not mud, sir."

The voice seemed weak.

"Speak up," Epstein demanded.

"I have no strength sir. All around me are bodies...horses and men...and blood...blood... blood. It's...It's like a sea of blood. I can't speak sir...my tongue...I caaaan't...."

And the wine press was trodden outside the city, and blood came out from the wine press, [reaching] as high as horses' bridles, for a distance of one thousand and six hundred stadia [about 200 hundred miles].

(Revelation 14:20
Amplified Bible)

Then it dawned on him. Was what Sylvia had told him finally coming true? No, he couldn't believe such fantastic tales. There

*Epstein instructed the pilot to circle the Megiddo plains. What he saw was unbelievable.*

had to be an explanation to all of this. The sudden earthquakes ...falling stars...they must have been a chain reaction from the air pollutants. That's it. It can't be God...whoever he is or wherever he is.

The pilot turned to him.

"Sir, if I didn't know better I would say that battlefield looks like a sea of blood...and it looks like it covers miles and miles of the Plain of Esdraelon."

"Nonsense, head this crate for Jerusalem and let's get to Mt. Herzl as quickly as possible."

As Helicopter 1 approached Jerusalem, Epstein's heart sank in despair. He had not been a good Jew but he did remember his early years in Hebrew school... seven years of learning, reading the Talmud.

> For, behold, the Lord will come with fire, and with His chariots like a whirlwind, to render His anger with fury, and His rebuke with flames of fire.
>
> For by fire and by His sword will the Lord plead with all flesh: and the slain of the Lord shall be many.
>
> **(Isaiah 66:15-16)**

He hadn't remembered much. But in the Talmud, Gemarah Kiddushim 496 was a phrase of beauty he had remembered. It was so poetic and so true. As though in prayer he bowed his head and softly repeated it...

> Ten parts of beauty were allotted the world at large:
> out of these Jerusalem assumed nine measures
> and the rest of the world but one...
> Ten parts of suffering were visited upon the world —
> nine for Jerusalem and one for the world.

If there was any tenderness in Epstein's heart...this was the moment. But instead of an awakening towards the Messiah...as he saw the destruction...he became more bitter.

If there is a God, he thought, why did He allow this suffering ...this tragedy to "His" Jerusalem?

"Then he remembered that verse in Psalms...Psalm 137:5-6... and in derision he quoted it:

If I forget you, O Jerusalem,
May my right hand forget her skill
May my tongue cleave to the roof of my mouth,
If I do not remember you,
If I do not exalt Jerusalem
Above my chief joy.

In his bitterness he thought...the Hebrew school did me some good after all...he remembered that verse. To him it proved that God was not on the scene. For Jerusalem lay waste. The world was upside down.

Abel Epstein, who had come from selling records, to creating a laser ring, was not through yet! He was smarter than God... whoever he was. He, Epstein, would find a way out of this mess. Then he would live it up again!

The sudden descent of the helicopter engine brought him back to reality.

Flying over the Hebrew University the helicopter started its landing pattern onto Mount Herzl.

There was the Hill of Remembrance, on the ridge, dedicated to the six million European Jews killed by the Nazis in World War 2. The sight brought more bitterness to Epstein's heart. "Hitler was a saint compared to Brother Bartholomew," he thought, "why there must be at least 200 million dead out there at Megiddo!"

The helicopter landed atop Mount Herzl. Here Theodore Herzl was buried, the man who was first fired by the vision of a Jewish statehood and launched the movement. In 1949, forty-five years after his death, the body of Dr. Herzl had been brought in state from Vienna to Jerusalem.

The place seemed deserted.

Epstein quickly raced up the marble steps...each step echoing throughout the vast structure. It seemed eerie.

Running down a familiar hall, he came to Dr. Curter's office... swung open the door...and gasped in amazement and fright.

*Epstein angrily grabbed a book and hurled it at the bird.*

There in the chair was Dr. Curter. He looked alive. But the glassy stare of his eyes revealed differently. What eyes were left. There, perched on his head was a huge bird, gorging his belly as he pecked at Curter's eyes and took chunks from his swollen tongue.

Epstein angrily grabbed a book and hurled it at the bird. The sharp crack was heard throughout the hall as the book squarely hit Dr. Curter's head. His body

> And I saw an angel standing in the sun; and he cried with a loud voice, saying to all the fowls that fly in the midst of heaven, Come and gather yourselves together unto the supper of the great God;
> That ye may eat the flesh of kings, and the flesh of captains, and the flesh of mighty men, and the flesh of horses, and of them that sit on them, and the flesh of all men, both free and bond, both small and great.
> Revelation 19:17-18

slid awkwardly off the chair and sprawled on the floor. As other birds quickly flew in at the smell of open flesh...Epstein ran hysterically from the room and down to the waiting helicopter.

\* \* \*

Sylvia was noticeably worried. Standing there on the Mount of Olives with Terry she could sense something was wrong. Terry should have been overjoyed at this reunion. And she was...but.

Suddenly Sylvia realized in her concern for others and her witnessing this glorious reunion...she had forgotten about herself and Abel.

It was like hitting her with a ton of bricks. "Dear Jesus," she whispered to herself, "I want to be near you...and I want Abel to come to know you as Saviour and Lord."

Funny, she thought. She had thought of Abel as her lucky charm, her security blanket, her ace in the hole. After she married him she never wanted for money, perfume, or furs. Everywhere she went, she went first class. "Baby," he told her, "now that you've married me...you're going to travel first class!"

And first class she went. It was a cold, convenient love. There was never any warmth. Abel was all business in everything he did. He never even took time to eat properly or spend time with her. She was revolted by the way he gulped down a chicken sandwich and a soft drink...then dashed off to another business deal. When she complained, he would reply, "Make up your mind, baby, do you want me or money. You can't have them both."

And for a while, she was glad to settle for the money.

She attended all the social balls in New York. She thought nothing of spending $150 for a ticket to the Diamond Ball at the Plaza and dancing for hours to the bands of Meyer Davis and Peter Duchin.

She remembered even bidding for the Velazquez portrait at Wildenstein Gallery and seemed quite relieved when she was outbid by the final bid of $5.54 million!

Her greatest thrill, or so she thought, was when Abel sent her off on a worldwide cruise aboard the S.S. France. Her cabin cost $99,340 and she remembered filling her cigarette box in her suite with 500 crisp dollar bills for small tips.

And every August, without fail, she would head up to Saratoga Springs, New York for the Saratoga auction of yearling race horses.

But now, all the dazzle of money and society seemed to crumble into emptiness.

It's funny, she thought. Money can't buy happiness. Money couldn't win the war. Money couldn't bring peace. And when you die, money can not buy back one more minute of time.

> A rich man's wealth is his strong city, And like a high wall in his own imagination.
> (Proverbs 18:11 ASV)

The only thing that was real was her Saviour. Now, more than ever before, the reality of her salvation in Christ became apparent. And she clung to the precious promises she had learned as a child. But her heart ached. Why, oh why, didn't she learn more of these truths then. There it was...the entire blueprint of tomorrow laid out for her in the Bible. And she had squandered her time on charlatans and personal gain. The agony of regret seemed more than she could bear. The events around her were happening too fast. She could not think straight. She was like a little baby...helpless...waiting to be led.

Suddenly, a noise distracted her. Abel came bounding through the door. His face was ashen white.

She had never seen him this way. He looked pitiful. She felt so sorry for him. She wanted to hold him in her arms.

She had never felt like this before. Abel was always the master of his ship. But now it seemed like Abel's ship was without a rudder.

"Sylvia, grab your bags and hurry. We've got to get out of here!"

"Why, honey. Where can we go?"

"This place is a holocaust. Megiddo is one vast burial ground ...dead all over...sickening blood like a miry swamp. You should have seen it. I was lucky to get out alive. Even Dr. Curter is dead! Stop wasting time, Sylvia...let's get moving. There's a Concorde jet at Lod airport. I've given orders to hold the flight till we get there. We're flying to New York!"

"Abel, sit down and let's reappraise the situation. Don't you see there's nothing either of us can do. The King has arrived. Terry told me about it. It's all written in the Book of Revelation and it's actually coming true."

"Sylvia, stop listening to those fairy tales. Besides I don't accept the New Testament."

"I know that Abel, but the same prophecies are written in Daniel, Isaiah, Zechariah and Joel as well. You've witnessed the Battle of Armageddon. Tell me, where is Brother Bartholomew?"

"How did you know he disappeared?"

"I didn't, Abel, but if he did, he was Antichrist, and he's been cast into the Lake of Fire."

"Now I know you're having hallucinations, Sylvia. We've got to get out of here."

"Honey, listen to me...there's no time to lose. Let's get down on our knees now. Ask the Lord Jesus Christ to come into your heart. Accept Him as your Saviour...please darling."

> And he shall plant the tabernacles of his palace between the seas in the glorious holy mountain; yet he shall come to his end, and none shall help him.
> (Daniel 11:45)

Darling...funny, she had rarely called Abel darling. She slipped her arm about his waist. He seemed like a frightened boy now. For the first time in her life she felt a deep passionate love

*For the first time in her life she felt a deep passionate love for him. Abel, the cold, cool, millionaire now needed an understanding love.*

for him. Abel, the cold, cool, millionaire now needed an understanding love. She quietly tried to open the Word of God to him...as much as she could remember...she told him that his Messiah, his Redeemer had come...and soon for those who would not believe, would come an unbelievable and irreversible judgment. For a moment she thought he was on the verge of believing...his eyes moistened. Gently she brushed away a tear. He was about to speak.

A loud explosion outside their window jolted him to reality.

Cursing, he threw her down to the floor.

"Sylvia, you can have your heartless God. I've got my money in New York. And that's where I'm going. I'll buy my way into your Heaven...if there is one!"

The sleek Concorde supersonic airliner...all $35 million of it...was about to start its engines on the Lod airport runway when Abel Epstein rushed up to the gates. He was quickly waved on.

And again I say unto you, It is easier for a camel to go through the eye of a needle, than for a rich man to enter into the kingdom of God.
(Matthew 19:24)

He settled back in the soft, cushioned seats and ordered a cocktail from the stewardess. Abel Epstein had done it again. He'd show this God a lesson or two.

[God] who hath saved us... not according to our works... but according to His own purpose and grace.
(2 Timothy 1:9)

The stewardess came back. "Sorry, sir, we have no liquor anymore. All aircraft have been taken over by other personnel. Would you care for a glass of milk or a soft drink?"

For by grace are ye saved through faith; and that not of yourselves; it is the gift of God: Not of works, lest any man should boast.
(Ephesians 2:9)

Abel was furious and was about to vent his fury on the helpless stewardess. But he had second thoughts when he looked at her hand.

She was carrying a Bible.

He pushed his seat back into

And when Simon saw that through laying on of the apostles' hands the Holy Ghost was given, he offered them money,

Saying, Give me also this power, that on whomsoever I lay hands, he may receive the Holy Ghost.

But Peter said unto him, Thy money perish with thee, because thou hast thought that the gift of God may be purchased with money.
(Acts 8:18-20)

the reclining position and closed his eyes. Soon, he thought, I will be in New York with 10 million other sensible people and things will be back to normal. It was all a bad dream, he comforted himself...a bad dream.

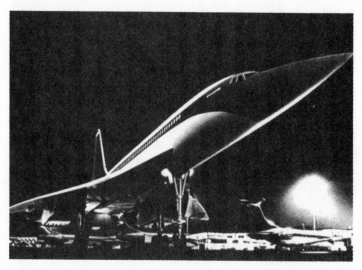

The Concorde Jet took off for the some 6000 mile journey. His face curled into a smile. He would be in New York in about 3 hours! Sylvia could quote all the verses she wanted to...but he wouldn't be there to hear them. She ought to read Proverbs 19:13. That was one verse he often quoted to her: "...a nagging wife annoys like constant dripping."

If Abel Epstein knew that this very moment his financial adviser, George Henderson, was winging his way to Jerusalem he would have lost every sense of security.

His slumber would not be for long. He was to find in New York an unforgettable picture of tragedy and terror.

He could stand no more surprises. But this one would be the biggest!

* * *

Sylvia looked into the mirror. Her hair was a mess. The tears had etched a path down her face. Yet she was no longer concerned about external beauty.

"Abel, dear Abel, why didn't you listen to me. Oh, God, please dear God, save him. I'll do anything for you. Just please save him."

It was some time later she finally found George and Faye with Terry Malone.

Between choking tears she poured out her story to them.

As she looked into their faces, she knew they understood... understood, perhaps too well.

"Sylvia, have you ever heard of Kadesh-Barnea?"

"No, George, why?"

"Well, just before Helen, Bill and Tom left us, they said they were accompanying the Redeemer to Ain Quedeirat."

"What's that?" Sylvia inquired.

"Ain Quedeirat is the Wilderness of Paran, known in Bible days as Kadesh-Barnea. It is in the area called the Arabah which means desert or plain. This is in the Sinai Peninsula. It is a desolate and nearly empty land. It has been the route for many armies. In this area Moses received the Ten Commandments. The Jews wandered here for 40 years.

The Sinai Peninsula itself is 260 miles long and 150 miles wide between the Gulf of Suez and Gulf of Aqaba. If you remember your Bible story, this was the site of the famous 'Grasshopper Retreat.' It was in Numbers, chapter 13, where God instructed Moses...I forget the rest."

> **And I will bring you into the wilderness of the people, and there will I plead with you face to face.**
>
> **(Ezekiel 20:35)**

"I know, Dad," Faye chimed in, "God told Moses to take one leader from each tribe and send spies into the land of Canaan. And 40 days later they came back to the wilderness of Paran at Kadesh. Caleb told the group to go up and possess the land... but they said, 'We felt like grasshoppers before them, they were so tall.' I remember Mom telling me that story."

"That's right, Faye, and they all cried to go back to Egypt. And that's when judgment fell."

"What's that have to do with what's happening now?" Sylvia pleadingly inquired.

*Mount Nebo, from which Moses viewed the Promised Land.*

Just then a messenger ran up to George Omega.

"You're wanted on the phone, sir. You may take it on the phone in the Intercontinental Hotel lobby. It's a transatlantic call, sir."

George picked up the phone. It was his boss at World Television network.

"Get over to Kadesh-Barnea," he screamed. "Some religious fanatics here have told me something's about to happen there."

"When did you get religion, Walter Brinks?"

"I didn't. Don't be stupid...but these characters have been hitting some predictions right on the button...as though they've been reading it in a book...all planned ahead. It's uncanny! And I want a scoop. They tell me the next big event is some kind of a judgment of the nation Israel. And its going to take place in Kadesh-Barnea...some forsaken place in the Sinai Peninsula. Their Redeemer is going to make a personal appearance."

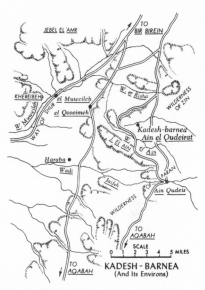

KADESH - BARNEA
(And Its Environs)

"You mean the Messiah, Jesus Christ?"

"Call Him what you want, Omega...but think of the ratings. We'll outpull the old Johnny Carson show. It'll be the scoop of the century. Get a couple mobile TV units there at the King David Hotel and high tail it down to this Kadesh place. As soon as you get there, I want you on the air. We'll telecast via orbiting satellite. I've cleared everything."

George related the entire conversation to Faye, Terry and Sylvia. And much against his will he let them accompany him to Kadesh-Barnea.

Their race against time seemed useless. For when they arrived at Kadesh-Barnea all was still. Occasionally a band of Bedouins with a troop of camels would pass, and one would hear his rhythmic Arabic voice prodding the camels on.

"I wonder if Moses knew then that the sons of his sons would wander here still contending with a Pharaoh?" George mused.

\* \* \*

Whatever was happening, Abel Epstein didn't like it. Suddenly it seemed like an invisible army was rounding up everyone of Jewish extraction...assigning them to ships in the harbor.

Epstein had gathered all his negotiable money and joined the others. Some were singing a song, "How the Oppressor has ceased!" It didn't make sense. Some

> ...thou shalt take up this proverb against the king of Babylon, and say, How hath the oppressor ceased! The golden city ceased!
> (Isaiah 14:4)

seemed hilariously happy. Others like Epstein were confused and sad. Where in the world was this ship going? Who in the world ever heard of this Kadesh place?

It didn't matter. He was tired of running. He fell asleep comforted by a money belt bulging with cash.

> Who are these that fly as a cloud, and as the doves to their windows?
> Surely the isles shall wait for me, and the ships of many lands first, to bring the sons of Israel home again from far away, their silver and their gold with them, unto the name of the Lord thy God, and to the Holy One of Israel, because He hath glorified thee.
> (Isaiah 60:8-9)

* * *

From George Omega's specially built TV booth he had a panorama picture of the action at Kadesh-Barnea. Soon the "ON" light would signal time for his telecast. How he wished he knew more about Bible prophecy. Outside of a few externals he had no idea what was about to happen.

Suddenly from nowhere, it seemed, Helen was by his side.

"But darling, where did you come from and how could you? The doors are closed and we're 50 feet high."

"Honey, you must remember I have been resurrected in Christ. Resurrected believers are not constrained by physical barriers. Besides you'll need help in this telecast."

With that the signal to broadcast lit up.

"This is George Omega reporting to you from Kadesh-Barnea, which is right outside of Israel, to the east. They say nothing is new under the sun. But what we are about to see today will not only be new, but to some, unbelievable. I understand the Redeemer...Christ, the Messiah, will actually be here. This will be His first appearance on television and certainly His first appearance on earth since the resurrection. It will be an historic occasion...yet one edged with much tragedy and also triumph. With me by my side is my wife, Helen."

"Helen is different...that is she was taken up in the Rapture... now she has a new resurrected body. It appears to look just like ours. I recognize her. Yet it is a perfect body, free from the ailments and the aging that still plague us."

"She is living in a new dimension without the restraints of time and space. Yet the marvelous thing about this is that I can communicate with her and she is still, and more so, my attractive Helen."

"You may ask how can I tell a resurrected believer from a living believer? Actually, it's very easy. Helen, as all resurrected believers, has an inner glow of perfection and somehow, don't ask me how, her entire silhouette is edged in a luminous glow."

> It is sown a natural body; it is raised a spiritual body. There is a natural body, and there is a spiritual body.
>
> For our conversation [citizenship] is in heaven: from whence also we look for the Saviour, the Lord Jesus Christ:
>
> Who shall change our vile body, that it may be fashioned like unto His glorious body, according to the working whereby He is able even to subdue all things unto Himself.
>
> **(1 Corinthians 15:44)**
> **(Philippians 3:20-21)**

"Helen, I am sure you can fill in the details of this occasion."

Helen, realizing far more the awe of this event, gently touched George's hand in understanding.

"I don't know how to begin," she started, "for what we are about to see here is not pleasant. The Millennium of 1000 years is soon to begin and what we will witness is often called the JUDGMENT OF THE NATION ISRAEL".

"God's chosen people are now back in Israel to stay. Their long years of wandering are over. Their Messiah, and ours, will never again hide His face from His people."

"What we are about to see here is the Judgment of Israel in fulfillment of Ezekiel 20:33-38 which tells us:

> ...it shall come to pass, when all these things are come upon thee, the blessing and the curse, which I have set before thee, and thou shalt call them to mind among all the nations, whither the Lord thy God hath driven thee,
>
> And shalt return unto the Lord thy God, and shalt obey His voice according to all that I command thee this day, thou and thy children, with all thine heart, and with all thy soul;

'...I shall be king over you. And I shall bring you out from the peoples and gather you from the lands where you are scattered...

And I shall bring you into the wilderness of the peoples, and there I shall enter into judgment with you face to face.

As I entered into judgment with your fathers in the wilderness of the land of Egypt, so I will enter into judgment with you...

And I shall make you pass under the rod, and I shall bring you into the bond of the covenant;

And I shall purge from you the rebels and those who transgress against Me...they will not enter the land of Israel. Thus you will know that I am the Lord.'"

Helen turned to continue but Sylvia's tears broke the silence.

"Not my Abel, not my precious Abel...God can't be that cruel!" she sobbed.

Startled, George Omega grabbed the microphone. "I'm sorry for that interruption, and yet God's judgments are sure. Sylvia is one of our best friends, yet her husband failed to accept the Redeemer as King."

Sylvia frustrated and angry dashed to the elevator that quickly whisked her to the ground level.

She could never forget what she saw. All over the plain were what appeared to be millions of people,

That THEN the Lord thy God will turn thy captivity, [restore your fortunes] and have compassion upon thee, and will return and gather thee from all the nations whither the Lord thy God hath scattered thee.

If any of thine be driven out unto the outmost parts of heaven, from thence will the Lord thy God gather thee, and from thence will he fetch thee:

And the Lord thy God will bring thee into the land which thy fathers possessed, and thou shalt possess it; and He will do thee good, and multiply thee above thy fathers.

And the Lord thy God will cleanse thine heart, and the heart of thy seed, to love the Lord thy God with all thine heart, and with all thy soul, that thou mayest live.

(Deuteronomy 30:1-6)

...Thus saith the Lord God; Behold, I will take the children of Israel from among the heathen, whither they be gone, and will gather them on every side, and bring them into their own land:

And I will make them one nation in the land upon the mountains of Israel; and one king shall be king to them all: and they shall be no more two nations, neither shall they be divided into two kingdoms any more at all;

And David my servant shall be king over them; and they all shall have one shepherd: they shall also walk in my judgments, and observe my statutes, and do them.

And they shall dwell in the land that I have given unto Jacob my servant, wherein your lined in formation according to their final residence. Quickly she ran to the New York line. Almost instantly she spotted Abel.

Breaking through the barriers, it seemed with superhuman effort, she grabbed Abel's arm and pulled him away from the crowd. Hysterically she half carried him to an open place directly in front of the TV cameras.

fathers have dwelt; and they shall dwell therein, even they, and their children, and their children's children for ever: and my servant David shall be their prince for ever.
(Ezekiel 37:21-22,24-25,28)

And I will plant them upon their land, and they shall no more be pulled up out of their land which I have given them, saith the Lord thy God.
(Amos 9:15)

There in splendor beyond words was a Throne. Her eyes so filled with tears, she looked up at the person on the Throne. Though her vision blurred, no one had to tell her. Little Sylvia Epstein was face to face with her Saviour.

She knew what she must do. Tearing the buttons from Abel's shirt she yanked the money belt from around his waist. Abel seemed in a trance, like a little boy, starry eyed and speechless.

She flung the belt at the foot of the Throne.

In an impassioned plea she cried: "Here, Abel, give your all... all your money...I love him, Lord. He doesn't deserve to die. He always gave to the United Jewish Appeal. He even bought Israeli bonds...Look at this money. There must be a million dollars... Abel, give it to the Lord for the rebuilding of Israel...Oh, Abel, repent."

And even as she hysterically spoke she saw no sign of repentance in Abel's stony face. Fear, yes; repentance, no. Her head bowed. It was too late!

Her Redeemer looked down. It was a look of both compassion and of judgment. The voice of what sounded like an angel then came from the side of the throne and thundered across the plains:

Why should I fear in days of adversity,
When the iniquity of my foes surrounds me,
Even those who trust in their wealth,
And boast in the abundance of their riches
No man can by any means redeem his brother,

*She flung the money belt at the foot of the Throne. In an impassioned plea she cried: "...I love him, Lord. He doesn't deserve to die."*

Or give to God a ransom for him —
For the redemption of his soul is costly...
For he sees that even wise men die...
And leave their wealth to others.
This is the way of those who are foolish
As sheep they are appointed for the realm of the dead
And their form shall be for Sheol to consume. [1]

The One upon the throne then waved His arm. George Omega continued the telecast, saying,

"Two men are escorting Abel Epstein to a judgment platform whose ceiling is one that appears to be luminous rod. There are two runways extending out, as one passes through...almost like separating sheep. Epstein is now under the rod...."

"George", Helen added, "if I may interrupt. This is the final fulfillment of the Old Testament Scripture from Malachi 3:2-5. Let me read it to our audience:

'...who can endure the day of His coming? And who can stand when He appears? For He is like a refiner's fire and like fullers' soap (bleaching the dirtiest garments).

He will sit as a...purifier of silver, and He will purify the Levites (the ministers of God). At that time my punishments will be quick and certain.'"

"This is exactly what we are seeing here."

"Yes, Helen, Abel Epstein is now being led away and off of the platform. The swinging door to life and freedom on the right has closed. The only possible route now is the runway to the left. This leads to a transportation column of what appears to be an endless chain of busses. It's hard to describe. Epstein seems meek and unresponsive as though all life has suddenly left him."

"What we have witnessed here is sorrow at Sinai!"

Amid the tears, Faye whispered something into Terry's ear.

Those few words she uttered took but a few seconds, but they were going to have their effect for 1000 years!

[1] Psalm 49:5-15

### No Light . . . No Sound!

Abel Epstein was no longer a proud man. He was in Hades . . . the unseen world . . . awaiting **the Great White Throne Judgment**.

How often he had kidded Sylvia when Sylvia tried to tell him about her Christ.

"Sylvia," he would say, "so I'll go to Hell . . . at least I'll meet all my friends there. We'll be so busy drinking, we won't have any time for regrets."

Yet, never before had Abel felt so helpless and so hopeless. Money had been his servant before. He could have anything he wanted. When he was sick . . . he summoned the best doctors . . . when he was restless, he hired an entire plane to fly him to Acapulco. He loved the warmth of light. His apartment was bathed in walls of luminescent light . . . and he could turn to any imaginable hue at the flip of a switch. "A hue for every mood," he used to boast to Sylvia.

Now, he had no idea where he was. The terror of complete darkness was punishment enough. Dark . . . dark . . . midnight dark . . . pitch dark . . . eerie dark . . . a darkness so black that it conjured countless images of fright in his mind.

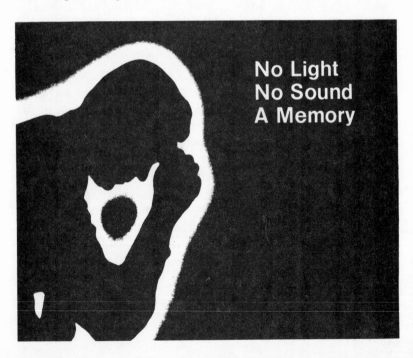

No Light
No Sound
A Memory

Instinctively, he would reach for a switch . . . hoping that all of this was a dream from which he would soon awake . . . a cruel dream. But there was no switch. He found himself grappling helplessly in the air, reaching frantically . . . for a switch nowhere to be found.

The reality struck him time and time again. There was no switch. There would never be a switch. There was no light. **There would never be any light.** Just total and complete darkness.

How often he tried to talk and communicate with others. He would open his mouth but nothing seemed to come out. Was their sound coming out? He mouthed the words carefully . . . enunciating clearly. Then in frenzy . . . he shouted until his throat became hoarse . . . and yet **no sound** . . . and no reply.

Was Hades so big that the human voice found no reflecting wall to bounce back the sound?

He could not even hear himself. It was like talking in a vacuum.

### First No Light!
### Then No Sound!

What else could there be?

He REMEMBERED and for a while this consoled him. He remembered *The Wall Street Journal.* It was in June, 1972 when he had first read about the Black Holes in space. Time Tunnels . . . that's what they called them. There were mysterious signals coming from these deep recesses of space. These signals were picked up by Explorer 42. He recalled that the computers related that the signals came from an object in our galaxy that was many thousands of billions of miles from earth. And what amazed the researchers was that this unknown object seemed to have a diameter *smaller* than that of the earth. Yet the energy it was producing made it 1000 times more powerful than the sun. Bewildered scientists named it Cygnus X-1. Some even believed it to be a time tunnel.

*And death and hell were cast the Lake of Fire. This is the second death [the Lake of Fire].* **(Revelation 20:14)**

What could this be? Abel searched his mind without any solution. Was this heaven? Would it become the Lake of Fire? He knew enough Bible to know that the Lake of Fire would become his next and final destination. Or was Cygnus X-1 where he was right now . . . Hades?

Then, suddenly, his thoughts came back to Sylvia. He had taken her for granted. Women were to be used . . . that was his motto. He had cruelly taunted her about the bevy of beauties he had on a string, while Sylvia quietly went on praying for him. She wasn't perfect, he knew that. She loved money and the things it could buy. But the last few months she had suddenly changed . . . and he loved her . . . and he loved her . . . oh, how he loved her. If only he could hold her in his arms . . . just once . . . and kiss her and tell her he loved her.

*And if thy hand offend thee, cut it off: it is better for thee to enter into life maimed, than having two hands to go into hell, into the fire that never shall be quenched: Where their worm dieth not, and the fire is nor quenched.*
**(Mark 9:43-44)**

The darkness seemed to carry a cloak of dampness that enveloped Abel Epstein. He cried but there were no sobs. The tears that normally would come . . . just never came. It was a hollow cry.

Suddenly he realized Hades had played a cruel trick on him. For not only now, but throughout eternity he would be plagued constantly with the torment of a **MEMORY.**

The picture the world had conjured up of the devil with a pitchfork constantly prodding everyone . . . this would be a relief, he thought to himself.

Facing him was a penalty far more unfathomable.

**No Light**
**No Sound**
**and**
**A Memory**

# 7

## WHAT ARE YOUR PLANS FOR ETERNITY?
### Your Lack Of Decision Destines You For Hell!

**Your
Choice!**

God has given you as an individual a CHOICE.

1. You may determine your own personal opinions about Heaven and Hell or you may believe the opinions of others.
2. Or you may accept God's Word as it is written and accept the Lord Jesus Christ as your personal Saviour and Lord.

This is your choice. Only you can make this decision. And it *must* be made while you are *living*. Otherwise it will be too late. Your lack of decision to accept Christ as Saviour and Lord will leave you to an eternity in Hell . . . regardless of what your personal opinions may be. THERE IS AN ANSWER! And that answer is GOD! Before you were born . . . Christ has told us in the Bible:

> . . . Come, ye blessed of my Father
> (Believers), inherit the Kingdom prepared for
> you from the foundation of the world. . . .
> (Matthew 25:34)

... I am afraid,
   lest as the serpent deceived Eve
   by his craftiness,
   your minds should be led astray
   from the simplicity and purity
   of devotion to Christ.

Such men (who preach another Gospel)
   are false apostles,
   deceitful workers,
   disguising themselves as apostles of
   Christ.

And no wonder,
   for even Satan disguises himself
   as an angel of light.

Therefore it is not surprising
   if his servants
   also disguise themselves
   as servants of righteousness;
   whose end shall be according to their
   deeds.

                    (2 Corinthians 11:3, 13-15)

## YOU CANNOT EARN YOUR WAY INTO HEAVEN!

**Works
Do Not
Gain You
Entrance!**

You do not automatically go to Heaven. And your works, no matter how good they are, will not earn your way into Heaven. For you cannot earn your way into Heaven . . . regardless of how good your intentions are! Eternal life in Heaven is a *gift* of God:

> . . . *God commendeth His love toward us, in that, while we were yet sinners. Christ died for us.*
>
> . . . *as by one man (Adam) sin entered into the world, and death by sin; and so death passed upon all men, for that all have sinned. . . .*
>
> *For as in Adam all die, even so in Christ shall all be made alive. . . .*
>
> *For the wages of sin is death; but the gift of God is eternal life through Jesus Christ our Lord.*
>
> (Romans 5:8, 12; 1 Corinthians 15:22; Romans 6:23)

That gift of eternal life is yours . . . by acceptance of Jesus Christ in your heart as your personal Saviour and Lord. The *wages* you have earned as a sinner is *death*; but the gift which God will give to you if you repent of your sins and turn to Him in faith is *eternal life*.

That is the decision you must make for eternal life. It is the only decision you have to make. Don't fear coming to God, for Jesus has promised, "Him that cometh unto me shall in no wise be cast out" (John 6:37).

**The
Sad
Fact!**

If you do not make this decision, your lack of decision automatically leaves you condemned already because of your sins to eternal damnation in a real, tormenting Hell.

## YOUR MOST IMPORTANT DECISION IN LIFE

**God
Hates
Sin!**

Because sin entered the world in the days of our first parents and because God hates sin, God sent His Son Jesus Christ to die on the cross to pay the price for your sins and mine.

If you place your trust in Him, God will freely forgive you of your sins.

> For by grace are ye saved through faith; and that not of yourselves: it is the gift of God: (8)
>
> Not of works, lest any man should boast (9) —(Ephesians 2:8, 9).
>
> . . . He that heareth my word, and believeth on Him that sent me, hath everlasting life, and shall not come into condemnation: but is passed from death unto life—(John 5:24).

What about you? Have you accepted Christ as your personal Saviour?

By delaying your decision you forget that the clock of your life may stop suddenly, and your obstinate clinging to your still unforgiven sin will rob you of your inheritance of Heaven.

## YOU CAN BE ASSURED OF ETERNAL LIFE!

**You
Can
Be Saved
Right NOW!**

Do you realize that right now you can know the reality of this new life in Christ Jesus? Right now you can dispel the doubt that is in your mind concerning your future. Right now you can ask Christ to come into your heart. And right now you can be assured of eternal life in Heaven.

All of your riches here on earth—all of your financial security—all of your material wealth, your houses, your land will crumble into nothingness in a few years.

And as God has told us:

> As it is appointed unto men once to die, but after this the judgment: (27)

> So Christ was once offered to bear the sins of many; and unto them that look for Him shall He appear the second time without sin unto salvation (28)—(Hebrews 9:27, 28).

Are you willing to sacrifice an eternity with Christ in Heaven for a few years of questionable material gain that will lead to death and destruction? If you do not accept Christ as your personal Saviour, you have only yourself to blame for the consequences.

Or would you right now, as you are reading these very words of this book, like to know without a shadow of a doubt that you are on the road to Heaven—that death is not the end of life but actually the climactic beginning of the most wonderful existence that will ever be—a life with the Lord Jesus Christ and with your friends, your relatives, and your loved ones who have accepted Christ as their Saviour.

**Come
To Him
As You Are!**

It's not a difficult thing to do. So many religions and so many people have tried to make the simple Gospel message of Christ complex. You can not work your way into Heaven—*Heaven is the gift of God to those who believe in Jesus Christ.*

No matter how great your works—no matter how kind you are—no matter how philanthropic you are—it means nothing in the sight of God, because in the sight of God, your riches are as filthy rags.

> *. . . all our righteousnesses are as filthy rags . . .*
> —(Isaiah 64:6).

Christ expects you to come as you are, a sinner, recognizing your need of a Saviour, the Lord Jesus Christ.

Understanding this, why not bow your head right now and give the prayer on the next page. It is a simple prayer of faith to the Lord.

Say it in your own words.

It does not have to be a beautiful oratorical prayer—just a prayer of humble contrition.

## My Personal Decision for CHRIST

"Lord Jesus, I know that I'm a sinner and that I cannot save myself by good works.

I believe that you died for me and that you shed your blood for my sins.

I believe that you rose again from the dead.

And now I am receiving you as my personal Saviour, my Lord, my only hope of salvation.

I know that I'm a sinner and deserve to go to Hell.

I know that I cannot save myself.

Lord, be merciful to me, a sinner, and save me according to the promise of Your Word.

I want Christ to come into my heart now to be my Saviour, Lord and Master."

Signed . . . . . . . . . . . . . . . . . . . . . . . . . . . . . . . . . . . . . . . . . . . . . ·

Date . . . . . . . . . . . . . . . . . . . . . . . . . . . . . . . . . . . . . . . .

---

If you have signed the above, having just taken Christ as your personal Saviour and Lord . . . I would like to rejoice with you in your new found faith.

Write to me . . . SALEM KIRBAN, **SECOND COMING, INC.,** Box 278, Montrose, Pennsylvania 18801 . . . and I'll send you an informative booklet to help you start living your new life in Christ.

---

NAME _____
      (Please PRINT)

Address _____

City _____

State _____ Zip _____

**235**

# QUESTIONS OFTEN ASKED
# ABOUT HEAVEN and HELL

---

## ONCE SAVED . . . ARE YOU ALWAYS SAVED?
## EXPLAIN THE TWO VIEWS ON ETERNAL SECURITY.

---

### CALVINISM

After the start of the Protestant Reformation (1517 AD) the writings of both Luther and Calvin both explained the doctrine of salvation similar to Augustine (5th Century AD).

The Dutch theologians of Holland in the late 16th and early 17th Centuries made these teachings their prime emphasis. Because of their fondness for quoting Calvin, these became known as the system called **Calvinism.**

> Here the stress is that man's salvation
> is totally by "grace" [unmerited favor].

I am indebted to

**Dr. GARY G. COHEN**

for writing **Questions Often Asked About Heaven and Hell.**

Dr. Cohen is both a Hebrew and Greek scholar. He is Program Coordinator at Miami Christian College.

Dr. Cohen is the author of many books and co-authored **Revelation Visualized** with Salem Kirban.

1. That is to say that God's sovereign mercy and kindness is given totally to underserving man on the basis of Christ's finished work at the cross. Thus God . . . in the words of Romans 8:29,30

> "foreknew" those who were to be saved
> by His Sovereign decision in eternity past
> to love them, and hence to know them in advance.

2. Then He "predestined" them (Romans 8:29) . . . that is, liter- He foreordained these whom He foreknew, that they were, in eternity future, ". . . to be conformed to the image of Christ."

3. These He "also called" . . . that is,

> the Holy Spirit did effectually call them
> irresistibly to come to Christ.

This was accomplished through the Spirit acting when the Scriptures were proclaimed and these, of their own free agency, believed.

4. Then He "justified" or pronounced as forgiven, saved, and in His family all who were called . . . that is . . . the believing people.

5. Finally, all of these were or are "glorified" upon death or upon His glorious coming for His Church [The Rapture].

This is perceived as an unbroken chain which transports, by the will of God, all the "foreknown" . . . that is, foreloved [compare Amos 3:2] to the status of being "glorified," safe in Heaven forever as God's redeemed children.

> Therefore, it is impossible for anyone
> to fall out of this or to walk away
> if they are truly foreknown
> and hence predestinated (or elected).

Verses such as John 10:29:

> "No man is able to pluck them out
> of my Father's hand,"

support this and hence the teaching that "once saved always saved."

# ARMINIANISM

Joseph Arminius (1560-1609) put forth a set of writings disputing the Calvinistic understanding of Paul's writings. He also disputed Luther's writings on the subject. [Luther was possibly a greater "Calvinist" than was Calvin!]

The Dutch Church met at the <u>Council of Dort</u> (17th century) and debated these issues.

Arminius taught that:

> God's foreknowledge extended to
> His knowing
> who would favorably believe in the Gospel,
> and that God predestinated
> only those <u>He knew</u> would believe.

This rests the <u>ultimate decision</u> on who would be saved . . . on **man's choice** and **man's will**. This is the keystone of Arminianism!

# THE FIVE POINTS OF CALVINISM

While these two differing positions [Calvinism vs. Arminianism] are certainly good cause to separate into different denominations or churches . . . to prevent endless arguments . . . neither position should be considered by adherents of the other as heretical.

Both sides quote a multitude of verses to buttress their position and there is not space in this brief answer to analyze them here. Let it, however, be noted that at the Council of Dort, the Dutch theologians expressed five points to refute the writings of Arminius. These are often called **"The Five Points of Calvinism"** . . . or **TULIP** which is an acrostic as follows:

### Total depravity
> or inability of man to do anything good
> in the sense of meriting him salvation.

### Unconditional Election
> God chose those to be saved
> by His own Sovereign grace . . .
> not because He saw in any man
> a future goodness of belief.

### Limited Atonement
> Christ came to die to bring the elect ones
> surely into heavenly glorification,
> not merely to provide
> a potential atonement for all . . .
> [although the merit of the atonement
>    to save all is clear].

### Irresistible Grace
> Those who God foreknew
> and predestinated [Romans 8:29,30]
> would indeed find the call
> of God's Spirit to faith irresistible.

### Perserverance of the Saints
> All whom God called to faith
> would be preserved by God
> to remain in the saving faith
> until their glorification.

A final caution must be given, reminding the reader that in all cases theological . . . some will add elements and/or explanations to Calvinism. Some will also make additions to any other acceptable creed so as to make the doctrine offensive, or questionable at best. So be on guard! Not everyone who labels himself as a Calvinist or Arminian [be he a scholar or layman] means the same thing or necessarily refers to the same set of explanations.

Also too, let us know that there is absolutely no <u>connection</u> between Arminianism and being an Armenian [that is, of the ethnic people located in Western Asia southeast of the Black Sea].

## ARE THESE DEGREES OF PUNISHMENT IN HELL?

The answer is **YES!**

Our Lord, in Luke 12:47,48, spoke of those who would be *". . . beaten with many stripes . . ."* and those who would be *". . . beaten with few."*

For your background information . . . there are **two** Judgments:

1. **The Judgment Seat of Christ**
   [where believers receive rewards
   based on what they did for Christ on earth]

   The Bible clearly denies a weighing of people's deeds as the condition of entrance into Heaven . . .

   *"For by grace are ye saved"* (Ephesians 2:8,9)

   The Scriptures clearly teach, however, that there will be different degrees of **rewards** for believers for their works. (See 1 Corinthians 3:12-15, 1 Corinthians 15:40,41)

2. **The Great White Throne Judgment**
   [where unbelievers are cast into the Lake of Fire]

   The Bible clearly reveals that there are differing degrees of **punishments** for unbelievers in Hell. See Luke 12:47,48.

   While our sins are equally a breaking of God's law . . .
   yet quantitatively . . .
   some sins are referred to in the Bible
   with great hatred ["abominations"].

Those who commit the more outrageously wicked or evil sins clearly are to receive the "many stripes" in the eternity of Hell. This is the Lake of Fire where **all** the lost abide forever separated from God's mercy and grace which they chose to refuse and reject.

## IF YOU ARE LIVING NOW . . .
## AND THE RAPTURE OCCURS . . .
## AND YOU REMAIN ON EARTH . . .
## CAN YOU BE SAVED IN THE TRIBULATION PERIOD?
## ALSO . . . IS THERE NO SECOND CHANCE?

First . . . God's Word teaches us that there is "no second chance".

This is in direct opposition to the unscriptural Catholic doctrine of purgatory [a place where those go who have died with only minor, venial sins on their souls]. In purgatory, the Catholic church teaches that there they are cleansed . . . purged . . . of these sins before they can enter heaven. This is not biblical! Scripture reveals "no second chance" . . . a teaching of denial of any type of a after-death opportunity to believe and enter heaven . . . for the lost.

At the Rapture (1 Thessalonians 4:17), **all believers** will join the resurrected saints of the past and rise to be with Christ forever after . . . first in the heavenlies and then for an eternity upon the New Earth and in the New Jerusalem.

> [See 1 Thessalonians 4:13-18;
> 1 Corinthians 15:51-52; and Revelation 21:1-3]

After this, God will pour out His judgments upon the earth as described in Revelation chapters 8 and 15.

Those still **alive** . . . as long as they remain alive . . . have yet opportunity to repent . . . and are still in their "first chance."

> We refer to those who believe during this period
> as "tribulation saints"
> and martyrdom awaits many of them
> at the hands of Antichrist and his False Prophet.
> See Revelation 13:15.

Those, however, who have once taken the Mark of Antichrist have committed the "unpardonable sin" against the Holy Ghost for this period [Matthew 12:31], and these cannot be saved. God's Holy Spirit will no longer call out to these blasphemers. Revelation 14:9-11 clearly states that *"If any man . . . receive his mark* [Antichrist's] *. . . the same shall drink of the wine of the wrath of God . . ."* See Revelation 15:9-11.

## WE ARE TOLD THAT THERE WILL BE "LIVING BELIEVERS" DURING THE MILLENNIUM. THESE MUST HAVE BEEN SAVED DURING THE TRIBULATION PERIOD. DOES THIS CONTRADICT THE TEACHING OF "No Second Chance" MENTIONED PREVIOUSLY?

It is difficult for us to imagine the details of the 1000 year Millennial Period. Looking back just 200 some years . . . it would have been hard for George Washington to understand our world of television, automobiles and huge jumbo jets.

This is no doubt part of the reason God has chosen to not reveal more of the details of this future Millennial age. God also no doubt desired us to have our debates with unbelievers over the resurrection of Christ, and not over details of the Millennium . . . which scoffers would be quick to ridicule.

Matthew 25:31-46, nevertheless, shows Christ ushering the faithful survivors of the Tribulation Period into the 1000 year Millennium . . . while shutting out the wicked.

The Living Believers were indeed the ones judged to be righteous during the Tribulation Period. This righteousness will be demonstrated by their faith . . . at risk, no doubt, of their lives when Antichrist and his False Prophet rule. See Revelation 13:5,15.

Again, as stated in the previous answer, this does not contradict the Scriptural teaching against any "second chance" as that teaching specifically denies a second chance for belief in Christ to those who died rejecting the Saviour.

## DOES THE BIBLE GIVE ANY INDICATION
## AS TO EXACTLY WHEN THE TRIBULATION PERIOD BEGINS
## AFTER THE RAPTURE OF THE CHURCH?
## IMMEDIATELY? ONE YEAR LATER? FIVE YEARS LATER?

This question needs to be answered by an entire book with various chapters beginning with the words:

"If such and such is true . . . then. . . .

Most prophetic students today would probably say that the Rapture will occur . . . and then, the Tribulation Period will begin immediately after it.

What they actually mean is that Daniel's 70th Week (Daniel 9:27) will begin after the Rapture of the Church. To be more in keeping with biblical terminology, the **"Great Tribulation"** begins at the midpoint of this seven years (Daniel 9:27; Matthew 24:15,21; Revelation 13:5) when *"the man of sin"* (Antichrist) *is revealed"* and begins his persecution in Judea (2 Thessalonians 2:3; Matthew 24:15-21). Using this more correct terminology, the **70th week of Daniel** begins after the Rapture, and the **"Great Tribulation"** begins 3½ years later.

Recently some have suggested
        that the 70th Week of Daniel
                [7 years actually because Daniel 9:27
                is in a context of seven's of **years**]
        may be delayed for a while
                so as to give either Antichrist, Israel,
                or the leaders of the world
        time to sign the peace treaty between Antichrist
        and Israel.

This is a speculative guess which may or may not have any validity. Others, of course, who do not hold to the pretribulation Rapture position suggest that the Rapture could take place in the middle or sometime during Daniel's 70th week of years.

Thus, the answer is that the Church will be raptured . . . Daniel's 70th week of seven years will start . . . 3½ years later the "Great Tribulation" of Matthew 24:21 will begin when Antichrist is revealed as the evil one. And, at the close of the seven years, Christ will come **with** His saints at Armageddon to destroy the Antichrist, bind Satan and begin His Millennial 1000 year reign.

# WHAT
# IS
# HEAVEN
# LIKE?

# SALEM KIRBAN

# WHAT IS HEAVEN LIKE ?

## Table of Contents

This book is divided into five sections.
This is the **Fourth** Section
## WHAT IS HEAVEN LIKE ?

I Shall Never Forget This Moment!

# DEDICATION

In Memory of

# CATHERINE JORDAN FRICK

Still Born
February 25, 1984

*She Bypassed Earth and Went Straight To HEAVEN*

The early part of 1984 was a very difficult time for both my wife
and I. It was a time of trials, testings and tears. I believe we ran
through the entire spectrum of emotions.

> But through it all...
> we learned to lean on God <u>fully</u> in <u>all</u> wisdom.
> He knows the path that we take and promises that
>     though we walk through the valley
>     of the shadow of death...
> it is only a <u>shadow</u>.
>
> And beyond that shadow, God promises an eternity of
> *"goodness and mercy...dwelling in the house of the Lord*
> *forever"* [Psalm 23:6].

As you may know, our daughter, Doreen and her husband, Wes,
lived in the State of Washington in the early 1980's. They have
four children: Jessica, Joshua, Piper and Joel. The home they built
was in Valley, Washington...about 35 miles north of Spokane. This
home was way out in the country surrounded by mountains...next
to an old, neglected cemetery.

In 1982, Doreen walked through this cemetery while having her
devotions. It was overgrown with weeds that covered the worn
tombstones. Some markers were knocked over. Years had faded
the memories there.

Doreen moved away some of the overgrown brush from some of the
tombstones and her heart was touched. The inscriptions revealed
heartaches of children who had died over 100 years ago...some at
age 3, some at 2 and some at age 0.

Wes and Doreen decided to devote some time to clean up all the underbrush and weeds and restore the cemetery as much as possible. Since this small cemetery was next to their home...they were able to spend many hours in weeding and raking and cleaning. **Little did they realize at that time that God was preparing them for a tragedy and triumph!**

Mary and I visited them in Valley, Washington many times. And often they told us of how many older folk travelled for miles...some as far away as California...to make their annual pilgrimage to this cemetery to honor their loved ones. Those who came were grateful for the way Wes and Doreen tenderly restored this resting place.

On that wintry February day in 1984, we committed Catherine Jordan Frick to the Lord. [Left to right: our daughter, Dawn, Salem, Mary, Doreen, Joshua, Jessica.] Wes took the photograph.

Mary and I were planning to visit Doreen and Wes in February, 1984 to await their birth of their fifth child. It was to be a time of happy reunion.

Then, one evening,
two days before the child was due to be delivered...
Doreen called us.
Mary could tell by the sound of her voice...
    something was wrong.

Just the day before, Doreen had been to the doctor...and everything was fine. Then, one day later, somehow, the baby became entangled in the umbilical cord and died...just 2 days before birth!

We were all shocked by the news!
Yet through our tears
    we saw the sovereignty of God!
And we know **HE MAKES NO MISTAKES**!

Jessica placing flowers on grave as Joshua looks on.

Instead of Mary and I flying to Washington for the joy of a new birth...we flew out to provide both comfort and love to Wes, Doreen and the children. As we asked God *"Why?"*...God's promises flooded our soul and gave us peace.

Both Wes and Doreen agreed that this little dark haired girl, **CATHERINE JORDAN**, should be buried in the same cemetery they had so lovingly cared for. So the arrangements were made. And they asked me to perform the simple service at the cemetery.

It was the most difficult thing I have ever done!

We walked out the back door of their home just a few steps to the burial plot. It was a crisp, cold day. Snow was on the ground. Five of us [Wes, Doreen, our daughter, Dawn, Mary and I] plus two of their children, Jessica and Joshua, were there. Wes and Doreen wanted a private and quiet funeral. We were ringed by mountains and stately pine and spruce trees. Ever green...these trees were silent witnesses of the security of an eternity with Him.

Left to right: Wes Frick, Jessica, Joshua, Doreen, Mary and Dawn.

As I conducted the short service, I reminded them that our citizenship is in Heaven...that one day soon, Christ will call His own...the dead first...and that Catherine Jordan is already rejoicing with Christ. I shared with them the fact that, in a sense, Catherine Jordan is far better with Jesus...for **she bypassed earth and went straight to Heaven**. She will not have to experience the trials, the testings, the disappointments and the tears of this ever complex world in which we live.

But I must confess...I cried through much of the burial service. Somehow, the awesomeness of that moment overwhelmed me. As I tried to be a comfort to Wes and Doreen...God washed my eyes with tears...that I might see! And through these tears God revealed to me three vital truths:

1.  I understood, in part,
    what a great sacrifice it was for God to send His Son
    to die for my sins...
    so that I might have eternal life.

    I can understand, in part,
    the anguish as Christ called out on the cross:
    *My God, my God,*
    *why hast thou forsaken me?*   [Mark 15:34]

The immensity of it all! That God would send His Son, His ONLY Son, to die for an unloving world of sinners. How great is our loving God!

2.  I rejoiced in the fact that God has already
    prepared a place for us in Glory  [John 14:2,3].
    And that He is coming SOON!

3.  On that cold, snowy day, February 25, 1984...
    at that cemetery plot, I came to understand

    [a] How short our life span is on earth
    [b] How we do not know what tomorrow
        will bring and
    [c] In light of all this...
        **how we must put eternal priorities**
        **above temporal, selfish gains!**

For Jesus Christ, Himself will be our judge at the Judgment Seat of Christ  [John 5:22].   And our rewards for an eternity will depend on our works on earth  [2 Corinthians 5:10].

Be very honest with yourself.
IF CHRIST SHOULD COME RIGHT NOW...
   would you have **REGRETS**
   [because you lived for SELF]...
   or would you be **REJOICING**
   [because much of your life
      is in giving to tell others the Good News] ?

Mary and I would never trade this experience for anything. It was a moment in time we shall never forget. And to a sweet little dark haired girl whom we shall meet and fellowship with throughout an eternity...**CATHERINE JORDAN FRICK**...this book on Heaven is humbly dedicated.

December, 1991                    **Salem Kirban**

Mary and I fly to Washington state almost every year to visit our daughter, Dawn and her husband Ron and two children, Melissa and Laura. Each time we visit Catherine's resting place. This photo was taken January, 1986. We placed a teddy bear and a bouquet of flowers at the site in the snow.

# 1

## THE DAY THAT NEVER ENDS
### Heaven Is The Place Where Time Stands Still!

He the pearly gates will open
So that I may enter in,

For He purchased my redemption
And forgave me all my sin!

**Final**
**Fulfilment**
**Of**
**God's Promise**

There is no subject that gives me a greater thrill to write than this one. The event that we will now describe will fulfill all of the aspirations of the Old Testament saints, of the New Testament saints and of the Tribulation and Millennial saints.

No earthly pen can hope to convey the completeness of joy and the fullness of peace that will be ours as Christians, born-again believers, in God's New Heaven and New Earth!

But some day, God will reveal our Heavenly inheritance and it will be beyond human words . . .

The false and empty shadows
The life of sin, are past—
God gives me mine inheritance,
The land of life at last.

Prior events that occur are these. We have seen Satan loosed from his prison at the end of the 1000 year Millennial Period; and *"numerous as the sands of the sea"* are those that follow him, not satisfied with Christ.

To have a fulfilled life

One must have...

Something to do

Someone to love

Something to hope for.

**Judgments Begin**

And as the rebels encircled Jerusalem, God, in a judgment from Heaven itself, reaches down and slays them (Revelation 20:7-9).

At this point no unsaved are left alive!

Satan is then cast into the Lake of Fire to join Antichrist and the False Prophet forever (Revelation 20:10).

The unsaved dead are then raised from the dead in what is commonly referred to as the "second resurrection" (the first resurrection being when the believers were raised to life eternal with Christ. Revelation 20:5-14).

Then—the saddest verse of all:

> And whosoever was not found
> written in the book of life
> was cast into the lake of fire.
> (Revelation 20:15)

Then God seeks to purge even the physical earth and heavens of any evidences of sin. He does this by sending a fire so intense that it melts the elements with a fervent heat and burns the earth. The heavens also pass away with a great noise (2 Peter 3:10-12).

Now God has rid the universe of the last vestige of man's pollutions through sin.

## HEAVEN
## WILL OCCUPY ALL OUR THOUGHTS

**Great
Expectation**

And now every Christian is about to enter into the greatest glory that God has prepared—the NEW HEAVEN and the NEW EARTH!

One of the first inklings that God gives us about this Divine inheritance for us is found in the Old Testament book of Isaiah:

> For behold,
>   I create new heavens and a new earth:
>   and the former
>   shall not be remembered,
>   nor come into mind.
> (Isaiah 65:17)

I wonder if you can grasp the full significance of this verse? What God is revealing to us is that not only is He going to create a New Heaven and a New Earth . . . but it will be so wonderful, so breathless in sight that it will <u>occupy all of our thoughts</u> and we will not even remember this old world we call Earth . . . nor will we even recall it! It simply will not come into our minds! Can you imagine such peace of mind?

There will be no homesickness for the old things of Earth—such will be the dazzling splendor of this New Earth!

The New Heavens and New Earth do *not* come into being until

1. After the battle of Armageddon
   *(Revelation 16:16; 19)*
2. After the Millennial reign of Christ
   *(Revelation 20)*
3. After the judgment of sinners at the Great White Throne *(Revelation 20)*
4. After the present earth is burned up
   *(2 Peter 3; Revelation 21)*

**258**

## OUR NEW BODY

**Goodbye
Sickness!**

Scriptures indicate that we will be the same person having the same soul as we now have. We will also have a new glorified body.

The characteristics of this new body will no doubt bear a relationship to our former body much the same as the qualities of Christ's resurrection body bore to His same pre-resurrection body.

The Bible tells us that when we accept Christ as Saviour and Lord we too are spiritually a new creation:

> . . . if any man be in Christ,
> he is a new creature:
> old things are passed away;
> behold, all things are become new.
>                                  (2 Corinthians 5:17)

All will be new in that day . . . New Heavens, New Earth, and New Jerusalem (Revelation 21:1,2).

Here will be a place finally without corruption. No decay, no rust. Many people think that silver won't rust, but rust, which is iron-oxide, also has its counterpart even in silver-oxide and silver-sulfide. All metals today corrode in one way or another. As an example, for every hour of plane flight in Vietnam, it required 25 man-hours of anti-corrosion maintenance. NASA and the military together spend $10 billion per year fighting corrosion damage.

God tells us:

> Your gold and silver is cankered;
> and the rust of them
> shall be a witness against you . . .
>                                  (James 5:3)

**259**

**1000**

**LIFE
IN THE
MILLENNIUM**

The Millennium will not yet be heaven. Compare Isaiah 65:20 with Revelation 21:4 to see this. The government of the Millennium will be a *theocracy.*

A *theocracy* is a government in which God is recognized as the supreme civil ruler and His laws are taken as the laws of the state. And the Lord will choose Jerusalem to be the center of all spiritual blessing (Zechariah 2:12; 8:22; 14:16).

In the Millennium will be **3** classes of people:

1. All the **saved** of **Israel alive**
   at the end of the 7-year Tribulation Period.

2. All the **saved** of the **Gentiles alive**
   at the end of the 7-year Tribulation Period.

These people in listings **1** and **2** will have **natural bodies.**

3. **The Believers who have died before the Rapture.** These resurrected saints will have positions of responsibility in the Millennium (Matthew 19:28; Luke 19:12-27). They will have **resurrected bodies.**

Living believers (Listing 1 and 2) will be able to marry and be given in marriage. The women will reproduce and have children. These children born in the Millennium will be given an opportunity to accept Christ or reject Him at the end of the Millennium. A vast number will reject Him and follow Satan (Revelation 20:7, 8).

Life in the Millennium will be one of **peace** (Isaiah 11:6-9), **happiness** (Isaiah 11:6-9; Revelation 20:3) and **long life and health** (Isaiah 33:24; 35:5, 6; 65:20; Jeremiah 30:19, 20).

The New Heavens and New Earth follow the Millennium.

**Complete
Fulfillment!**

Thus, believers, who through acceptance of Christ, are now new creatures, will be completely fulfilled in all of God's glory in the New Heavens and the New Earth.

You will recall that the relationship between Christ and His saints is revealed in Christ's prayer of intercession in Gethsemane when He prayed:

> *Father, I will that they also,
>   whom thou hast given me,
>   be with me where I am;
>   that they may behold my glory,
>   which thou hast given me . . . .*
>
>                                   (John 17:24)

There will be no need of hospitals. Nor will there be pain and sorrow. Heart disease, arthritis, diabetes, cancer, headaches and nervous tension will forever be gone! We will have a new body . . . a glorified body!

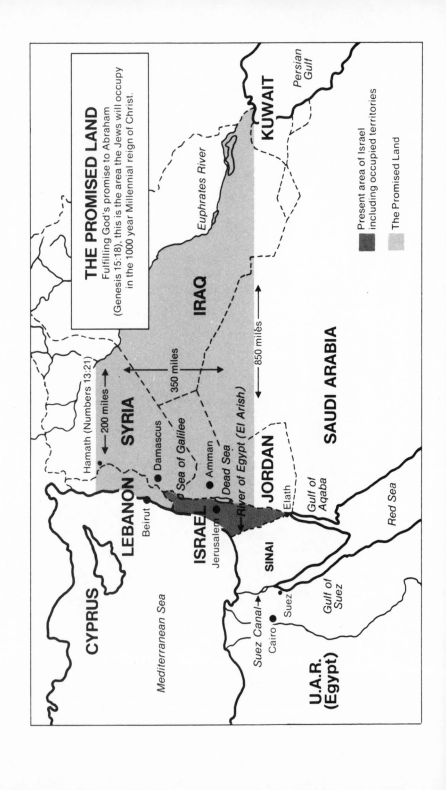

## THE PROMISED LAND

Fulfilling God's promise to Abraham (Genesis 15:18), this is the area the Jews will occupy in the 1000 year Millennial reign of Christ.

Present area of Israel including occupied territories

The Promised Land

Persian Gulf

KUWAIT

Euphrates River

IRAQ

850 miles

350 miles

SAUDI ARABIA

200 miles

Hamath (Numbers 13:21)

SYRIA

Damascus

Sea of Galilee

Amman

River of Egypt (El Arish)

Dead Sea

JORDAN

LEBANON

Beirut

ISRAEL

Jerusalem

Elath

Gulf of Aqaba

Red Sea

SINAI

CYPRUS

Mediterranean Sea

Suez Canal

Cairo

Suez

Gulf of Suez

U.A.R. (Egypt)

**New Jerusalem
To Be
Suspended
Over The
Earth!**

Let's read in Revelation about our new inheritance:

> *And I saw a new heaven and a new earth;*
> *for the first heaven and the first earth*
> *were passed away;*
> *and there was no more sea.*
>
> *And I John saw the holy city,*
> *new Jerusalem,*
> *coming down from God out of heaven,*
> *prepared as a bride*
> *adorned for her husband.*
>
> (Revelation 21:1,2)

It is important to remember that this New City, JERUSALEM, will not be the identical city on this present earth that we know as Jerusalem.

(For a further study on this subject we would recommend that every Christian read THE BIBLICAL DOCTRINE OF HEAVEN by Dr. Wilbur M. Smith).

> *. . . and (He) showed me that great city,*
> *the holy Jerusalem,*
> *descending out of Heaven from God . . .*
>
> (Revelation 21:10)

Here, God is revealing to John, the author of this inspired Book of Revelation, that great city, Jerusalem, descending out of Heaven.

This New City, Jerusalem, is suspended over the earth as John sees it in the future!

One of the very interesting aspects of these new things is that while God chose to reveal to us in one single verse the creation of the New Heavens and Earth . . . there are at least 25 verses which describe in very great detail the *"great city, the holy Jerusalem"* (Revelation chapters 21 and 22).

**1.**
**No**
**Temple!**

It is hard for man to fathom the characteristics of this New City, Jerusalem. It is also an eternal city without a Temple!

You will recall that there will be a Temple in the Millennial earth. But here in the New City, Jerusalem, there will be no need for a Temple. Christ will be that Temple. The entire city will be that Temple—a vast cubical Holy of Holies wherein God dwells (Revelation 21:16). Since there will be no sin and our conversation and thoughts will be holy we will be dwelling with God in that Holy City.

**2.**
**No**
**Night!**

There will be no darkness there. Christ will be the light that illumines that City.

> . . . I am the light of the world:
> he that followeth me
> shall not walk in darkness,
> but shall have the light of life.
>
> (John 8:12)

With sin gone and with the saints being in the physical presence of God His Light will be our light and there will be no night there.

> . . . for there shall be no night there.
> (Revelation 21:25)

**3.**
**No Tears!**
**No Death!**

There will be no tears in Heaven. There will be no more pain in Heaven. There will be no more sorrow, no crying in Heaven. There will be no more death in Heaven! Hear God's promises to every Christian who has placed his faith and trust in Him:

*. . . God shall wipe away all tears
from their eyes;
and there shall be no more death,
neither sorrow, nor crying,
neither shall there be any more pain:
FOR THE FORMER THINGS
ARE PASSED AWAY.*

(Revelation 21:4)

What a glorious transformation . . . when His blessed face I see . . . no more pain and no more sorrow . . . O what glory that will be!

**In Heaven** . . . no more sorrow . . . no more tears . . . no more pain!

## THINGS THAT WILL NOT EXIST IN HEAVEN!

Heaven is a place of positive joys! There will be nothing in Heaven that will be able to cast a gloom over it. In fact, in Heaven there will be

| NO MORE | Revelation |
|---|---|
| Tears | 21:4 |
| Death | 21:4 |
| Mourning | 21:4 |
| Crying | 21:4 |
| Pain | 21:4 |
| Sickness | 22:2 |
| Hunger | 7:16 |
| Thirst | 7:16 |
| Insecurity | 21:25 |
| Sea | 21:1 |
| Sun | 21:23 |
| Moon | 21:23 |
| Night | 21:25 |
| Sin | 21:27 |
| Deceiver | 20:10 |
| Condemnation | Romans 8:1 |
| Separation | Romans 8:38,39 |
| Time | Revelation 10:6 |

In Heaven, time will continue forever as eternity begins.

*"And there shall be no night there; and they need no lamp, neither light of the sun; for the Lord God giveth them light, and they shall reign forever and ever"*

(Revelation 21:5).

**4.
No More
Separation!**

All the saints of all the ages will be there. No more will friends have to part again. No more will families have to have tearful farewells. What a grand reunion saints in Christ will enjoy forever and forever. As Dr. Wilbur M. Smith has so wonderfully reminded us . . . there will be no need to carry photographs of our absent loved ones in order for us to renew our memory of them . . . for those who have been absent for years . . . will now be ever present. No more disagreements, or misunderstandings, with our loved ones. Together, the believers will rejoice in everlasting joy and companionship.

Joyful relatives greeted this arrival of a loved one from Cuba. But the mother on the right, in tears, waits in vain for her son to show up. In Heaven . . . there will be no more tears . . . but a glad, joyous reunion . . . forever!

**Heaven will be a place of everlasting joy and fellowship.**

# 2

## WELCOME TO YOUR NEW HOME!
### All That We Hoped For Will Be Realized!

**No Disappointments!**

Have you experienced the thrill of . . . for the first time . . . walking into your new home! It is an event of happiness and contentment . . . as well as fulfillment! Over the years, however, that feeling fades away especially when the roof needs repairing or the furnace needs replacing. But in Heaven . . . that initial joy will continue throughout eternity. There will be no disappointments in Heaven! Let's look at some of Heaven's characteristics.

**The Temple:** *The Lord God Almighty and the Lamb . . . The tabernacle of God is with men.* (Revelation 21:22 and 21:3)

**The Sunlight:** *The Glory of God and the Lamb*

*And the city had no need of the sun, neither of the moon, to shine in it: for the glory of God did lighten it, and the Lamb is the light thereof.* (Revelation 21:23)

**The River:** *A pure river, clear as crystal*

*This is the river of paradise with its fountainhead being God and the Lamb.*

*While the streams of earth are polluted, this river of life is pure and clear as crystal.* (Revelation 22:1)

**Food At Its Best!**

**The Tree:** *The Tree of Life*

*Through the middle of the broad way of the city; also, on either side of the river, the tree of life with its twelve varieties of fruit, yielding each month its fresh crop . . .* (Revelation 22:2)

**The
Perfect
Harmony
Of
Healing!**

*Fed by the pure waters of the crystal river, this tree offers 12 varieties of fruit to satisfy every taste. It is never barren.*

**The Leaves of the Tree:** *Healing*

*You may recall in Genesis 2:9 that "out of the ground the Lord God made to grow every tree that is pleasant to the sight or to be desired . . ." But, of course, by disobeying God's law Adam caused sin to enter the world. Now, this Tree in the New Jerusalem has healing in its leaves, forgiveness to all who believe.*

**No Temptation:** *NO MORE CURSE*

*Satan is no longer present . . . and the curse has been removed as promised:*

*"And there shall be no more curse: but the Throne of God and of the Lamb shall be in it. . . ."* (Revelation 22:3)

**No Night:** *GOD is the Light*

*There will be no need for candles, light bulbs or even sunlight for the Lord God will by His very presence illuminate this New Jerusalem.* (Revelation 22:5)

**The City:** *TRANSPARENT GOLD*

*This may be hard to imagine now as nothing on earth can presently duplicate a pure gold, clear and transparent like glass.*

*Yet, God showed John in the Revelation a sight of this new city, New Jerusalem, which he could only describe as having streets of Gold so clear and transparent that it resembled glass.* (Revelation 21:18).

**A Home
Only
For The
Redeemed!**

What a marvelous revelation of our new home!
And what a marvelous promise:

> . . . the gates of it shall not be shut at all by day:
> for there shall be no night there . . .
> but nothing and no one
> . . . shall ever enter it . . .
> but they which are written
> in the Lamb's book of life.
>
> (Revelation 21:25,27)

No unsaved person will be in Heaven . . . nothing
that would defile this Heavenly Kingdom. How
true that old things will have passed away and all
things will then be new!

As Dr. J. Dwight Pentecost has so excellently
pointed out in his fine book, THINGS TO COME,
life in that eternal city of the New Jerusalem will
include:

1. A life of fellowship with Him
2. A life of rest
3. A life of full knowledge
4. A life of holiness
5. A life of joy
6. A life of service
7. A life of abundance
8. A life of glory
9. A life of worship

What greater promise is there than that found in
I John:

> . . . we know that when He shall appear,
> we shall be like Him . . .
>
> (I John 3:2)

## HOW LONG IS ETERNITY?

Eternity is forever. In this world, man must either decide to accept Christ as personal Lord and Saviour . . . or by sinful indecision, reject Him.

Based on that decision he destines himself either for God's forgiveness and an eternity in Heaven or for God's judgment and an eternity in Hell.

Try to imagine that this earth upon which we dwell is nothing but sand. Now try to imagine that a little bird could fly through space from a far-away planet to ours and carry back with him a tiny grain of sand, and that the round trip would take a thousand years.

Now try to imagine how long it would take for that little bird to carry away this entire earth, a grain of sand each thousand years!

The time required for this would be *but a moment* in comparison to eternity!

Where do you want to spend ETERNITY?

# 3

## IN HEAVEN ALL THINGS WILL BE NEW!
### Earth's Greatest Joys Will Not Compare!

**That
Initial
Joy**

Remember the overwhelming joy you experienced when:

1. Christmas became a reality of presents!
2. You learned to drive a car!
3. You finally graduated from High School!
4. You first met the girl who was to become your wife!
5. You became one on your wedding day!
6. Together you welcomed your first child!
7. You bought your first brand new car!
8. You bought your first home!
9. You welcomed your first grandchild!
10. You accepted Jesus Christ as your Saviour and Lord!

These were all new experiences . . . experiences that brought real joy into your life. In Revelation 21:5, Christ tells us that in Heaven all things will be new! There's no earthly way to describe the complete joy and inner happiness of Heaven. But think of:

1. That first train set or doll you received.
2. That day you were finally able to ride a two wheel bike.
3. That perfumed aroma that captivated you when on your first date.
4. That enticing freshness of mom's baked bread. [Nothing says loving like baking in the oven]
5. The smell of luxurious leather in your brand new car.

| | |
|---|---|
| **Everlasting Joy!** | And you have just a peak at not only the initial but also everlasting joy you will experience in Heaven where all things will be new! If you can capture those moments just listed . . . heaven will be much more than this and that feeling will last forever! What are these new things that we will share in for an eternity? |
| **A New Song** | When the New Jerusalem descends from Heaven we will be singing a new song. While the hymns of this world offer us comfort and joy . . . Heaven's songs will bring us peace and eternal happiness. [Revelation 21:1,2] |
| **A New Jerusalem** | We shall have the privilege of entering a new and eternal home, the city of the living God, which He has prepared especially for us. [Hebrews 12:22, Revelation 21:10-27] |
| **A New Wealth** | The city will be built of the best materials since the builder is God. Our dwelling place will be composed of pure gold, pearls and precious varicolored stones . . . symbols of beauty and never-changing wealth! While on earth homes can deteriorate, stocks and bonds can go up and down . . . our heavenly wealth is constant forever! [Isaiah 54:11,12] |
| **A New Security** | The New Jerusalem will have a wall of jasper completely surrounding it. See Revelation 21:17, 18. These walls will be 216 feet thick! While jasper is usually red, brown or yellow . . . this jasper quartz will be different. It will be crystal clear according to Revelation 21:11. It will be protected by God as though there were a wall of fire completely surrounding it. [Zechariah 2:5] |
| **A New Home** | The New Jerusalem will be a transparent cube, 1500 miles high, 1500 miles wide and 1500 miles long. It will be big enough to contain all the past generations of all time. [Revelation 21:16] |

**A New Entrance**  There will be 12 gates (three on each side). This will provide abundant access to those who come from all points of the horizon. [Revelation 21:13, 14] Each gate is formed of one single pearl (Revelation 21:21). This pearl symbolizes purity, unity, beauty and worth. The gates are never closed. And since an angel stands at each of the 12 gates allowing only the elect to enter, there is no enemy to be feared! [Revelation 21:12,25,27]

**A New Thorofare**  No more clogged highways, auto accidents or traffic jams or potholes! The streets of the New Jerusalem are made of pure gold . . . so pure it will look like transparent glass!

[Revelation 21:21]

**A New Ruler**  No more elections nor crooked politicians nor tyrant rulers! The throne of God will be in the New Jerusalem and Christ will be there. The Lord will rule without any rivals. [Revelation 22:3]

**A New Light**  We will not need the sun nor the reflected light of the moon to give us light. Instead the glory of God will light up all of this New Jerusalem. The whole city will shine as light reflects from the clear jasper stone of the walls and the transparent-like gold of streets.

[Revelation 21:11,18,21]

**A New Home**  Here is a city with streets of metallic gold, gates of precious pearl and foundations of valued mineral jewels! It is beautiful beyond description. And think of this . . . there are no mortgage payments! Our Saviour paid the full price at Calvary. No taxes! No lawn that requires mowing! No weeds to pull! No leaky roof to repair. A perfect home! [Revelation 21:10,11]

**A New Menu**      Four times the Tree of Life [Genesis 3:22] is mentioned in Revelation. In Revelation 2:7 it is promised as a reward to the believer. And in Revelation 22:2,14,19 it is a part of the city of God. You recall in Genesis 3:22 God expelled Adam and Eve from the Garden lest they eat from the Tree of Life and live forever. But in the New Jerusalem, believers will eat from this Tree as it now becomes for them an emblem of eternal life! No more hamburgers and french fries! We will eat from the Trees of Life that will have twelve types of fruit and produce every month! The leaves of the tree are enough to assure perpetual health.

**A New Direction**      On earth our directions are different and also very temporary . . . school . . . marriage . . . a home . . . children . . . a good job . . . retirement. Everything on this present earth is limited by time. Everything has a beginning and an ending! Our most treasured things last but for a season . . . and we wish we could enjoy them forever.

But in Heaven . . . all this will change. For as believers we know that our citizenship is not on earth but in Heaven [Philippians 3:20]. And when we accept Jesus Christ as our personal Saviour and Lord, we know that we have an inheritance that can never perish. We also have a home in Heaven that is undefiled and that will never fade away [1 Peter 1:4]. We know that this heavenly inheritance is already reserved for us. And though we are in the world, as Christians we are not of the world. Therefore our direction in life is changed from the temporary earthly goals to an eternal heavenly inheritance! A new direction! And realizing this we ". . . seek the things that are above . . . and set our minds on the things above, not on things that are upon the earth." See Colossians 3:1,2. In Heaven, time will never end. Each joy will last throughout all eternity!

**A New Jerusalem** It is interesting to compare the first Jerusalem that we know on this earth with the Heavenly Jerusalem.

| Present JERUSALEM: | Heavenly JERUSALEM: |
|---|---|
| Built by man's hands | Built without hands— hence built by God |
| Built of stones, mortar, wood | Built of transparent gold, precious stones |
| Home for a few generations of people | An everlasting home for all in Christ |
| Embroiled in conflict | Peace forevermore |

The glory of the Holy City, the new city of Jerusalem, will lie in the fact that it is the city wherein God dwells—with the redeemed. Here ALL THINGS NEW, not all new things. The things that God once made and called good are not now abandoned never again to come into being— light, trees, water, animals . . . they are rather now made anew, afresh.

Photo of the Dome of the Rock. Jerusalem today is torn by strife. The New Jerusalem will be a city of everlasting peace and safety.

# THE NEW JERUSALEM

The Bible tells us the measurements of the New City, JERUSALEM in Revelation 21:16-21.

*Size:* 1500 miles in each direction

Dr. Wilbur M. Smith, in his book, THE BIBLICAL DOCTRINE OF HEAVEN gives us some insight from an Australian engineer.

The City will give you an area 2,250,000 square miles. This makes it 15,000 times as big as London; 20 times as big as New Zealand; 10 times as big as Germany and 10 times as big as France.

And it is 40 times as big as all England and even much bigger than India!

Taking the number of people to a square mile in the city of London, this Australian engineer, computed that the City Foursquare (the New Jerusalem) could hold 100 thousand MILLIONS—or about 70 times the present population of the globe!

Skyline of present day Jerusalem.

Now it must be kept in mind, however, that this New City, Jerusalem will **not** initially be located on earth, but rather, above the earth. It descends to the New Earth after the New Earth is brought forth by God *(Revelation 21:1,2)*.

*Wall:* The wall is approximately 216 feet high.

*Gates:* It will have 12 gates.

The 12 gates are as 12 pearls in appearance, glistening!
There are 3 gates facing in each direction. They are guarded by 12 angels. The names of the 12 tribes of Israel are on these gates.

*Foundations:* There are 12 foundations to the City, each named for one of the Apostles.

*For he looked for a city which hath foundations, whose builder and maker is God.* (Hebrews 11:10)

Stones in Foundation
(with the meanings traditionally assigned to them).

JASPER, an indication of wisdom
SAPPHIRE, repentence
CHALCEDONY (white agate), drives away sadness
EMERALD, fidelity, indicating no counterfeits in Heaven
SARDONYX (onyx), married happiness
CHRYSOLITE, freedom from evil passions
BERYL, everlasting happiness
TOPAZ, fidelity and friendship
CHRYSOPRASE (green agate)
JACINTH (a reddish orange gem)
AMETHYST (violet quartz)

One commentator described the size of the New Jerusalem as follows:

The New Jerusalem will be in the shape of a square:

1500 milles wide
1500 miles high
1500 miles long

That means it would stretch from Maine to Florida. That means if every story were 15 feet high . . . it would be 528,000 stories or floors high! That means that on every floor, there would be 2 million square miles plus! It means that in all of that wonderful place called Heaven there is 1 Billion, 188 million square miles in Heaven.

According to the Department of Eugenics at Carnegie Institute that there has been approximately 30 Billion people who have lived on the face of the earth since time began. If every one of them were going to Heaven . . . every person in that wonderful place would have over 39 miles to live in by themselves! So don't worry about Heaven being big enough. It's more than big enough and you'll have plenty of elbow room . . . because the Lord has made a marvelous, expansive place for those He calls His children.

# THREE HEAVENS

The word *heaven* is used hundreds of times in the Bible. The primary meaning of *heaven* is *"that which is above."*
In God's Word *heaven* refers to one of three major realms as noted below.

| THE HEAVENS | WHERE IS IT | SOME REFERENCES IN SCRIPTURE |
|---|---|---|
| **THE ATMOSPHERIC HEAVENS** | The atmosphere which surrounds the globe. Our troposphere is a blanket of air around earth. It is no higher than 20 miles above the earth. Most clouds are within 7 miles of the earth. | The Israelites were told that the land they were to possess "is a land of hills and valleys and drinketh water of the rain from heaven" (Deut. 11:11).<br><br>See also Deut. 11:17, II Chron. 7:13, Isa. 55:9-11, Psalm 147:8, Matthew 24:30, Zach. 2:6. |
| **THE CELESTIAL HEAVENS** | This is the sphere in which the sun and moon and stars appear.<br><br>I Kings 8:27 speaks of the Celestial Heavens when it says, "Behold, the heaven of heavens cannot contain God." | "And God said, Let there be lights in the firmament of the heaven to divide the day from the night..." (Genesis 1:14).<br><br>"... Look now toward heaven, and tell the stars, if thou be able to number them..." (Genesis 15:5).<br><br>See also Hebrews 1:10, Psalm 33:6, Isaiah 14:12, Amos 5:26 and Jeremiah 23:24. |
| **THE BELIEVERS HEAVEN (The Abode of God)** | This is characterized by holiness because God dwells there. Believers also will dwell in God's heaven because they have been made holy by the grace of God. Jesus assured us of the *reality* of this place (John 14:2). | "... I dwell in the high and holy place, with him also that is of a contrite and humble spirit..." (Isaiah 57:15).<br><br>"Look down from heaven, and behold from the habitation of thy holiness and of thy glory..." (Isaiah 63:15).<br><br>See also Exodus 20:22, Deut. 4:36, Matthew 3:17, Matthew 14:19, Acts 7:55 and John 3:27. |

For a fuller treatment of this subject we recommend: THE BIBLICAL DOCTRINE OF HEAVEN, Wilbur M. Smith, Published by MOODY PRESS, Chicago, Illinois

# 4

## WHAT IS HEAVEN LIKE?
### Earth's Trials and Testings Will Disappear!

**Heaven
Is A
Prepared Place
For
Prepared People!**

Heaven is a place where Mansions have already been prepared for us:

> *In my Father's house are many mansions . . . I go
> to prepare a place for you . . . that where I am,
> there ye may be also . . .*    (John 14:2,3)

Heaven is a place where all our saved loved ones will be:

> *Then we which are alive and remain shall be caught
> up together with them [our saved loved ones] in
> the clouds, to meet the Lord in the air: and so
> shall we [all of the saved] ever be with the Lord.*
> (I Thessalonians 4:17)

Heaven is a place where we shall see God:

> *Then we . . . shall be caught up . . . to meet the
> Lord in the air and so shall we ever be with the
> Lord.*    (I Thessalonians 4:17)

Heaven is a place where we will have new bodies:

> *So also is the resurrection of the dead.
> It [the body] is sown [planted] in corruption;
> it is raised in incorruption.*
> (I Corinthians 15:42)

Heaven is a place where we will receive awards:

> *If any man's work abide
> which he hath built thereupon,
> he shall receive a reward.*
> (I Corinthians 3:14)

**281**

282 • WHAT IS HEAVEN LIKE?

Heaven is a place where we will be given wonderful rewards. The Bible describes these as crowns, wreaths of victory (*stephanos* in Greek), as those given to the winners of the Grecian games.

However the crowns of the Christian are eternal, enduring, and golden.

> *Now they*
> *[those who participate in the Grecian games]*
> *do it to obtain a corruptible crown,*
> *but we an incorruptible.*
>
> (I Corinthians 9:25)

---

## BEHOLD THE ETERNAL CROWNS:

---

**5 Crowns
Of
Reward**

1. A Crown of Life
   *. . . he* (the Christian) *shall receive the crown of life, which the Lord hath promised to them that love Him.*

   (James 1:12)

2. A Crown of Righteousness
   *Henceforth there is laid up for me a crown of righteousness, which the Lord, the righteous judge, shall give me at that day: and not to me only, but unto all them also that love His appearing.*

   (II Timothy 4:8)

3. A Crown of Glory
   *And when the chief Shepherd shall appear, ye shall receive a crown of glory that fadeth not away.*

   (I Peter 5:4)

4. A Crown for Soul Winners
   *For what is our hope, or joy, or crown of rejoicing—is it not even yourselves [Paul's converts]—in the presence of our Lord Jesus at His appearing?*

   (I Thessalonians 2:19 From the Greek)

5. A Crown for Martyrs

*. . . behold, the devil shall cast some of you into prison . . . be thou faithful unto death, and I will give thee a crown of life.*

(Revelation 2:10)

**Claim His Promises!**

And Christ promises that He will come quickly to call for His own, and He thus urges us in the Scriptures to be strong in the Last Days, not to give in to false doctrine nor to those who would say, "Where is the promise of His Coming?" But rather, Christ tells His followers:

*. . . hold that fast which thou hast,
that no man take thy crown.*

and promises

*Him that overcometh
will I make a pillar
in the temple of my God. . . .*
(Revelation 3:11,12)

And so overjoyed will we be in this New Jerusalem that we will cast our crowns at His pierced feet (Revelation 4:10).

*And when the battle's over,
We shall wear a crown!
We shall wear a crown!
We shall wear a crown!
And when the battle's over.
We shall wear a crown in the New Jerusalem!*

What joy will be ours, eternally, in the Day that Never Ends!

**Have
Christ
Directed
Priorities!**

We are reminded in 2 Peter 3:10,11 that this present heaven and present earth will pass away with a great noise, the elements will be destroyed by fire, and the earth and everything in it will be burned by fire.

Therefore, if we understand that all these things will melt away, how important it is for us to lead godly lives, productive for Jesus Christ. And we should look forward as believers to a New Heaven and a New Earth.

### *Behold, I Make All Things New!*
[Revelation 21:5]

Christ promises that He will come quickly to call for His own, and He thus urges us in the scriptures to be strong in the Last Days, not to give in to false doctrine nor to those who would say, "Where is the promise of His Coming?" But rather, Christ tells His followers:

*". . . hold that fast which thou hast, that no man take thy crown,"*

and Christ promises

*"Him that overcometh will I make a pillar in the temple of my God . . . "*
(Revelation 3:11,12)

How overjoyed we will be in this New Jerusalem!
Then we shall be
where we would be
Then we shall be
what we should be
Things that are not now
nor could be
Soon shall be our own!

What joy will be ours, eternally, in the Day that Never Ends!

# 5

## THE DAY WHEN TIME STANDS STILL
### A Thousand Years Is As One Day!

**Stopping
The
Aging Process!**

Looking at it from a human standpoint, the only way we can stop the aging process is for TIME TO STAND STILL.

Of course you would not want time to stand still at a disappointing time of your life or a time of deep struggles or testing. That certainly would be tragic!

Therefore, if you were preparing a Heaven . . . you would **(1)** WANT TIME TO STAND STILL and **(2)** WANT TIME TO STAND STILL AT YOUR HAPPIEST MOMENT IN LIFE.

It appears from reading Scripture that Heaven will be a place where TIME WILL STAND STILL. The ravages of aging will cease. The toll of illness will no longer be weakening the saints. If we right now had the power to make time stand still . . . would we not achieve eternity?

For many years, space scientist C.R. Camplejohn was an atheist. And he was bothered every time he read 2 Peter 3:8 . . . *beloved, be not ignorant of this one thing, that one day is with the Lord as a 1000 years and a 1000 years as one day.*

If today's trees are beautiful . . . Heaven's trees will not only be beauty beyond description but also very fruitful. (Revelation 22:2)

## A REVEALING EXAMPLE

**30 Days
and
30,000 YEARS!**

But the more he investigated the velocity of light the more he was convinced there is a God. Now, as a Christian, Camplejohn makes these observations.

Suppose you went
on a **30**-day trip into outer space . . .

(**15** days traveling out into space
**15** days returning to earth)

Let's assume you could
come near to the velocity of
the speed of light . . .
to **99** and **99/100's** near
the velocity of the speed of light . . .

When you returned to earth . . .
your time clock
would have slowed down sufficiently
at that speed
for **30,000** years
of earth's time to have gone by . . .
but you were only gone
for **30** days!

Thus,
in **30** days . . . **30,000** years elapsed!
That's called "Time Dilation!"

Peter said in 2 Peter 3:8 that ". . . *one day is with the Lord as 1000 years and 1000 years as one day.*" Who told Peter? GOD DID! Yet it was not until 1905 that Albert Einstein had uncovered this secret that time dilation is possible! How many more mysteries have yet to be unfolded to us from God's Word!

## ENERGY IS LIGHT!

**We Enter
The
Fourth
Dimension!**

Paul writes in 1 Timothy 6:15, 16:

> ". . . the King of Kings . . .
> who only hath immortality,
> dwelling in the light
> which no man can approach unto . . . "

Paul is saying that no man can approach God physically.

This is true! Man, in his body (in his material structure) cannot get into or surpass **THE LIGHT** in which God lives.

**MATTER** (and we are matter) cannot surpass the velocity (speed) of light. As soon as it does, it is no longer matter, as we know it. It becomes **E/N/E/R/G/Y** at this point! And it will exist forever because it has gone into what we call the Fourth Dimension!

## MATTER BECOMES ENERGY

**Time
Stops!**

At this point . . .            **TIME HAS STOPPED!**
Then,
whatever that matter is . . .
       it has become immortal!
God tells us that
    ". . . *to be absent from the body*
        *is to be present with the Lord*"
            (2 Corinthians 5:8).

In sub-atomic physics, scientists now realize that everything in this world is made of **E/N/E/R/G/Y.**

ENERGY, in science,
is embodied in one word called
**LIGHT**.

In 1 John 1:5, the Bible reveals that
    *"God is Light."*

According to the time differential (between our time and God's time) . . . a day with God is as 1000 years!

How long ago did Jesus Christ leave this earth?

By His time . . . about 1.989 days!

**He has not been gone 2 days yet!** (by His clock).

Now, do you think that He has had time to forget about you? Has He not still bore the memory of the cross . . . if it occurred less than 2 days ago?

# UNDERSTANDING IMMORTALITY

### By William Jennings Bryan

A grain of wheat has the power to discard its body and from earth and air fashion a new body so much like the old one that we cannot tell one from the other. If this invisible germ of life in the grain of wheat can thus pass unimpaired through three thousand resurrections, I shall not doubt that my soul has the power to clothe itself with a new body, suited to its new existence, when this earthly frame has crumbled into dust.

In Cairo I secured a few grains of wheat that had slumbered for more than three thousand years in an Egyptian tomb. As I looked at them, this thought came into my mind: if one of those grains had been planted upon the banks of the Nile the year after it grew, and all its lineal descendants planted and replanted from that time until now, its progeny would today be sufficiently numerous to feed the seething millions of the world.

To every created thing, God has given a tongue that proclaims a resurrection. If the Father deigns to touch with Divine power the cold and pulseless heart of the buried acorn and make it burst forth from its prison walls, will He leave neglected in the earth the soul of man, made in the image of his Creator?

If He stoops to give the rose bush, whose withered blossoms float upon the autumn breeze, the sweet assurance of another spring time, will He refuse the word of hope to the sons of men when the frost of another winter comes? If matter, mute and inanimate, though changed by the force of nature into a multitude of forms can never die, will the spirit of man suffer annihilation when it has paid a brief visit, like a royal guest, to the tenement of clay?

No. I am as sure there is another life as I am that I live today.

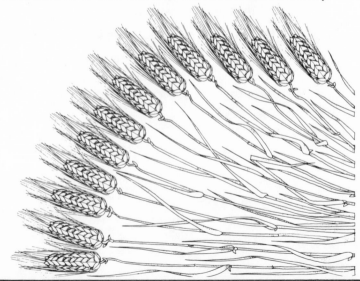

## A GLORIOUS REALIZATION!

**A
New
Challenge!**

Realizing this,
doesn't this bring our Saviour a little closer to
us. He is not somebody who died 2000 years
ago. In God's time, this only happened about 2
days ago! In this time frame, just the day before
yesterday, Christ died for me!

God is LIGHT!
And as believers, we are the
*". . . children of LIGHT."*
(I Thessalonians 5:5)

Because we are
*". . . light in the Lord,"*
we are directed to
*". . . walk as children of Light."*
(Ephesians 5:8)

And we are commanded to
*". . . put on the armour of Light."*
(Romans 13:12)

## THE *"NO MORE'S"* OF SCRIPTURE

How often have you sung the first verse of WHEN
THE ROLL IS CALLED UP YONDER . . .

*When the trumpet of the Lord shall sound,
and time shall be no more,*

and never realized the full importance of that
phrase *"time shall be no more!"*

**TIME WILL BE NO MORE because TIME WILL
STAND STILL.** God, who is Light, has abolished
death and brought life and immortality to light
through the Gospel. Read 2 Timothy 1:10. As believers we are called out of darkness into His marvelous LIGHT. 1 Peter 2:9. We then are looking
for that blessed hope (Titus 2:13) because we are
made heirs according to that hope (Titus 3:7).

291

# THE MINISTRY OF ANGELS

"Angel" primarily means "messenger." Angels bear a relationship in some ways similar to sonship because of having their origin from Him. Because of their personal nearness to God they enjoy His special friendship and love. Read Psalm 91:11.

## THE NATURE OF ANGELS

They are spirits, normally without bodies. At times, however, they assume bodily form (Ezekiel 9:2; Genesis 18:2).

They are holy (Mark 8:38).

They are sexless and innumerable. In Matthew 26:53 Christ could have called 72,000 angels in the Garden of Gethsemane. See also Hebrews 12:22, Matthew 22:30.

At the time of Christ's earthly ministry they did not know the time of His Second Coming (Rapture). "But of that day and hour knoweth no man, no, not the angels for heaven, but my Father only" (Matthew 24:36).

The Bible reveals that the angels, like mankind, also experienced a moral testing. It appears that 1/3 of the angels fell with Satan (Revelation 12:7-9 and 12:4 where "stars" here seem to figuratively represent angels which once glistened in glory; Job 38:7). That not all of the angelic host fell, but only 1/3, is possible because they, unlike mankind, are apparently not a race but individual sons of God (Job 38:7).

## ARCHANGELS

Only two archangels are revealed to us in Scriptures by their names: Gabriel (Name in Hebrew means, "Strong One of God") who announced the birth of Christ; Michael (Name in Hebrew means, "Who is like God") who predicts the Tribulation Period (Daniel 12:1).

Archangels are believed to be rulers of large groups of angels.

## CHERUBIM AND SERAPHIM

Cherubims are first mentioned in Genesis when God drives man out from the Garden of Eden and ". . . He placed at the east of the garden of Eden Cherubims, and a flaming sword which turned every way, to keep the way of the tree of life" (Genesis 3:24). Both J. G. Murphy and Wilbur M. Smith as well as other evangelical scholars believe Cherubims are real creatures, not symbols, with a special office in the general administration of the divine will of God.

The Cherubim is closely related to the Seraphim. See Isaiah 6. *Saraph* in Hebrew means *"to burn"* and it may be that they impart a cleansing fire from God (Isaiah 6:5, 6).

# THE MINISTRY OF ANGELS

| MAJOR ANGELIC ACTIVITIES | EXAMPLES IN THE SCRIPTURES | SCRIPTURE REFERENCES |
|---|---|---|
| **REVEAL THINGS TO COME** | More of the activities of angels are seen in Revelation than in any other book of the Bible. | Revelation 1:1,2<br>10:2<br>14:6-8<br>17:7 |
| | "The Revelation of Jesus Christ, which God gave unto him, to show unto his servants things which must shortly come to pass; and he sent and signified it by his *angel* unto his servant John" (Revelation 1:1). | |
| | An angel reveals the vision of the New Heaven and New Earth. | 21:9,15 |
| | There are 12 angels at the 12 gates of the Holy City. | 21:12 |
| **EXECUTORS IN CARRYING OUT JUDGMENTS OF GOD** | Seven angels announce the seven Trumpet judgments. Two angels participate in harvest of souls of men. | Revelation 8:1-9:1, 13-14<br>14:7-8 |
| | An angel looses other angels at the sound of the Sixth Trumpet Judgment. These latter angels (perhaps Satan's?) slay ⅓ of men. | 9:13-15 |
| | In the battle of Armageddon an angel beckons the birds to feast on the flesh of men on the battlefield. | 19:17-18 |
| | An angel binds Satan in prison for 1000 years during the Millennial Reign of Christ on Earth. | 20:1 |

For a fuller treatment of this subject we recommend:
THE BIBLICAL DOCTRINE OF HEAVEN, Wilbur M. Smith, Published by MOODY PRESS, Chicago, Illinois.         Copyright © 1969, Salem Kirban, Inc.

# QUESTIONS OFTEN ASKED ABOUT HEAVEN

## DO SCRIPTURES TELL US
## HOW LONG THE MARRIAGE SUPPER WILL LAST?

The Scriptures reveal that just as the official joining of a man to a women is celebrated by a Marriage Supper, a banquet of rejoicing, so the union of Christ to the Church will have its banquet of rejoicing. Suggestions as to its length have varied from those who feel that it is a single festive meal at the start of the Millennium to those who liken it to a 1000 years of rejoicing with Christ during the entire Millennial Age. Some say it will be entirely in Heaven, while the last half of the Tribulation is going on in the earth; but others have it as an affair on the earth.

The exact answer seems not to be revealed in Scripture in its details. Thus the opinions on such details becomes theoretical deduction at best. Such suggestions must be examined cautiously (not ridiculed—but examined).

Suffice it to say that scripture is crystal clear in revealing that there will be a grand and glorious supper celebrating Christ and the Church's forever being bodily together. All the redeemed will be there, it will be sometime after the Rapture (when at last Christ takes His Church to Himself), and it will coincide with the joyous inauguration of the promised Kingdom of God.

## WILL WE BE REUNITED WITH OUR LOVED ONES IN HEAVEN? WILL WE LIVE AGAIN WITH OUR MATES?

Scripture indicates that there will be no more separation in Heaven! All those who have accepted Christ as Saviour will be there. No more will friends and loved ones have to part again. No more will families have to have tearful farewells (Revelation 21:4). What a grand reunion saints in Christ will enjoy forever and forever (1 Thessalonians 4:15)!

In 1 Corinthians 15:44 we are told that in Heaven our bodies will be entirely different in nature. In Luke 20:35-36 the Lord tells us that the marriage relationship as we know it today has no place there, for there is no longer any need for the bearing of new children—death is no more and countless thousands and millions will be there who have been redeemed by Christ.

In 2 Corinthians 5:16, a key verse, we are told, *"Henceforth know we no man after the flesh: yea, though we have known Christ after the flesh, yet now henceforth know we him no more."* This is saying that consequently, from now on we estimate and regard no one from a purely human point of view . . . even though we once estimated Christ from a human viewpoint. We shall know one another in Heaven and be able to rejoice together in the memories of God's grace to us.

The husband will recognize his wife and the wife her husband, and it will be a loving recognition . . . they will doubtless love and be in the presence of one another as well as others in a lasting perfect love. All will be absorbed in the spiritual delights of their new condition in Christ.

There will be no need to carry photographs of loved ones in order to renew memories . . . for those Christians who have been absent for years will now be present in Heaven.

Thus, we will recognize our saved loved ones and be with them in Heaven but there is no Scripture which indicates we will live together as husband and wife precisely as we did on earth. Since Revelation 21:4 assures us of perfect bliss in the future world let no child of God be fearful. God made heaven for us, He loves us, He knows our needs—it will not disappoint us. It will be wonderful, and there we shall at last be with Christ unseparated forever.

## ARE THERE SCRIPTURES THAT SHOW THAT A BELIEVER GOES TO BE WITH THE LORD IMMEDIATELY AFTER DEATH?

Yes. A number of Scriptures teach this.

You recall the Lord's words of assurance to the thief who turned to Him in faith on the cross:

> *"Today shalt thou be with me in paradise"* (Luke 23:43).

Read also our Lord's account of the rich man and Lazarus (Luke 16:22).

Another evidence is found in 2 Corinthians 5:6-8:

> *"Therefore we are always confident, knowing that,*
>   *whilst we are at home in the body,*
>   *we are absent from the Lord . . .*
>   *we are . . . willing rather*
>   *to be absent from the body,*
>   *and to be present with the Lord."*

These Scriptures indicate clearly that when a believer dies, he or she goes at once to be with the Lord. Absence from the body means present with the Lord! How wonderful! This scripture alone refutes the false doctrine of soul sleep. For, if the dead in Christ remain unconscious in some long sleep of the soul until the resurrection, then Paul could *never* have said that he was "willing rather to be absent from the body," that is, dead. Then it would be better for him to live as long as possible before the slumber of death. No, the moment a believer dies he or she is with their Lord. That is the Biblical teaching.

## DOES A BELIEVER WHO DIES AND GOES TO BE WITH CHRIST RECOGNIZE AND KNOW THOSE WHO HAVE GONE BEFORE?

This appears to be so. Those with Jesus on the Mount of Transfiguration knew each other, even though they had never met Moses and Elijah (Matthew 17:1-8).

1 Corinthians 13:12 says *"Then shall I know, even as also I am known."* The word *know* here means "to know fully."

Our powers of perception, it would appear, will be enhanced and not diminished in Heaven.

## WHAT ABOUT THOSE
## WHO HAVE ALREADY GONE TO BE WITH CHRIST?
## DO THEY KNOW WHAT IS GOING ON HERE ON EARTH?

The wife of the president of a very fine theological seminary once declared that the answer to this must certainly be Yes. Her husband then assured her that the answer must be No. The truth is that we do not know for sure. Revelation 6:10, however, shows the early martyrs of the Tribulation Period asking the Lord.

> *"How long, O Lord, holy and true,*
> *dost thou not judge and avenge our blood*
> *on them that dwell on the earth?"*

This shows that these in heaven have both an interest and a degree of knowledge concerning earthly happenings. This would seem to be the answer.

**We shall meet again our saved husbands and wives. And the loving joys will be even greater than we can imagine!**

## WILL THERE BE MALE AND FEMALE IN HEAVEN?
## WHAT ABOUT SEXUAL UNION IN MARRIAGE?

Yes, there will be male and female in Heaven. If you are a male on earth [having accepted Christ as your personal Saviour and Lord] . . . in Heaven you will also have the same male characteristics. If you are a female you will be endowed with the same female body differences as you now have.

However, our bodies will not be subject to the ills and aging which we experience here on earth. Instead our bodies will be eternally transformed into a perfect heaven-oriented body.

While on earth, the sexual union between husband and wife is the ultimate culmination of fulfilled joy . . . what will replace this joy in Heaven? The Bible does not reveal this to us.

However, this is certain. The heart relationship will not be changed. We shall meet again our saved husbands and wives and our parents and children. And, since this will be Heaven, we shall love them even more than we did on earth! Since in Heaven we are immortal and never die, there is no need for sexual union to procreate.

God created man [and out of man, woman] and the physical characteristics and inner emotional motivation that make the mutual attraction possible and desirable.

And since in Heaven everything is perfect, it is only reasonable to believe that Heaven's emotional, loving joys will be even greater than one could possibly imagine!

One of my favorite photographs. I took this picture in Bethany near Jerusalem in 1973. Two little Arab girls on their way home with freshly baked bread. In the New Jerusalem Arab and Jew will dwell together in complete peace feasting on the Bread of Life!

## WILL THERE BE OLD AND YOUNG IN HEAVEN, ACCORDING TO THE AGE AT WHICH THEY DIE? OR WILL ALL PEOPLE IN HEAVEN BE THE SAME AGE?

The Bible does not give an explicit answer on this. However in 1 Corinthians 15:42-44 we are told that the resurrection body will be different from our present body.

| Our Present Body | Our Spiritual Body |
|---|---|
| Sown in corruption | Raised in Incorruption |
| Sown in dishonor | Raised in glory |
| Sown in weakness | Raised in power |
| Sown a natural body | Raised a spiritual body |

These verses show clearly that we shall not carry any physical defects into Heaven. Whatever disabilities this physical body may suffer in this life, they will be completely corrected and overcome in the resurrection.

Since all who go to Heaven will share in physical perfection it would appear that there will be no physical "growing up" in Heaven and thus no infants; but rather those who died as infants will have or soon come to have mature bodies. Likewise the aged will have what would be equal to a youthful, mature, vigorous body.

We can be confident, however, that God will allow sufficient physical difference—all of them attractive in their own way—so as to preserve our ability of clearly recognizing individuals.

## HEAVEN: A GUIDE FOR TRAVELERS

**ACCOMMODATION:** Arrangements for first-class accommodation have been made in advance.

> *In My Father's house are many mansions . . .*
> *I go to prepare a place for you (John 14:2).*

**PASSPORTS:** Persons seeking entry will not be permitted past the gates without having proper credentials and having their names registered with the ruling Authority.

> *There shall in no wise enter into it anything that defileth . . . but they which are written in the Lamb's book of life (Revelation 21:27).*

**DEPARTURE TIMES:** The exact date of departure has not been announced. Travelers are advised to be prepared to leave at short notice.

> *It is not for you to know the times or the seasons, which the Father hath put in His own power (Acts 1:7).*

**TICKETS:** Your ticket is a written pledge that guarantees your journey. It should be claimed and its promises kept firmly in hand.

> *He that heareth My word, and believeth on Him that sent Me, hath everlasting life, and shall not come into condemnation, but is passed from death unto life (John 5:24).*

**CUSTOMS:** Only one declaration is required while going through customs.

> *That if thou shalt confess with thy mouth the Lord Jesus, and shalt believe in thine heart that God hath raised Him from the dead, thou shalt be saved (Romans 10:9).*

**IMMIGRATION:** All passengers are classified as immigrants, since they are taking up permanent residence in a new country. The quota is unlimited.

> *They desire a better country, that is, an heavenly . . .*
> *for He hath prepared for them a city (Hebrews 11:16).*

**LUGGAGE:** No luggage whatsoever can be taken.

> *We brought nothing into this world, and it is certain we can carry nothing out (1 Timothy 6:7).*

**AIR PASSAGE:** Travelers going directly by air are advised to watch daily for indications of imminent departure.

> *We which are alive and remain shall be caught up together with them in the clouds, to meet the Lord in the air: and so shall we ever be with the Lord. (1 Thessalonians 4:17)*

**VACCINATION AND INOCULATION:** Injections are not needed, as diseases are unknown at the destination.

> *God shall wipe away all tears from their eyes; and there shall be no more death, neither sorrow, nor crying, neither shall there be any more pain. (Revelation 21:4)*

**CURRENCY:** Supplies of currency may be forwarded ahead to await the passenger's arrival. Deposits should be as large as possible.

> *Lay up for yourselves treasures in heaven, where neither moth nor rust doth corrupt, and where thieves do not break through nor steal (Matthew 6:20).*

**CLOTHING:** A complete and appropriate new wardrobe is provided for each traveler.

> *He hath clothed me with the garments of salvation, He hath covered me with the robe of righteousness. (Isaiah 61:10)*

**TIME CHANGES:** Resetting of watches will not be necessary to adjust to any day/night schedule.

> *The city had not need of the sun, neither of the moon, to shine in it: for the glory of God did lighten it, and the Lamb is the light thereof . . . there shall be no night there (Revelation 21:23, 25).*

**RESERVATIONS:** Booking is now open. Apply at once.

> *Now is the accepted time; behold, now is the day of salvation (2 Corinthians 6:2).*

**CORONATION CEREMONY:** The highlight of the journey is the welcoming reception and coronation which await each new arrival.

> *There is laid up for me a crown of righteousness, which the Lord, the righteous judge, shall give me at that day: and not to me only, but unto all them also that love His appearing (2 Timothy 4:8).*

*by MARCELLE PRICE*

A little boy, after mowing the lawn, ran into the kitchen and presented his mother with the following bill:

| | |
|---|---|
| For mowing the lawn | $5.00 |
| Sitting with baby brother | .50 |
| Going to the store | 1.00 |
| Cleaning the attic | 2.00 |
| Weeding the garden | 4.00 |
| Taking out the trash | 1.00 |
| **Total due me** | **$13.50** |

The mother, who was washing the dishes, dried her hands on her apron, turned the bill over and wrote this note:

*I carried you in my womb. NO CHARGE!*

*I gave you life. NO CHARGE!*

*I nursed you when you were hungry. NO CHARGE!*

*I took care of your every need. NO CHARGE!*

*In the wee hours of the morning I rocked you to sleep in my arms. NO CHARGE!*

*When you were sick, I pleaded in prayer hour after hour for the Great Physician to heal you. NO CHARGE!*

*I have sacrificed all I have so you can have all I never had at NO CHARGE!*

*And even though you would disown me, I would do it all over again at NO CHARGE!*

*Because I love you*

The boy, upon reading this, wrote on his bill **PAID IN FULL!**

What many of us seem to forget is that: God created

| | The Heavens | **NO CHARGE!** |
| | The Earth | **NO CHARGE!** |
| | The Universe | **NO CHARGE!** |
| | The Waters | **NO CHARGE!** |
| | The Plants and fruit trees | **NO CHARGE!** |
| | The Sun | **NO CHARGE!** |
| | The Moon | **NO CHARGE!** |
| | The Birds | **NO CHARGE!** |
| | Every Living Creature | **NO CHARGE!** |

Then He brought forth Man . . . . . . . . . . . . . . . . . . . . . **NO CHARGE!**

And for man He gave him Woman . . . . . . . . . . . . . . **NO CHARGE!**

Then God sent His Son to tell us of His
Father and to die for our sins . . . . . . . . . . . . . . . . . . . **NO CHARGE!**

And all we have to do is to believe and
He promises to Give us Eternal Life at . . . . . . . . . . . **NO CHARGE!**

And, now, for His saints, Christ is
preparing a mansion in Heaven for us at . . . . . . . . . . **NO CHARGE!**

How can I do less than give Him my best... and live for Him
completely **AFTER ALL HE'S DONE FOR ME!**

# DISCOVERING LIFE'S TRUE VALUES

## MY MATERIAL POSSESSIONS

(List items of material value here such as Clothes - $450, Automobile - $9500, Camera - $70, Furniture - $5200, House, Hobby and Sport equipment, Bank Account, Insurance, etc.)

On this side, list items of material value you *now* possess and estimate their dollar value.

On this side, list items of material value you are striving or desire to possess (such as: New Job, Promotion, New Car, Television Set, Golf Clubs, Refrigerator, Bedroom Set, Rugs, etc.)

| ITEMS I NOW POSSESS | | ITEMS I DESIRE TO POSSESS | |
|---|---|---|---|
| ITEM | $ VALUE | ITEM | $ VALUE |
| 1. House | $ | 1. | $ |
| 2. Automobile | | 2. | |
| 3. Furniture | | 3. | |
| 4. Clothing | | 4. | |
| 5. Television | | 5. | |
| 6. Savings Account | | 6. | |
| 7. Investments | | 7. | |
| 8. | | 8. | |
| 9. | | 9. | |
| 10. | | 10. | |
| 11. | | 11. | |
| 12. | | 12. | |
| 13. | | 13. | |
| 14. | | 14. | |
| 15. | | 15. | |
| TOTAL VALUE | $ | TOTAL VALUE | $ |

Place here Total of **BOTH** Columns   $

*Do not be afraid when a man becomes rich, When the glory of his house is increased; For when he dies he will carry nothing away; His glory will not descend after him.*   *(Psalm 49:16-17)*

# DISCOVERING LIFE'S TRUE VALUES

## POSSESSIONS
## MONEY CANNOT BUY

On a Marking Scale of 1 to 3, grade your estimate of achievement in accumulating possessions that money cannot buy.

Place a **1** under Sale of Achievement if you have **not** achieved this goal. Place a **2** under Scale of Achievement if you **occasionally** achieve this goal. Place a **3** under Scale of Achievement if you have **successfully** achieved this goal.

| POSSESSIONS MONEY CANNOT BUY | Scale of Achievement |
|---|---|
| 1. Eternal Life, (John 3:16; Romans 6:23; 10:9) | |
| 2. Harmony in Your Home | |
| 3. A Fulfilled Happy Marriage | |
| 4. Love and Respect from your Children | |
| 5. Family Devotions | |
| 6. Personal Morning and Evening Devotions | |
| 7. Attend Church Faithfully | |
| 8. The ability to say: "I'm sorry." | |
| 9. The ability to say: "I made a mistake." | |
| 10. Peace of Mind | |
| 11. Abundant Health | |
| 12. Freedom from Fear | |
| 13. Freedom from Worry | |
| 14. Exhibit Joy through Trials | |
| 15. A Thankful Happy Heart | |

Total Scale of Achievement ➤⟶

| | |
|---|---|
| 40 - 45 | You have discovered Life's true values! |
| 35 - 39 | You are making progress. Check your weak points and strive to bring them up to Scale 3 level. |
| 25 - 34 | You need to realign your priorities in life. Are you seeking the best of both worlds? You can't serve two masters! Honestly appraise your life's direction and plan to change your priorities. |
| Under 25 | You should very seriously reexamine your life and your goals in light of eternal values. Your priorities are mis-appropriated. Make major changes now while you still have time. |

# WHAT IN THE WORLD WILL HAPPEN NEXT?

## BY SALEM KIRBAN

World history changed overnight on November 9, 1989 when the Berlin Wall came tumbling down. Suddenly Eastern bloc nations overthrew their communist yoke of bondage. Mikhail Gorbachev, head of the Russian empire, embraced the Pope and encouraged German reunification! The U.S. became the world's largest debtor nation! Is this the beginning of the end? This book tells **WHAT IN THE WORLD WILL HAPPEN NEXT!**

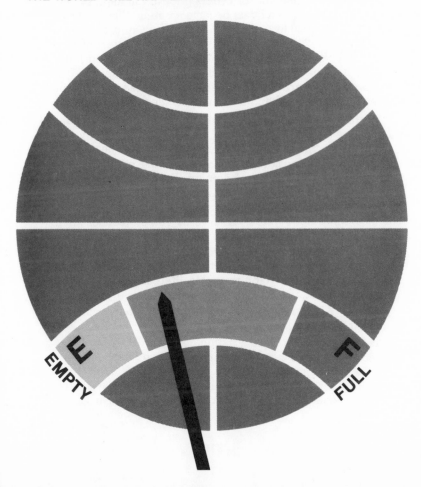

### What is the Rapture?

This refers to the time, prior to the start of the 7 year Tribulation Period, when believing Christians (both dead and alive) will "in the twinkling of an eye" be caught up ("raptured") to meet Christ in the air.

### When will it Occur?

The Bible says in Matthew 24:34, "...This generation shall not pass, till all these things be fulfilled." To some, the start of this Timetable of Events prior to the Rapture began May 14, 1948 when Israel became a nation. Since a generation is about 30 to 33 years, they say, the Rapture will occur between 1978 to 1981. Others feel that the start of Israel should begin at the 6-Day War in June, 1967 when Jerusalem became a part of Israel. Both views, however, are speculative, arriving at conclusions based on personal opinions, rather than on clear Bible teaching.

Matthew 24:34, Mark 13:28-31 and Luke 21:29-33 and Luke 21:24 may well indicate that the Rapture Countdown begins when the time of the Gentiles ends. Whether a countdown can be considered as starting in 1948 or 1967 or some other date is a matter of opinion. Even, however, if 1948 were an acceptable date...one cannot use the phrase of Matthew 24:34 "This generation..." and state that this means 30 or 33 years. This verse rather teaches that... those living in that time will not die until they see these things come to a final consummation. Thus, if someone were 1 year old in 1948, conceivably...he would see the fulfillment of the Rapture in his lifetime (and that's the key phrase)...and this could be some 70 or 80 years later.

IF WE ARE in the Rapture Countdown the events will progress like lightening.

1948    Israel becomes a nation.

1967    Jerusalem at last again belongs to Israel.

1973    Nations the world over hate Israel.

19?? or 2???...How long will it be until the Messiah comes again to deliver Israel and the Earth...?

### What is the Tribulation?

This is the term commonly given to the period also known as "Daniel's 70th Week" of years (Daniel 9:27). Precisely speaking, however, the Biblical period denoted by Jesus as that characterized by "Great Tribulation" is the last half of this 7 years — from the Antichrist's committing the horrible Temple desecration called "the Abomination of Desolation" to Christ's coming to destroy the armies of Antichrist gathered in the Armageddon Valley (Esdraelon-Jezreel) of Israel.

This seven years will be a period of phenomenal world trial and suffering. It is at this time that Antichrist will reign over a federation of 10 nations which quite possibly could include the United States. See Daniel 9:27 and Matthew 24:15,21.

### When will it Occur?

Although no one knows the exact time that it will begin, many Scriptural promises cause us to believe that it will follow the Rapture. Whether it begins the very minute after the Rapture or several years after the Rapture we do not know. It should, however, begin in a time span soon after the Rapture. It will last 7 years.

### What will Happen?

There will be 21 judgments, divided into 3 units of 7 judgments each — the 7 Seals, the 7 Trumpets, and finally the 7 Bowls of God's wrath. The first of these series of judgments are the **Seven Seal Judgments.** Christ allows a man to appear on earth who will pose as the "Saviour of the World." He will be Antichrist. War, famine, death, persecution and catastrophic changes on earth will mark these judgments. Antichrist will pretend to be a friend of Israel. After 3½ years, however, he will turn on them and persecute them severely.

# THE JUDGMENTS OF THE TRIBULATION PERIOD

| | First Seal | Second Seal | Third Seal | Fourth Seal | Fifth Seal | Sixth Seal | Seventh Seal |
|---|---|---|---|---|---|---|---|
| After The Rapture comes... <br><br> **The Seven Seal Judgments** | Rider on White Horse <br> Peace—Antichrist | Rider on Red Horse <br> War | Rider on Black Horse <br> Famine | Rider on Pale Horse <br> Death | Martyred Souls <br> Persecution | Changes on Earth <br> Destruction | Silence |

*First 3½ Years*

| | First Trumpet | Second Trumpet | Third Trumpet | Fourth Trumpet | Fifth Trumpet | Sixth Trumpet | Seventh Trumpet |
|---|---|---|---|---|---|---|---|
| From out of the Seventh Seal comes... <br><br> **The Seven Trumpet Judgments** | ⅓ Earth afire <br> ⅓ Trees burned <br> All grass burned | Meteor destroys ⅓ ships, fish—⅓ sea—blood filled | Falling Star poisons ⅓ of all water | ⅓ of sun, moon and stars darkened | 5 months of torture by Scorpion stings | Satan's 200 million army kills ⅓ Mankind | Earthquake 7000 die in Jerusalem |

| | First Vial | Second Vial | Third Vial | Fourth Vial | Fifth Vial | Sixth Vial | Seventh Vial |
|---|---|---|---|---|---|---|---|
| From out of the Seventh Trumpet comes... <br><br> **The Seven Vial Judgments** | Boils affect those with Mark of Antichrist | Sea of Blood Everything in ocean dies | Rivers of Blood Rivers, springs turn to blood | Heat from Sun scorches all Mankind | Darkness Earth plunged into darkness | River Euphrates Dried up—Army attacks Israel | Hail Cities crumble |

*Last 3½ Years*

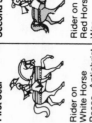

### What is Armageddon?

Armageddon — a strange sounding name — will be the battle ground for the greatest blood bath that the world has ever seen.

### Where is Armageddon located?

Armageddon (Hebrew for: "Mount Megiddo") represents a strategic valley in Northern Israel named for the nearby ancient city of Megiddo. This city built upon a hill, Mt. Megiddo, commands the Jezreel Valley and the Plain of Esdraelon. This is the gateway through the mountains from the North to Jerusalem.

### When will the Battle of Armageddon occur?

It will occur at the **end** of the 7-year Tribulation Period.

### How will events bring about this Battle?

During the Tribulation Period the war machine of Russian Communism will be destroyed (Ezekiel 38:1-39:16). Two world leaders will emerge. The 10-nation European Federation will elect a powerful, personable man to lead them. He will be able to bring peace in the Middle East. He will be the **Antichrist.** A religious leader will direct all worship only to the Antichrist. He will be the **False Prophet.**

Antichrist will persecute Israel, and his power will become worldwide. China and her allies, called the "Kings of the East" in Revelation 16:12, will bring an army of 200 million towards Israel with the intent of destroying Jerusalem and taking over world leadership. Antichrist, for some diabolical cause, also causes armies from all over the earth to invade Israel. Perhaps Antichrist seeks to fight the Asian alliance. Suddenly, against both the armies of Antichrist and the armies of the East, something unusual happens. The Heavens open. Jesus Christ appears on a white horse with the armies of heaven, and destroys all these armies gathered in central Israel. More than 200 million die! The blood bath covers 185 miles of Israel! Antichrist and the False Prophet are cast into the Lake of Fire.

### What is the Judgment Seat of Christ?

This is a time when believers, who have been raptured into Heaven, will stand before their Lord to receive crowns and rewards.

### When will this Occur?

This will occur after the Rapture and during the Tribulation Period. The Judgement Seat of Christ will occur in Heaven (it is sometimes called "the day of Christ"). See Philippians 1:10 and 2:16. At the same time there will begin on earth what is called "the day of the Lord." This is the Tribulation Period.

### Is this different than the Great White Throne Judgment?

YES! The Judgment Seat of Christ occurs immediately after the Rapture and is for believers. Believers will receive rewards. Whereas the Great White Throne Judgment is for unbelievers. This latter judgment will destine unbelievers to an eternity in Hell.

### What happens at The Judgment Seat of Christ?

Each believer will appear before the judgment seat of Christ (2 Corinthians 5:10). No question of divine or eternal penalty will be raised. The believer's works will be examined. Rewards will be given based on the Lord's estimate of their value. See 1 Corinthians 3:10—4:5. Not only will our works be examined but also how well we have done these works and for what motives. The entire depth of our spiritual life, while on earth, will come up for review. If we were "surface Christians" who attended church on Sunday and were active in all types of social church activity...our rewards will be very limited. Our works have no value if they are not built on Christ. Five different crown rewards will be given. Each person will receive rewards in relation to their individual service while on earth. 1 Corinthians 3:8.

### What is the Marriage of the Lamb?

It is that moment when the church (believers) is united with Christ in Heaven.

### When does it Occur?

The Marriage of the Lamb occurs <u>after</u> the Rapture and <u>after</u> the Judgment Seat of Christ. It occurs in Heaven.

### What Happens?

This marks a time when Christ, the heavenly bridegroom, forever will be with His beloved Church (believers). The Bride is the Church, and the Church is all the redeemed of Jesus Christ.

There will be two principals at the Marriage of the Lamb:

The Heavenly Bridegroom: Jesus Christ
The Bride: The Church, which is all the redeemed of
Jesus Christ to the moment of the Rapture.

There will be great rejoicing as this long awaited true marriage between Jesus Christ and the Church is fulfilled ...a union that will last through eternity.

### Will there be a Marriage Supper?

YES! Every marriage has its feast filled with joy and happiness...where everyone fellowships around a table laden with food. At this banquet of banquets will come the prophets, the Old Testament patriarchs and all the redeemed. You may be sitting next to Moses or Nehemiah or Paul or Timothy!

### What will Happen Then?

After the marriage feast Christ will present His Church to the earth to reign in the 1000 year Millennium.

### What is the Judgment of the Nation Israel?

This is a time when all **living** people of Jewish heritage will be judged.

### When does this judgment of living Israel occur?

This occurs <u>after</u> the Battle of Armageddon and <u>before</u> the 1000 Year Millennium.

### Where does it occur?

The place of judgment will be on earth. All **living** Israel will be regathered, possibly at Kadesh-Barnea or at a similar location. Kadesh-Barnea is about 65 miles south of Gaza in the Negev desert. It was here that the Israelites spent many years after their exodus from Egypt. When the Israelites reached this place, Moses sent 12 spies to scout southern Canaan. Encouraged by the Lord to invade Canaan, the Israelites rebelled. See Deuteronomy 9:23. God judged them by not permitting the rebels to enter the Promised Land.

Thus, the area of Kadesh-Barnea quite possibly, based on Ezekiel 20:34-38, could be the area where all living Jews from the four corners of the earth will be regathered.

### What will happen there?

Malachi 3:2-5 speaks of the Lord's First Coming and then of His later judgment. It is described as a refiner's fire that will purify and purge living Israel. God will judge each individual separating the saved from the unsaved.

The unsaved will be cut-off and cast into Hell (Ezekiel 20:37 and Matthew 25:30).

The saved of living Israel will be taken into the 1000 year Millennium, will be resettled into Jerusalem and the Promised Land, and will reign with the Lord Jesus Christ forever.

### What is the Judgment of the Gentiles?

This is a time when all **living** Gentiles who have survived the 7 year Tribulation Period will be judged. See Matthew 25:31-46.

### When does this judgment occur?

This occurs after the Battle of Armageddon and before the 1000 year Millennium.

### Where does it occur?

The Old Testament pictures in Joel 3:2 that God's Armageddon judgments will take place in the Valley of Jehoshaphat. The exact boundaries of this location cannot be determined. We do know that when the Lord returns to the Mount of Olives at the end of the Battle of Armageddon, a great valley will be opened (Zechariah 14:4). Jehoshaphat means "Jehovah judges." This newly opened valley, symbolic of God's judgment could be the area where the Gentiles are judged.

### What will happen there?

The **living** Gentiles at this judgment who showed by their sinful lives that they had rejected the message of Christ's witnesses during the Tribulation Period will go to Hell (Matthew 25:41). Those who showed by their righteous lives that they had accepted Christ during this Period will live on earth for the Millennium Period, and then they will enter the New Heavens and New Earth.

The saved who have accepted Christ up to the point of the Rapture become **Resurrected** Believers...along with the resurrected martyrs of the Tribulation Period. Those who accept Christ after the Rapture in the 7 year Tribulation period and who survive the Tribulation alive are **Living** Believers who live on **Earth** during the Millennium prior to receiving their eternal bodies.

### Why this additional resurrection?

Before the Tribulation Period of 7 years begins, the Rapture occurs. At this point all the Saints, living and dead...are caught up to be with Christ.

When the Tribulation Period begins many people on earth will refuse to accept the Mark of Antichrist. They will refuse to pay homage to him. In fact they will become Christians and will unashamedly testify to others about the redeeming blood of Jesus Christ. Because of their testimony, many will be beheaded. See Revelation 20:4,5.

Thus, this additional resurrection so the Tribulation Saints can join the Raptured Saints.

### What about the Old Testament Saints?

The Bible does not reveal every detail of God's Plan for the future. And because of this Biblical scholars differ on exactly when the Old Testament Saints will be resurrected. Some say they will be resurrected at the Rapture...**prior** to the Tribulation Period. Others say the Old Testament Saints will be resurrected **after** the Tribulation Period **with** the Tribulation Saints. In either case, they will participate in the Marriage of Lamb...since this event continues on up to the Millennium. Daniel 12:2, Isaiah 26:19 and John 5:28,29 are good references here.

### Then how many resurrections are there?

The Bible speaks of **two** great resurrections, the **First** and the **Second.** The one is unto life and the other is unto judgment. The First Resurrection has at least two parts.

**First.** (a) The resurrection of believers at the Rapture (1 Thessalonians 4:16; 1 Corinthians 15:51-53)

     (b) The resurrection of Tribulation Saints (Revelation 20:4,5)

**Second.** The resurrection of the unsaved at the Great White Throne Judgment (Revelation 20:5, 11-14)

### Who are the Evil Ones?

They are the three major leaders during the Tribulation Period...Antichrist and his associate, The False Prophet, and, of course, Satan. This is the False Trinity which will fully manifest itself during the end of this age.

### When does judgment fall on them?

At the <u>end</u> of the 7 year Tribulation Period.

### What actually happens?

Jesus Christ, after destroying the armies of the world at the battle of Armageddon...then turns to take care of the leaders of this evil plan.

Antichrist, whose 42 months of world power began when he desecrated the Temple in Jerusalem in the middle of the 7 year Tribulation Period, now must face the consequences of his sins. He is cast into the Lake of Fire (Rev. 19:20).

The False Prophet, a religious leader, who directed allegiance to Antichrist, is also cast into the Lake of Fire (Revelation 19:20).

They are not merely slain...as the multitudes are who took part in the Battle of Armageddon. Both of these masterminds of iniquity are actually cast **alive** into the Lake of Fire without waiting for any final judgment.

### What is the Lake of Fire?

It is the place of eternal suffering burning with brimstone, a place of perpetual darkness with no hope of deliverance.

### What happens to Satan?

Satan at this time is bound in the bottomless pit for 1000 years. He does not reappear until the end of the Millennium Period. The bottomless pit is not necessarily Hades or Hell but a holding place where Satan is bound by a "*great chain*" (Revelation 20:1-3).

### What is the Millennium?

This is a period when earth again is placed under the direct rule of God, and when all the believers of all the ages reign with Christ. It is not yet, however, the perfect state of the New Earth and the New Heavens which comes later.

Those previously resurrected at the Rapture and those saints who died in the Tribulation and were resurrected along with Old Testament saints...will reign with Christ in the Millennial Age as **Resurrected Believers.** This includes all of the believers who, alive at the time of the Rapture, were then changed "in the twinkling of an eye."

### When will this occur?

The Millennium will occur **after** the Tribulation Period.

### Are there two types of Believers at that time?

YES. There are **Resurrected Believers** and **Living Believers.** **Resurrected Believers**, those already raised from the dead, have been previously described above. They will be given positions of responsibility in the Millennial Kingdom (Matthew 19:28, Luke 19: 12-27).

**Living Believers** will be Gentiles and Jews alike who are still living at the close of Armageddon, and who are permitted to enter the Millennial Kingdom. These were not raptured (they were not believers at the time of the Rapture), nor did they die in the Tribulation Period (they survived). They are still in their human unresurrected bodies.

### Will Living Believers still have children?

YES. During the Millennium these **Living Believers** will still be fully normal people who are able to reproduce children. Children born of these Living Believers will still be born with a sin nature. And for them, as for all humans born at any time, salvation is still required. They must individually make a decision whether to accept Jesus Christ as Saviour and Lord...or to deny Him.

### What is the Final Rebellion?

This is a time when Satan will have a brief and last opportunity to deceive people.

### When does this occur?

This will happen at the **end** of the 1000 year Period.

### How can Satan get a following after 1000 years of peace and happiness?

You must remember that many will be born during this 1000 years. And, as ideal as the Millennium will be it still will not be Heaven. Many born during this 1000 years will not become believers. Sin will still be possible. Although the majority of those born during the Millennium will no doubt follow Christ, yet other multitudes will not believe. Some will refuse to go up to Jerusalem to worship the Lord (Zechariah 14:17-19). Christ rules with an "iron rod" in a theocratic government during this Millennial reign. Because of this some will inwardly rebel. Once and for all, God will give them this last opportunity to voluntarily choose between His Kingdom or Satan's. Like Adam and Eve, they will be given an opportunity to choose life or death.

### How many decide to follow Satan?

The Bible says in Revelation 20:7,8 "...Satan shall be loosed out of his prison...to gather them (the unbelievers) together to battle: the number of whom is as the sand of the sea." This could involve millions of people.

### What is the outcome of this revolt?

This vast number of people will completely encircle the Living Believers within the capital city, Jerusalem, in a state of siege. When this occurs, God brings fire down from Heaven killing the millions of Satan's army (Revelation 20). Satan is then cast into the Lake of Fire where Antichrist and The False Prophet already are.

### What is the Great White Throne Judgment?

This is the final judgment of the unsaved, non-believers, of **all** of the ages. These are resurrected for this event and they are judged before God.

### When does this Judgment occur?

This occurs **after** the Final Rebellion at the end of the Millennial Period.

### What actually happens?

Immediately prior to this, at the close of the Millennium Satan was cast into the Lake of Fire where the Antichrist and the False Prophet have already been for 1000 years.

Now, before the Great White Throne are arraigned all of the unrepentent sinners of the ages. This throne is different from the throne of the Tribulation Period. That throne had a rainbow around it (Revelation 4:3) indicating God would show mercy and many would be saved during the Tribulation Period (Revelation 7).

But the Great White Throne has **no rainbow.** No more mercy will be extended. The God of love is now a God of JUDGMENT. The whiteness of the throne stands for God's unspotted holiness. This holiness condemns all of the unrepentent sinners of all of the ages.

Not only do the living unbelievers face this judgment but **all** the lost dead of all the ages are raised from the dead to face this same judgment. **Here is the saddest roll call in history!** No matter how rich you are in today's world . . . money does not buy your way into Heaven . . . no more than good works!

All these unbelievers are then cast in the Lake of Fire (Revelation 20:15). Thus ends . . . and begins . . . the most tragic moment in history . . . a moment that for the unbeliever will begin an eternity in constant torment and eternal separation from God, called in the Bible, "the Second Death" (Revelation 20:14).

 **13** Earth Burns Up

### When does this present Earth burn up?

This present earth is purified **after** the Final rebellion which closes the Millennium of 1000 years.

### Why is the earth destroyed?

It is **not** really destroyed. It is purified through burning. Because the earth has become so polluted with sin, God desires to wipe the slate entirely clean from every trace of that sin. He will do this by purging the earth by fire... giving His Saints a New Heaven and a New Earth.

### What does occur?

In the New Testament 2 Peter 3:3-12 we are told five important facts:

1. This event will occur SUDDENLY
2. The Heavens will pass away WITH A GREAT NOISE
3. The Elements will melt with a FERVENT HEAT
4. The Earth will be BURNED UP
5. Everything on the Earth will be BURNED UP

The Sun, 100 times the diameter of the earth, has the capacity to generate a heat so intense it could set the entire earth afire. If you could build a cake of ice 1½ miles square and 93 million miles high...it would reach from earth to sun. Scientists tell us, if the full power of the sun were focused on this cake of ice it would be completely melted in just 30 seconds!

In this, God's final judgment, the intensive fire will melt all the elements of the earth, burn the earth, set the atmospheric heavens on fire and in that fire...dissolve those heavens! Some have suggested that this final fire of purification when "the elements shall melt with fervent heat" will be a divinely originated nuclear inferno — refining by fire the former sin cursed planet (2 Peter 3:10).

## RELATED VERSES

**The Rapture**
John 14:1-3 • Acts 1:11 • 1 Thessalonians 4:13-18 • 1 Corinthians 10:1, 15:51-52
**The Tribulation**
Jeremiah 30:7-10 • Daniel 9:27 • Daniel 12:1 • Matthew 24:15-29 • Revelation 12:6-17
**The Battle of Armageddon**
Isaiah 63:1-6 • Joel 3:1,2,9-17 • Zechariah 12:8-14 • Revelation 14:14-20; 16:12-16; 19:11-21
**The Judgment Seat of Christ**
Romans 14:10-12 • 1 Corinthians 3:12-15; 4:4-5 • 2 Corinthians 5:9-11 • Revelation 19:7b
**The Marriage of the Lamb**
2 Corinthians 11:2 • Revelation 19:7-9
**The Judgment of the Nation ISRAEL**
Ezekiel 20:34-38 • Zechariah 13:1-2 • Malachi 3:2-5
**The Judgment of the GENTILES**
Matthew 25:31-46
**Resurrection of Tribulation Saints**
Isaiah 26:19-21 • Daniel 12:1-3 • John 5:28-29 • Revelation 20:4-6
**Disposition of Evil Ones**
Daniel 7:19-28; 9:27 • John 5:43 • Revelation 13:1-18; 19:19-21
**The 1000 Year Millennium**
Isaiah 65:19-25 • Jeremiah 30:19-20 • Ezekiel 36:33-38 • Zechariah 8:20-23; 14:16-21 • Revelation 20:1-7
**The Final Rebellion**
Revelation 20:3-7,10
**The Great White Throne Judgment**
Revelation 20:11-15
**Earth Burns Up**
2 Peter 3:3-12
**The New Heavens and the New Earth**
Isaiah 65:17-19 • 2 Peter 3:13-14 • Revelation 21:1 to 22:5

### When do the New Heavens and New Earth become a reality?

The New Heavens and the New Earth will be formed after this present Earth burns up and is purified. This is the **LAST** and final part of God's eternal plan for mankind.

### Who will be in the New Heavens and the New Earth?

All the Old Testament saints, all the New Testament saints, and all of the Tribulation and Millennial saints. In other words all the redeemed (saved) of all the ages will be there! This will be the ultimate in glory reigning forever with Christ in a New Heaven and a New Earth (Revelation 21).

### How will the New Earth be different from this present Earth?

1. Every believer will have a NEW BODY.
   It will be an imperishable body. No longer will we be plagued with illness or death; nor will there be any tears in Heaven but rather, eternal joy!
2. There will be NO NIGHT.
   Christ will be the light that illumines all.
3. There will be NO MORE SEPARATION.
   All our loved ones who are believers will be there.
4. There will be NO HUNGER NOR FAMINE.
   The Tree of Life will provide sufficient for all.

### Where will the New City of Jerusalem be?

The New City, JERUSALEM, will not be identical in size or boundaries to the city on this present earth that we know today as Jerusalem. The New Jerusalem will be approximately 1500 miles on each side and could conceivably hold according to some theoretical calculations 53 billion people. Revelation 21:1-22:5 gives the most extensive revelation of the eternal home of the redeemed. Will you be there?

## WHAT WILL YOU DO WITH JESUS ?

After reading this book, it should become evident to you that the world is **not** getting better and better. What happens when it comes time for you to depart from this earth? Then...**WHAT WILL YOU DO WITH JESUS ?**

Here are five basic observations in the Bible of which you should be aware:

1. ALL SIN — For all have sinned, and come short of the glory of God. (Romans 3:23)
2. ALL LOVED — For God so loved the world, that He gave His only begotten Son, that whosoever believeth in Him should not perish, but have everlasting life (John 3:16)
3. ALL RAISED — Marvel not at this: for the hour is coming, in which all that are in the graves shall hear his voice.

   And shall come forth; they that have done good, unto the resurrection of life; and they that have done evil, unto the resurrection of damnation. (John 5:28,29)
4. ALL JUDGED — ...we shall all stand before the judgment seat of Christ. (Romans 14:10)

   And I saw the dead, small and great, stand before God; and the books were opened...(Revelation 20:12)
5. ALL BOW — ...at the name of Jesus every knee should bow...(Philippians 2:10)

Right now, in simple faith, you can have the wonderful assurance of eternal life.

Ask yourself, honestly, the question....WHAT WILL I DO WITH JESUS?
God tells us the following:
"...him that cometh to me I will in no wise cast out. (37) Verily, verily (truly) I say unto you, He that believeth on me (Christ) *hath* everlasting life" (47)—(John 6:37, 47).

He also is a righteous God and a God of indignation to those who reject Him....
"...he that believeth not is condemned already, because he hath not believed in the name of the only begotten Son of God"—(John 3:18).

"And whosoever was not found written in the book of life was cast into the lake of fire"—(Revelation 20:15).

# YOUR MOST IMPORTANT DECISION IN LIFE

All of your riches here on earth—all of your financial security—all of your material wealth, your houses, your land will crumble into nothingness in a few years.

No matter how great your works—no matter how kind you are—no matter how philanthropic you are—it means nothing in the sight of God, because in the sight of God, your riches are as filthy rags.

"...all our righteousnesses are as filthy rags..." (Isaiah 64:6)

Christ expects you to come as you are, a sinner, recognizing your need of a Saviour, the Lord Jesus Christ.

Understanding this, why not bow your head right now and give this simple prayer of faith to the Lord.

---

### My Personal Decision for CHRIST

"Lord Jesus, I know that I'm a sinner and that I cannot save myself by good works. I believe that you died for me and that you shed your blood for my sins. I believe that you rose again from the dead. And now I am receiving you as my personal Saviour, my Lord, my only hope of salvation. I know that I cannot save myself. Lord, be merciful to me, a sinner, and save me according to the promise of Your Word. I want Christ to come into my heart now to be my Saviour, Lord and Master."

Signed . . . . . . . . . . . . . . . . . . . . . . . . . . . . . . . . . . . .

Date . . . . . . . . . . . . . . . . . . . . . . . . . . . . . . . . .

---

If you have signed the above, having just taken Christ as your personal Saviour and Lord...I would like to rejoice with you in your new found faith.

Write to me... Salem Kirban, Second Coming/Missions, Box 278, Montrose, Pennsylvania 18801... and I will send you an informative booklet to help you start living your new life in Christ.

# Catalog of SALEM KIRBAN Books and Cassettes

In July, 1967, I took a trip around the world. As an investigative reporter I covered the war in Vietnam and the aftermath of the Six Day war. From the American dead in Vietnam to the dying in Calcutta . . . the final leg of my journey was to witness the living dead in Jordan.

In a refugee camp in Shuneh (50 miles from Amman, Jordan), I came across a tent city. These were Arabs . . . many originally from Jerusalem and Bethlehem . . . now without a home or homeland. The scene above particularly moved me . . . an Arab father and his child. Their home was a few poles and a tattered rag, just sufficient to provide a little shade. This scene challenged me to reach **both** Arab and Jew and the *world* for Christ through the power of the **PRINTED WORD!**

## SECOND COMING / Missions
Box 278, Montrose, Penna. 18801

Your Gift is TAX DEDUCTIBLE

Since **1970, SECOND COMING/Missions** has been distributing the
Word of God worldwide by way of the printed page. My interest in Bible
prophecy began in **1938**. As a young child I attended a little missionary
church in Clarks Summit, Pennsylvania. [Clarks Summit is a small town
about 10 miles above Scranton]

Church services were held in a rented room on the 2nd floor of the Fire Hall
in the center of town. Rev. Pryce was the Pastor. It was here my brother,
Lafayette, my sister Elsie and I were brought to church each Sunday.

The photograph **below** was taken in **1938** at the annual church picnic at
Covey's Farm in Clarks Summit. I am that little boy in the circle on the
front row. I can remember vividly at this picnic the various church members
discussing the book of Revelation and prophecy. And, remember, this was
**1938**! This discussion was the first spark that kindled a flaming desire for
me to understand God's prophetic promises better.

And it was from this beginning that eventually led me to start **SECOND
COMING/*Missions*** in 1970. My desire was to make sure that Bibles and
books on Bible prophecy would be available to seeking souls worldwide. By
your faithful giving...you are making this dream come true...year after year!

## HOW TO ORDER FROM
## The CATALOG Of
## CHRISTIAN GROWTH HELPS

On the following pages are
items that will help you grow in
your spiritual life. Each item
has an Order Number.

1. **SELECT** items you desire.
2. Then **TURN** to the
   Back Order Page.
3. In the **BOX** provided
   **INSERT** the
   **Order Number[s]** of
   items you desire.
4. **MAIL Response Form**
   with your Gift to
   **SECOND COMING.**

Salem & Mary Kirban

---

## BIBLE PROPHECY Message
## by SALEM KIRBAN on Cassette

Hear Noted Author SALEM KIRBAN
in a Bible prophecy message that was
given in over 300 churches nationwide!

## COUNTDOWN TO RAPTURE

Answers these questions and much more:

- Will Russia Invade Israel?
- Will We See World War 3?
- Is Antichrist Alive Today?
- Is The Marking System Already Here?
- Who Lives In The Millennium?
- How Will Time Actually Stand Still?
- How our farms are being taken over by global food chains...
    how this will one day force people to wear The Mark!
- Is The Marking System Already Here?
- The Day BREAD is $5 a Loaf and COFFEE is $45 a Jar!
- Has The Rapture Countdown Begun?
- What is the Judgment Seat of Christ and
    How does it differ from the Great White Throne Judgment?

---

| To Receive | **COUNTDOWN TO RAPTURE Cassette** | |
|---|---|---|
| One Cassette | For a Gift of $10 | Order No. 9 |

## WHAT IS LIFE?

Explores the questions:
**Why did God create you?** •
What is your purpose on earth?
• **What is the meaning of life on this earth?** •
Since your life span is under 100 years... what are your most vital priorities in light of an eternity?
• **Are the things you consider important *really* important?** Most people go through life never knowing what life *really* is! Discover how to have true joy, happiness, peace and contentment!

Excellent to give to unsaved loved ones!

**Order No. 137
For a Gift of $10**

# 666 And 1000

Two Best Selling novels by
**SALEM KIRBAN**
combined into One Book!
**666** vividly captures events of the Tribulation Period. **1000** is a sequel on the Millennium!

## 15 SUSPENSEFUL CHAPTERS in 666

1 I Saw The Saints Rise
2 The Great Reassurance
3 The Sinister Plot
4 Flight to Moscow
5 Cloud of Death
6 Invasion From North
7 Triumph and Tragedy
8 Secret Flight To Babylon
9 Startling Pronouncement
10 Search for Safety
11 The Shocking Spectacle
12 The Strange Destroyer
13 The Sound of Death
14 March on Megiddo
15 SEARCH FOR TOMORROW

## 10 CLIMATIC, SHOCKING CHAPTERS in 1000

[Sequel to the book **666**]

1 The Great Reunion
2 Sorrow At Sinai
3 Valley of Tears
4 Journey To Jerusalem
5 Life in the Leaf
6 Marriage at Megiddo
7 To Lick the Dust
8 The Secret at Sodom
9 Point of No Return
10 The CHOICE

Both Books Are Filled With Photos & Illustrations

| **TO RECEIVE** | **666 and 1000** | |
|---|---|---|
| One Copy | For a Gift of $25 | Order No. 4 |

# WHAT IS SECOND COMING/*Missions*?

**SECOND COMING, Inc.** is a Non-Profit ministry dedicated primarily to printing Bibles and prophetic portions of Scripture for <u>FREE</u> distribution throughout Asia, Africa, the Middle East and the far unreached areas of the world. Salem Kirban is President of **SECOND COMING, Inc.** This Non-Profit global ministry began in 1970.

Salem Kirban is the author of over 50 books including GUIDE TO SURVIVAL, 666, YOUR LAST GOODBYE, THE RISE OF ANTICHRIST, SATAN'S MARK EXPOSED and COUNTDOWN TO RAPTURE. He and his wife, Mary, have 5 children...Dennis, Doreen, Diane, Duane and Dawn. All but one is married. Diane is in full-time Christian service.

---

### SECOND COMING/Missions Began In JERUSALEM
### 125,000 Copies of GUIDE TO SURVIVAL
### Mailed Throughout All Of ISRAEL

---

When Mary and I began **SECOND COMING/*Missions***...I traveled around the world on a one-month journey. My first stop was Vietnam, where, as a war correspondent, I reported on the Vietnam War. I also stopped in Korea, Thailand, Cambodia, India and finally ended up in Jerusalem. The 6-Day War was just ending and I witnessed Arab refugees pouring out of Israel towards Jordan. As an Arab myself... [because my parents were born in Lebanon]...I had a heart of compassion for their plight.

And as a <u>Christian</u> Arab, I also realized the challenge to reach the people of Israel with the good news of eternal life. And that's how **SECOND COMING/*Missions*** began...by arranging with a missionary in Israel to translate **GUIDE TO SURVIVAL** into <u>Hebrew</u>. This book was printed right in Jerusalem. Over a 3-year period we printed **125,000** copies of **GUIDE TO SURVIVAL** and mailed them direct to Jewish people <u>throughout all of Israel</u>. The response was wonderful...and that's how **SECOND COMING/*Missions*** began its literature ministry of Bible distribution throughout the world.

In this Catalog...we make available to you CHRISTIAN GROWTH HELPS so you can better understand Bible Prophecy and God's Plan for you from the Rapture all the way up to the eternal New Heavens & New Earth.

We are **not** in the business of selling books and cassettes. We <u>ARE</u> in the ministry of <u>getting out the Word of God worldwide.</u> Therefore, when you send a Gift to SECOND COMING...we are happy to provide you with items in this Catalog to help you grow spiritually. And by your generous giving...you help this ministry reach out to lost souls worldwide.

# WHAT IN THE WORLD WILL HAPPEN NEXT ?

## By SALEM KIRBAN

☐ 28 Chapters ☐ 350 Pages ☐ Fully Illustrated

This book ranks among the most vital witnessing books to reach the world for Christ! It answers <u>in one book</u> every crucial answer to life's eternal destiny! Why not give to loved ones and friends.

---

### SALEM KIRBAN Answers Life's 5 Most Important Questions...

### WHAT IN THE WORLD WILL HAPPEN NEXT ?
At last! Here is a, clear, step by step explanation of the sequence of the **14** events that are **yet to occur** on God's Timetable! A page is devoted to each event...from the **Rapture** to the **New Heavens and New Earth**! And that's not all. There is a pictorial description of all **21** Tribulation judgments.

### WHAT IS LIFE?
Answers such questions as: Why did God create you? What is your purpose on earth? What is the meaning of life on this earth? Since your life span is under 100 years...what are your most vital priorities in light of an eternity? Are the things you consider important really important?

### WHAT IS THE RAPTURE ?
One of these days MILLIONS will suddenly DISAPPEAR from this earth without any warning *"...in the twinkling of an eye."* This is called **The RAPTURE** ! The Bible tells us that no one knows the day nor hour. However, God does give us clear indications of what to look for just before His coming for His saints! **We are now in that Time Period!**

### WHAT IS HELL?
Is there a real Hell? Is there real torment? Where is Hell? Is Hell a place of consciousness? Is it a place of darkness? What are the greatest torments one will suffer in Hell? Where are the unsaved dead <u>before</u> their Judgment Day? How can one escape an eternity of life in Hell? Must that decision be made while one is alive?

### WHAT IS HEAVEN?
You will find the answers to such questions as: What is life like in the 1000 year Millennium? Do our loved ones who are already in Heaven know what is happening on earth <u>now</u>? What type of body will we have in Heaven? Will we recognize our loved ones in Heaven? How do we become immortal? Where is Heaven? Revealing Charts and Photos!

---

| To Receive | WHAT IN THE WORLD WILL HAPPEN NEXT? | |
|---|---|---|
| **One Copy** | For a Gift of $10 | Order No. 282 |
| **Three Copies** | For a Gift of $25 | Order No. 283 |

## Taking The Gospel WORLDWIDE

*Mary and I in Fairbanks, Alaska*

To keep this ministry going... Mary and I have travelled hundreds of thousands of miles.  I spoke in Anchorage and Fairbanks, Alaska on two occasions in January when temperatures dropped to **30 <u>below</u>** zero and in Florida where they soared to over **100** degrees.  We have driven our car in snow, in rain, in hail, in fog and on the edge of a tornado!    Each speaking tour lasted from as little as a week to as much as **41** days.   Lifting Bibles and books in and out of our car was a challenge in itself.   **Each box weighs about 35 pounds!**   And, in my 60's...here I was lifting some **210** pounds of books into the church... and then [after the service] lifting boxes back into the car!  In the last 10 years I have spoken in <u>**over 400**</u> churches nationwide.    **We took on Church Speaking Tours for <u>two</u> reasons:**

**1.** To motivate Christian to get busy for the Lord in these Last Days.
**2.** To generate additional support for **SECOND COMING/*Missions***

To those who support **SECOND COMING/*Missions*** monthly we send our ***WORLDWIDE NEWS***...a newsletter written by Salem Kirban which shows how current events are the fulfillment of Bible prophecy.

By going on speaking engagements in Churches we were able to meet the shortfall of donor income so **Second Coming/*Missions*** could continue. Mary and I are both **68** years of age.   We feel led not to continue in church speaking engagements.   Sleeping in a different motel every night [often under  adverse conditions] carrying boxes in and out of over 400 Churches was both stressful and challenging.   We now feel our time is more wisely used both in writing Prophecy books and Newsletters and widening the literature outreach of **Second Coming/*Missions***.

**NOW!  Completely Updated, Revised and <u>ENLARGED!</u>**

by Salem Kirban

432 Pages!
36 Chapters!
56 Feature Pages!

**Over 100 ILLUSTRATIONS and CHARTS!**

Sometime in the near future several Million people will suddenly **disappear!** They will vanish *"in the twinkling of an eye."*  That's why this book was written originally in 1968.  But current world events are shaping up to complete chaos! Germany is reunified!  The Common Market nations are uniting as one major force with a common currency!  Russia is holding up her deceptive dove of peace.  The Middle East is a powder keg . . . ready to explode into a World War. **That's why I have completely updated, revised <u>and ENLARGED</u>** this <u>new</u> edition of **GUIDE TO SURVIVAL.**

---

**Some of The Exciting Chapters That Tell HOW THE WORLD WILL END!**

---

**Guide To Survival**
How Current News Events Reveal Shocking Fulfillment of Prophecy.

**Power That Destroys**
How the Nations of the World Now Have An Arsenal of Death.

**The Vanishing Christians**
How Christians Will Be Raptured and How The World Will React.

**Russia's Rise To Ruin**
How Russia and her allies, including Germany, will invade Israel!

**Is Antichrist Alive Today?**
Why The Time Is Ripe For Antichrist To Prepare His Entrance!

**Miracle Worker and Executioner**
How The World Is Already Welcoming A Coming False Prophet!

**Lulled Into A False Security**
How People Will Willingly Accept The Mark <u>666</u>!  Much more!

**The Day of Terror and Tragedy**
The **21** Tribulation Judgments and the terror that follows.

**The Battle of Armageddon**
The Monumental Death Toll and the Amazing Miracle That Occurs!

---

If you want to know what is going to happen in the near future you want to make sure both you and your loved ones get *GUIDE TO SURVIVAL.* The last chapter is a Decision chapter pointing the reader to Christ. Leave this book in a prominent place in your home so it serves as a constant witness even after you have been raptured.

**GUIDE TO SURVIVAL**          **Yours for a Gift of $25**          **Order No. 261**

## REVELATION VISUALIZED

### REVELATION VISUALIZED
By Gary G. Cohen
and Salem Kirban

<u>Never before</u>
so crystal clear
an explanation of
the last book of the Bible!

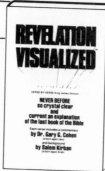

When you start feeling sorry for yourself, keep this photograph on the back of your mind. Perhaps it will change your thoughts from self-pity to praise as you say "Thank you, Jesus, for dying for my sins, for bearing my burdens, for providing eternal life, for meeting my every need." I took this photograph in 1971 in Hong Kong. I will never forget this scene. And it caused me to examine my life and to double my efforts in serving Christ.

The book of Revelation deals with future events. It is the most difficult book for many to understand. We have <u>**Visualized**</u> the book by **(1)** placing only 2 verses on each page **(2)** writing a clear Commentary on each page **(3)** including an explanatory illustration or Chart **(4)** tying the verse in to current events and **(5)** by a red arrow, pointing to the Time Period in which that particular verse relates. Full Color! 380 Pages!

To Order
Use this
Identifying
Number
①
Yours for
a Gift of
**$35**

---

## BIBLE PROPHECY Books    by Salem Kirban

Each of
These Books
Are Filled
with
**CHARTS**
and
**PHOTOS!**

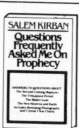

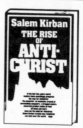

### QUESTIONS FREQUENTLY ASKED ME ON PROPHECY
This new updated version of a popular best-seller will answer those difficult questions many people sidestep. Answers clearly given to questions on Bible prophecy. Includes revealing photographs and crystal clear charts.  ②

### THE RISE OF ANTICHRIST
While the church sleeps…the advance forces of Antichrist have already arrived! Over 20 chapters include: *The Day They Reshape Man, The Plan to Control the Human Mind, The Day They Transplant Memories…*  ③

### HOW TO BE SURE OF CROWNS IN HEAVEN
Believers must appear before the Judgment Seat of Christ (2'Corinthians 5:10). Here their entire life will be reviewed before God (Romans 14:12). Shows how you can be **sure** of receiving Crowns in Heaven.  ⑬

**TO ORDER**…use Identifying Number in Circle.
Any book above for a Gift of $25 to SECOND COMING.

Below are four sample pages from **REVELATION VISUALIZED** showing the **five features** that make the book of Revelation easy to understand. ① Only two verses of Revelation are on a page, ② An explanatory commentary is below these two verses, ③ An illustration or chart adds to visual clarity of those two verses, ④ Plus more commentary shows how prophecy is being fulfilled ⑤ A Red Arrow points to Time Period in which those verse relate.

---

### Revelation 8

VERSES 6, 7

6 And the seven angels which had the seven trumpets prepared themselves to sound.
7 The first angel sounded, and there followed hail and fire mingled with blood, and they were cast upon the earth: and the third part of trees was burnt up, and all green grass was burnt up.

Exod. 9:23-25;
Ezek. 38:22

#### Commentary

6. More plagues now begin to fall upon the earth during this Tribulation Period already beset with false prophets, wars and revolutions, famine, death, martyrdom, and astounding signs in the sky. The seals begin the seven years and the bowls of wrath (chapters 15-16) are almost—as we shall later see—at the close of the seven years. It is the trumpets which fall in the middle. Thus commentators disagree as to which half of the period the trumpets should be assigned.
At present I am inclined to think that the trumpets occur in the latter half of the first 3 1/2 years. I think this to be so because they are introduced to us *before* the great parenthetical break of chapters 10 through 14 which reveals the worldwide kingdom of the Antichrist WHICH BEGINS ESSENTIALLY AT THE MIDPOINT OF THE SEVEN YEARS WHEN THE ABOMINATION OF DESOLATION IS COMMITTED.

THE FIRST TRUMPET

HAIL, FIRE, BLOOD
1/3 Earth on Fire
1/3 Trees Burned
All Grass Burned

#### Background ④

You will note that all these plagues have the element of fire in them. These initial plagues cause destruction of only a third part which would seem to indicate that God is still dealing with His people in mercy.

| PAST | PRESENT | RAPTURE | FIRST 3 1/2 TRIBULATION | LAST 3 1/2 | ARMA-GEDDON | MIL-LENNIUM | NEW HEAVENS & EARTH |
|------|---------|---------|-------------------------|------------|-------------|-------------|---------------------|

145

---

### Revelation 19

VERSES 17, 18

17 And I saw an angel standing in the sun; and he cried with a loud voice, saying to all the fowls that fly in the midst of heaven, Come and gather yourselves together unto the supper of the great God;
18 That ye may eat the flesh of kings, and the flesh of captains, and the flesh of mighty men, and the flesh of horses, and of them that sit on them, and the flesh of all *men, both* free and bond, both small and great.

Ezek. 39:17-24

#### Commentary

17-18. Here an angel standing with the sun as his background invites the carion of the sky to "THE SUPPER OF THE GREAT GOD." Thus this chapter speaks of two end-time contrasting suppers. In 19:9 we read of "THE MARRIAGE SUPPER OF THE LAMB" which will be a feast of unbounding joy as the redeemed partake of this feast together with their wonderful Lord. The armies of the redeemed who come with their Lord (19:14) will have a part in this grand banquet.

The armies of the wicked nations that in the end-time choose to follow Antichrist, the Beast, shall at this Revelation appearance of Jesus Christ be involved in this other supper (19:17-18). These shall be slain by "the brightness of His coming" and their dead bodies shall lie upon the ground lifeless to be picked at by the crows, hawks, and vultures 2 Thess. 2:8. This is a *Supper of Death* to which the followers of Antichrist will attend; while those who love Christ will attend the *Supper of Life!*

The description here in verses 17-18 perfectly matches that of Ezekiel 39:17-24, and the two passages I think must speak of this same Armageddon battle. Ezekiel 38:1-39:16, however, speaks of an earlier Russian invasion of Israel. The prophet, Ezekiel, first sees the Northern confederation's (Russia and her allies) invasion of Israel and then his vision moves right into this latter Armageddon. In both battles God in the latter days defeats a satanically inspired group of armies in the land of Palestine. Thus Ezekiel sees them both amid chapters 37-39 wherein the theme is the end-time deliverance and conversion of Israel by God.

*Israeli Cavalry unit on patrol on horses! Will horses play an important role in the Tribulation period?*

#### Background ④

At the end of the 7 year Tribulation Period there will occur the endtime Battle of Armageddon when evil armies from all over the world come up against Jerusalem for a diabolical purpose (Joel 3; Revelation 14 and 19).
While this is clear, all the details leading up to this battle have not been revealed to us. Antichrist, under the great coalition of western nations, may set up a headquarters in Jerusalem to reign over Israel. Not only will he reign over Israel and Europe but he will also control the entire world (Revelation 13:7,8)!
It will be at the close of the Tribulation Period that Israel will find itself under an invasion by an Army probably numbering into the millions of men - quite possibly this final armada will include the army of 200 million from the Sixth Trumpet (Revelation 9:16). These are those who must cross the River Euphrates (Revelation 9:14, 16; 16:12) - hence they come from ASIA!

| PAST | PRESENT | RAPTURE | FIRST 3 1/2 TRIBULATION | LAST 3 1/2 | ARMA-GEDDON | MIL-LENNIUM | NEW HEAVENS & EARTH |
|------|---------|---------|-------------------------|------------|-------------|-------------|---------------------|

---

# The Image of Daniel 2

**606 ± B.C.**
Gold — Nebuchadnezzar's
Babylon (Unquestioned
obedience to one absolute
sovereign)

**536 ± B.C.**
Silver — The dual Empire of
the Medes & Persians
(The 2 arms!)

**336 B.C.**
Copper — The Greek
Empire

**200 ± B.C.**
Iron Legs United —
Roman Republic & Empire

**300 ± A.D.**
Iron Legs Divided
Western & Eastern
Roman Empire

**476 & 1453 A.D.** (They fall)

Iron Legs Cracking —
European States

Iron & Clay Feet — End-time
Lawlessness (Communism)?

10 Toes — Revived Rome
Confederacy

**A.D.?**

**Sample Page from REVELATION VISUALIZED**
Feature No. 3 / Full Color illustrations and Charts
Feature No. 4 / Scripture verse is tied in with vivid explanation
Feature No. 5 / A red arrow points to Time Period of that Verse

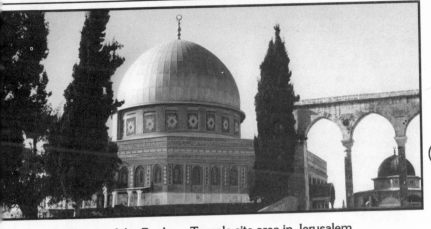
(3)

Dome of the Rock on Temple site area in Jerusalem

**BACKGROUND** The Bible tells us the measurements of the New City, JERUSALEM in Revelation 21:16-21

*Size:* About 1500 miles in each direction.

Dr. Wilbur M. Smith, in his book, THE BIBLICAL DOC-TRINE OF HEAVEN gives us some insight from an Australian engineer.

The City will give you an area 2,250,000 square miles. This makes it 15,000 times as big as London; 20 times as big as New Zealand; 10 times as big as Germany and 10 times as big as France.

And it is 40 times as big as all England and even much bigger than India!

(4) Taking the number of people to a square mile in the city of London, this Australian engineer, computed that the City Foursquare (the New Jerusalem) could hold 100 thousand MILLIONS - or about 70 times the present population of the globe!

(5)

▼

| PAST | PRESENT | RAPTURE | FIRST 3½ LAST 3½ TRIBULATION | ARMA-GEDDON | MIL-LENNIUM | NEW HEAVENS &EARTH |
|------|---------|---------|------|------|------|------|

| **To Receive** One Copy | **REVELATION VISUALIZED** For A Gift of $35 | Order No. **1** |
|---|---|---|

*Here are the revealing chapters in*
**THE NEW AGE SECRET PLAN FOR WORLD CONQUEST!**

**THE NEW AGE
SECRET PLAN
FOR
WORLD CONQUEST**

**By SALEM KIRBAN**
22 Chapters ☐ Fully Illustrated!

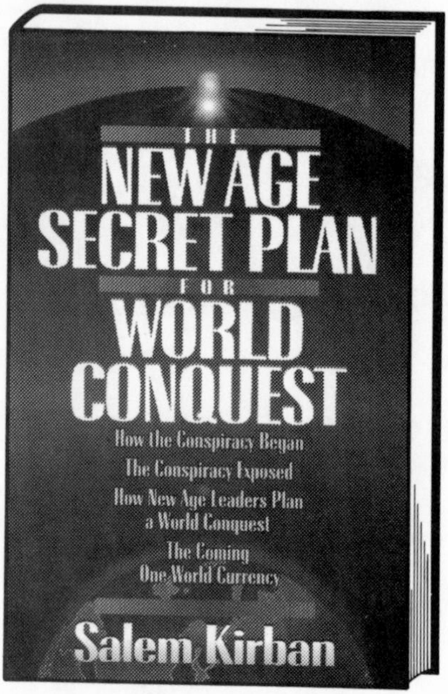

THE
**NEW AGE
SECRET PLAN
FOR
WORLD
CONQUEST**

How the Conspiracy Began
The Conspiracy Exposed
How New Age Leaders Plan
a World Conquest
The Coming
One-World Currency

**Salem Kirban**

---

Inflation
Made A
Hitler Possible!

What were the factors that made a Hitler possible?

1. The currency became worthless!
   · Inflation is making the U.S. dollar lose
   much of its purchasing power!

2. $6 Billion in foreign loans collapsed!
   · The United States gives some $10
   Billion in foreign aid annually!

3. 6 Million Germans were unemployed!
   · Today the United States has over 7
   Million unemployed!

4. Unfair taxes ...

---

**The Society for the Right to Die and
The Euthanasia Educational Council**

**Announce the adoption
of the Tokyo Declaration at the
First International
Euthanasia Conference**

The top illustration is the bird's head
from the first Great Seal of the United
States in 1782. The bottom illustration
is the Great Seal of 1902. The bird in
the first Seal bore little resemblance
to that of the eagle. This first so-called
eagle resembled the mythological phoenix of antiquity. The phoenix bird was
the Egyptian symbol of regeneration.
Thus, the new country (United States)
rising out of the old (Great Britain).

Contributions to the ................... City .............
Council are volunteer (tax deductible).

---

---

**To Receive    The NEW AGE SECRET PLAN For WORLD CONQUEST**
One Copy                    For a Gift of $25                    Order No. 270

# SECRET ORGANIZATIONS ACTIVE TODAY
invading even the Church
and Sunday School are part of

# SATAN'S ANGELS EXPOSED!
by Salem Kirban

**Salem Kirban**
# SATAN'S ANGELS EXPOSED

SPECIAL SECTION Reveals

The Illuminati
The Golden Dawn
Druid Witchcraft.
The Bilderbergers
The Trilateral Commission
Bancor Plan

## ILLUSTRATED

### AT LAST! SATAN'S STRATEGY REVEALED !

Most people are unaware that Satan's subtle deception has now infiltrated the Christian church. Many imagine Satan as a grotesque individual with horns. But Satan, who before his fall was an angel of light, now cleverly deceives even those who are born again by his "imitation holiness". **SATAN'S ANGELS EXPOSED** reveals how Satan is using an army of Judas Iscariots to undermine believers through "Christian" music, through false healers, through powerful religious groups that reach millions with polluted, watered down doctrine.

The "Angel of Light" as the Great imitator is the *"prince of this world"* and his successes in the Church and in high political places are exposed...clearly, concisely. Protect your children and those you love. **You need to get this book and know the facts!**

**From Baal worship**

**To Witchcraft**

**To Satan worship**

**And Now Even Infiltrating The Unsuspecting Church!**

**Satan's Symbols Explained**

How to recognize
doctrines of demons!

### SPECIAL SECTION Reveals

How secret organizations, whose threads of terror reach back centuries ago, are carefully weaving their power plot to control the world for Satan. Illustrated chapters reveal the behind-the-scenes manipulation of
**The Illuminati, The Golden Dawn and Druid Witchcraft. Plus!** Exposing the strange rise of political and economic power of **The Trilateral Commission, The Bilderbergers**, and the **Bancor Plan** for a universal money system!

| To Receive One Copy | SATAN'S ANGELS EXPOSED For a Gift of $25 | Order No. 6 |

# BEFORE IT HAPPENS

by Salem Kirban

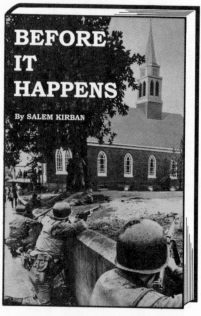

Christians in the United States live in a protective environment. They have not felt the sting of persecution because they named the name of Christ. They have not had to worship in secret nor have they been tortured for their faith. We are seeing a swelling tide of resentment against Christians directed by New Agers, secular humanists and environmentalists. **BEFORE IT HAPPENS** gives you a revealing insight into what Christians will soon face <u>even before the Rapture</u>!

---

One Sunday morning as Christians sing *"Onward Christian Soldiers"*...looking out the window of their Church...they will see <u>an army</u>...Satan's army of soldiers with drawn rifles ready to duplicate another *"Waco Incident"*. Read Salem Kirban's shocking new book **BEFORE IT HAPPENS**.

---

Here are the revealing chapters in **BEFORE IT HAPPENS**.

1 Satan's Insidious Invasion
2 The Shame of America
3 Christians Blamed
4 Rise of Antichrist...A Silver Tongued Orator
5 Except Those Days Be Shortened. The Plan To Persecute Christians
6 **FDA** Erodes Freedoms
7 **AMA 's** Powerful Lobby
8 When Wrong Becomes Right
9 Outrage Against Christians
10 **U.N.** Agenda: To Conform to New Age Theology
11 The Raw and Illegal Abuse of POWER!
12 Socialist Agenda for Control
13 **BEFORE IT HAPPENS**

---

### You Are NOT The Sole Parents
#### Now...The State and UN Are To Be Your CO-PARENTS !

5. The State and the U
   rendering "*appropri*
   *performance of thei*
   *ensure the developn*
   *care of children.*"

6. The creation of an i
   "*identification, repoi*
   *and follow-up*" of pa
   "rights," treat their c

---

### UNDERSTANDING THE FALSE TRINITY

SATAN is head of the False Trinity.

**SATAN** imitates the work of **GOD the FATHER**.

**ANTICHRIST** imitates the work of **CHRIST the SON**.

**The FALSE PROPHET** imitates the work of the **HOLY SPIRIT**.

---

### The State Will Make The Decisions About Your Child

**Use Response Form To Receive This Book**

---

### The NEW AGE AGENDA...
#### The Coming Persecutions of CHRISTIANS

What can we expect :
many knowledgeable

1. Military-style Poli
   agents will enjoy

2. Rights of individu
   unreasonable sea

3. Forfeiture laws w
   the property of ch

4. States will be forc
   authorities or face
   subsidies.

---

#### An Eye-Witness Account of Police Brutality

Below are excerpts of a letter written me from an individual who personally took part in the Pittsburgh, Pennsylvania Operation Rescue demonstration.   She was an eye-witness!

#### Women Dragged Nude On Their Stomachs

According to their testimony...inside the jail, they were photographed and then dragged with their shirts.  In many cases, women were dragged with their bras up around their necks.  They were taken one at a time up five flights of circular stairway through the center of the prison in this undressed condition.   Some were punched in both breasts.  Some had their breasts squeezed.   Women were dragged nude on their stomachs. They could hear the prisoners in the rows of stacked cells yelling as they watched.

At the top of the stairs they were strip searched by matrons.  Some were fondled and some beaten and verbally abused by the women guards.   A male guard watched.

#### Struggling For Breath...
#### They Blew Smoke In Her Face and Laughed!

Finally, they were put in the gymnasium on the top floor of the prison.  One woman had an asthma type attack and was almost killed by guards laughing and blowing smoke in her face.   The warden had been present during these events.  They were held in holding cells for **12** hours without food.

The men were not fed or given free access to drinking water for **29** hours.

---

**Th**

#### THE THEOLOG

1. Killing of babies
   Thus far we will ha
   The Government ev
   And we thought Hi

2. Killing of adults v
   Laws supporting ei
   Many states are no

3. Alternative lifesty
   Marriages between
   The Aids epidemic

---

| To Receive | BEFORE IT HAPPENS | |
|---|---|---|
| One Copy | For a Gift of $10 | Order No. 275 |

# IS THERE
# NO BALM
# IN GILEAD ?

## By SALEM KIRBAN

10 Chapters ◯ 88 Pages ◯ Fully Illustrated

This is the most unusual book I have ever written. It is the fulfillment of 25 years of study. You <u>personally</u> will benefit! Mary and I do all we possibly can to convey from God's Word *"...the Balm of Gilead"*.

---

## IS THERE NO BALM IN GILEAD ?

### Table of Contents

**1   AN OPEN LETTER TO THE PRESIDENT**
God Hath Chosen The Foolish Things of the World
To Confound The Wise...

**2   GET RID OF LOBBY GROUPS!**

**3   GOD MUST HAVE LOVED
      THE POOR PEOPLE...
            HE MADE SO MANY OF THEM!**

**4   HYPOCRISY REIGNS and
      THE DAY TRUTH DIED!**

**5   FDA...FRIEND OF SPECIAL INTERESTS ?**

**6   IS IT TIME FOR THE American MEDICAL
      Association TO "HEAL THYSELF" ?**

**7   WHAT IS THE *REAL* ANSWER
      TO Lowering HEALTH COSTS ?**

**8   WHAT ARE THE DRUG-FREE ALTERNATIVES
      TO BETTER HEALTH ?**

**9   *"THEY'VE MADE IT ILLEGAL TO SAY
      PRUNE JUICE IS A LAXATIVE"***

**10   IS THERE NO BALM IN GILEAD ?**

---

**I URGE YOU** to get this **88** page book. I can assure you that this book will be **VITALLY** important to you and to your loved ones.

If you have been blessed by any of the books I have written... I know *positively* you and your family [and unsaved loved ones] will *personally* be blessed and <u>greatly helped</u> by the information found in **IS THERE NO BALM IN GILEAD?**

Included in this book is a **most unusual Full Color photo** that I am sure you will agree is a rare and eye-catching revealing photograph!

---

**To Receive**
One Copy

**IS THERE NO BALM IN GILEAD?**
For a Gift of $10

Order No. 280

## Sample Pages from IS THERE NO BALM IN GILEAD?

### The Medical Establishment Has Brainwashed Our Senior Citizens

Put on a white coat and a stethoscope around your neck and most people will believe anything you say. To the average senior citizen the medical doctor is looked upon as a god.

### TOBACCO...A DISASTER THAT AFFECTS US ALL!

Tobacco is a nauseating plant consumed by only two creatures: a large green worm and man. The worm doesn't know any better!

### ARTHRITIS

There are several forms of arthritis: **Osteo**arthritis involves deterioration of the cartilage at the ends of the bones. When the smooth cartilage becomes rough, this friction brings pain. **Rheumatoid** arthritis is an inflammatory arthritis which attacks the synovial membranes which surrounds the lubricating fluid in the joints. **Lupus** and **gout** are other forms of arthritis.

| | |
|---|---|
| Cell Guard | As directed on bottle |
| [A free radical destroyer made by Biotec Foods and found in Health Food Stores] | |
| Primrose Oil | 2 capsules twice a day |
| Coenzyme $Q_{10}$ | 60 mg. daily |

### INSOMNIA

One thing that helped Rip Van Winkle sleep for 20 years was the fact that none of his neighbors owned a lawn mower! It was W.C. Fields who said "The best cure for insomnia is to get a lot of sleep." Insomnia can be the result of: hypoglycemia, asthma, stress or a lack of proper nutrients.

| | |
|---|---|
| Calcium [from Oyster shell] | 900 mg. at evening meal and at bedtime |
| Magnesium | 450 mg. at evening meal and at bedtime |
| Vitamin B Complex | 100 mg. at evening meal |
| plus extra | |

### MENOPAUSE

Menopause signals the end of menstruation. MEN-O-PAUSE, I believe, is when **MEN** should **PAUSE** and show greater love and understanding towards their wife. Symptoms may include: headaches, hot flashes, dizziness, depression and heart palpitations. If one is hypoglycemic, symptoms can increase in severity. Estrogen may cause an increase in symptoms associated with migraine headaches, asthma and heart disorders.

| | |
|---|---|
| Digestive Enzymes | This should include Hydrochloric acid [HCl] and should be taken with meals to aid digestion. |
| Lecithin | 1 Tablespoon before meals |
| Primrose Oil | As directed on label |
| Vitamin E | 400 I.U. daily as directed by physician |
| Vitamin B Complex | 100 mg. at evening meal / **Plus extra** |

| | | |
|---|---|---|
| **To Receive** One Copy | **IS THERE NO BALM IN GILEAD?** For a Gift of $10 | Order No. 280 |

# Here is the Harvest Your Gifts Make Possible!

Look at these faces pictured below. They each have ONE thing in common!
EACH has accepted Jesus Christ as their personal Saviour and Lord after
reading one of my books. Your Gifts make this harvest of souls possible!

Brenda Montgomery/New York

Jerry Kuck/Minnesota

Claire Young/Illinois

Gordon H. Coulter/Nebraska

Dear Mr Kirban,

    I received your book entitled
666 from a Christian friend of
mine last August. I always
thought of myself as being a
Christian by merely going to
church and being good but
I have since learned, there is
much more to it than that.
Since I have accepted Jesus
Christ as my personal Savior
there has been a whole new
meaning in my life. With the
Love He has given me I have
learned to love. This is the
reason I have dedicated my
life to helping people, not only
physically but spiritually also.

          Miss Jane Smith

Sandra K. Greens/New York

Julius Ajedo/Greece

# My MISSIONS Gift Response Form

Enclosed is my Gift to spread the Good News of Christ's soon return.    **Send Christian Growth Helps below.**

| ORDER NUMBER | DESCRIPTION | FOR A GIFT OF |
|---|---|---|
| _____ | _____ | $_____ |
| _____ | _____ | $_____ |
| _____ | _____ | $_____ |
| _____ | _____ | $_____ |
| _____ | _____ | $_____ |
| _____ | _____ | $_____ |

Send me **FOUR Hardback** *Salem Kirban* **REFERENCE BIBLES** for a one-time Special Price of **$100**   ➡   $ _____

**Total Enclosed**    $ _____

☐ Check or money order enclosed in the amount of $_____ payable to **SECOND COMING, Inc.** [U.S. funds only].    Sorry, no C.O.D.'s.

☐ **VISA**   ☐☐☐☐☐☐☐☐☐☐☐☐☐☐☐☐☐

Expiration Date ☐☐☐

☐ **master charge** WE HONOR / THE INTERBANK CARD   ☐☐☐☐☐☐☐☐☐☐☐☐☐☐☐☐☐

Expiration Date ☐☐☐

Signature X_____

Mr/Mrs/Miss_____
[Please PRINT]

Address_____

City_____State_____ZIP_____

**SECOND COMING/***Missions***       Your Gift Is
**Box 278, Montrose, PA. 18801**       *Tax Deductible*

All of our books have as their last chapter a Decision chapter. Those pictured here are a representative few of the many people worldwide who have signed the Decision Page and sent it in to **Second Coming Missions**. And it is your Gifts that make this harvest of souls possible!

You were the only author who penetrated the "SELF" + procrastinating pride of my husband! He served God 1 year after reading one or two books of yours, then died 1 year later at age 35.

Bette

Kaula McKitrick/Iowa

Samuel Missino/Conn.

Robert Martin,Jr./Kansas

This letter really Touched my heart!! God will honor and bless This SACRificial giving! Think what we can Accomplish for His MINISTRY if each ONE of us ARE DETERMINED To give As SACRificially As This college STUDENT!

Emma Woods/Illinois

Raymond Mule/U.S. Army

Dear Mr. Kirban,
The Lord has placed a burden on my hart to sell of my worldly possessions and place it instead in His work. Although, I know of a number of worthy Christian organizations, I am sure that my contributions will do the most good in Second Coming, Inc.

I am a college student and so most of my worldly needs are taken care of by my parents, but more importantly, I have faith that He shall supply all my needs.

Thus, enclosed is the money from my savings account, $350, which I trust will be put to work in witnessing, "...to the Jew first, and the Gentile,"    Also enclosed is $10 for the Arab refugees which I collected from students here at Carnegie-Melon U.

May the Peace of His Holy Name be with you,

**I CAN THINK OF NO GREATER nor LASTING <u>JOY</u>...**

than the joy of making your dollars work to winning lost souls to Christ. <u>What greater investment is there...than the investment in redeemed souls</u>...redeemed, <u>because you cared enough</u> to share a portion of that which God has entrusted to you! Who knows how many souls will be won to Christ because your Gift made possible the spreading of the Gospel! Only ETERNITY will reveal how many Crowns will be yours! And in eternity you will see and fellowship with those who are there because you care...you cared enough to pray... you cared enough to give! Mary and I thank you for <u>caring</u> and for, by your Gift... <u>sharing</u>!

To the left
is front cover
of
**GUIDE
TO SURVIVAL**
in Hebrew

Pictured on the right   >>>
A worker in Jerusalem
inserting the Hebrew edition of
**GUIDE TO SURVIVAL** into an
envelope to be mailed
throughout all of **ISRAEL!**

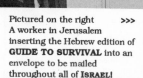

When we printed our First Edition of **GUIDE TO SURVIVAL** in Hebrew, we took several copies up on a hill overlooking Jerusalem. There, we dedicated this book to the Lord praying that it might bring forth much fruit for the Saviour. It is now our desire, when funds permit, to print **WHAT IN THE WORLD WILL HAPPEN NEXT?** in Hebrew...right in Jerusalem...mailing through all of Israel!

# My MISSIONS Gift Response Form

Enclosed is my Gift to spread the Good News of Christ's soon return.  **Send Christian Growth Helps below.**

| ORDER<br>NUMBER | DESCRIPTION | FOR A<br>GIFT OF |
|---|---|---|
| _____ | _____ | $_____ |
| _____ | _____ | $_____ |
| _____ | _____ | $_____ |
| _____ | _____ | $_____ |
| _____ | _____ | $_____ |
| _____ | _____ | $_____ |

Send me **FOUR Hardback**
*Salem Kirban* **REFERENCE BIBLES**
for a one-time Special Price of **$100**    ➤   $ _____

**Total Enclosed**    $ _____

☐ Check or money order enclosed in the amount of $_____ payable to **SECOND COMING, Inc.** [U.S. funds only].  Sorry, no C.O.D.'s.

☐ **VISA**  ⬚⬚⬚⬚⬚⬚⬚⬚⬚⬚⬚⬚⬚⬚⬚⬚

Expiration Date ◯◯◯

☐ **master charge**  ⬚⬚⬚⬚⬚⬚⬚⬚⬚⬚⬚⬚⬚⬚⬚⬚
THE INTERBANK CARD

Expiration Date ◯◯◯

Signature X_____

Mr/Mrs/Miss_____
[Please PRINT]

Address_____

City_____ State_____ ZIP_____

**SECOND COMING/*Missions*** **Your Gift Is**
Box 278, Montrose, PA. 18801 *Tax Deductible*